**PAOLO
BARON**
lyrics

**ERNESTO
CARBONETTI**
music

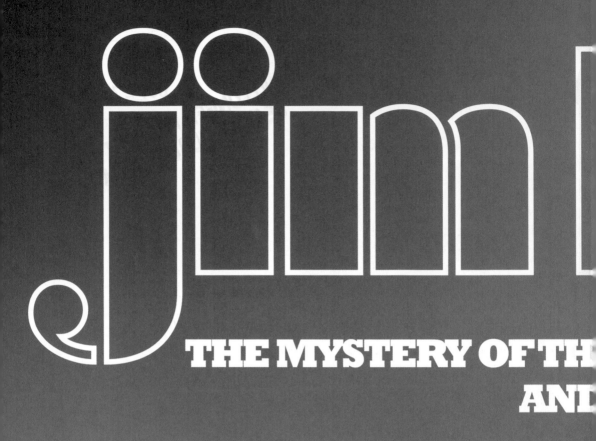

THE MYSTERY OF TH
ANI

STORY:
PAOLO BARON
ENGLISH TRANSLATION:
ADRIAN NATHAN WEST

JIM LIVES: THE MYSTERY OF THE LEAD SINGER OF THE DOORS & THE 27 CLUB. First printing. June 2021. Published by Image Comics, Inc. Office of publication: PO BOX 14457, Portland, OR 97293. Copyright © 2021 Paolo Baron & Ernesto Carbonetti. All rights reserved. "Jim Lives: The Mystery of the Lead Singer of The Doors & the 27 Club," its logos, and the likenesses of all characters herein are trademarks of Paolo Baron & Ernesto Carbonetti, unless otherwise noted. "Image" and the Image Comics logos are registered trademarks of Image Comics, Inc. No part of this publication may be reproduced or transmitted, in any form or by any means (except for short excerpts for journalistic or review purposes), without the express written permission of Paolo Baron & Ernesto Carbonetti or Image Comics, Inc. All names, characters, events, and locales in this publication are entirely fictional. Any resemblance to actual persons (living or dead), events, or places, without satirical intent, is coincidental. Printed in the USA. For international rights, contact: foreignlicensing@imagecomics.com. ISBN: 978-1-5343-1963-9.

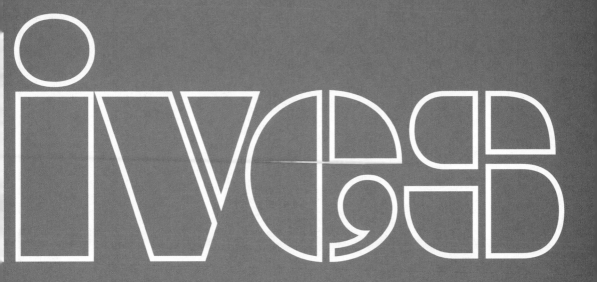

EAD SINGER OF THE DOORS

IE 27 CLUB

ART AND COVER:
ERNESTO CARBONETTI

SUPERVISOR:
MANFREDI GIFFONE

IMAGE COMICS, INC. • **Todd McFarlane**: President • **Jim Valentino**: Vice President • **Marc Silvestri**: Chief Executive Officer • **Erik Larsen**: Chief Financial Officer • **Robert Kirkman**: Chief Operating Officer • **Eric Stephenson**: Publisher / Chief Creative Officer • **Nicole Lapalme**: Controller • **Leanna Caunter**: Accounting Analyst • **Sue Korpela**: Accounting & HR Manager • **Marla Eizik**: Talent Liaison • **Jeff Boison**: Director of Sales & Publishing Planning • **Dirk Wood**: Director of International Sales & Licensing • **Alex Cox**: Director of Direct Market Sales • **Chloe Ramos**: Book Market & Library Sales Manager • **Emilio Bautista**: Digital Sales Coordinator • **Jon Schlaffman**: Specialty Sales Coordinator • **Kat Salazar**: Director of PR & Marketing • **Drew Fitzgerald**: Marketing Content Associate • **Heather Doornink**: Production Director • **Drew Gill**: Art Director • **Hilary DiLoreto**: Print Manager • **Tricia Ramos**: Traffic Manager • **Melissa Gifford**: Content Manager • **Erika Schnatz**: Senior Production Artist • **Ryan Brewer**: Production Artist • **Deanna Phelps**: Production Artist • **IMAGECOMICS.COM**

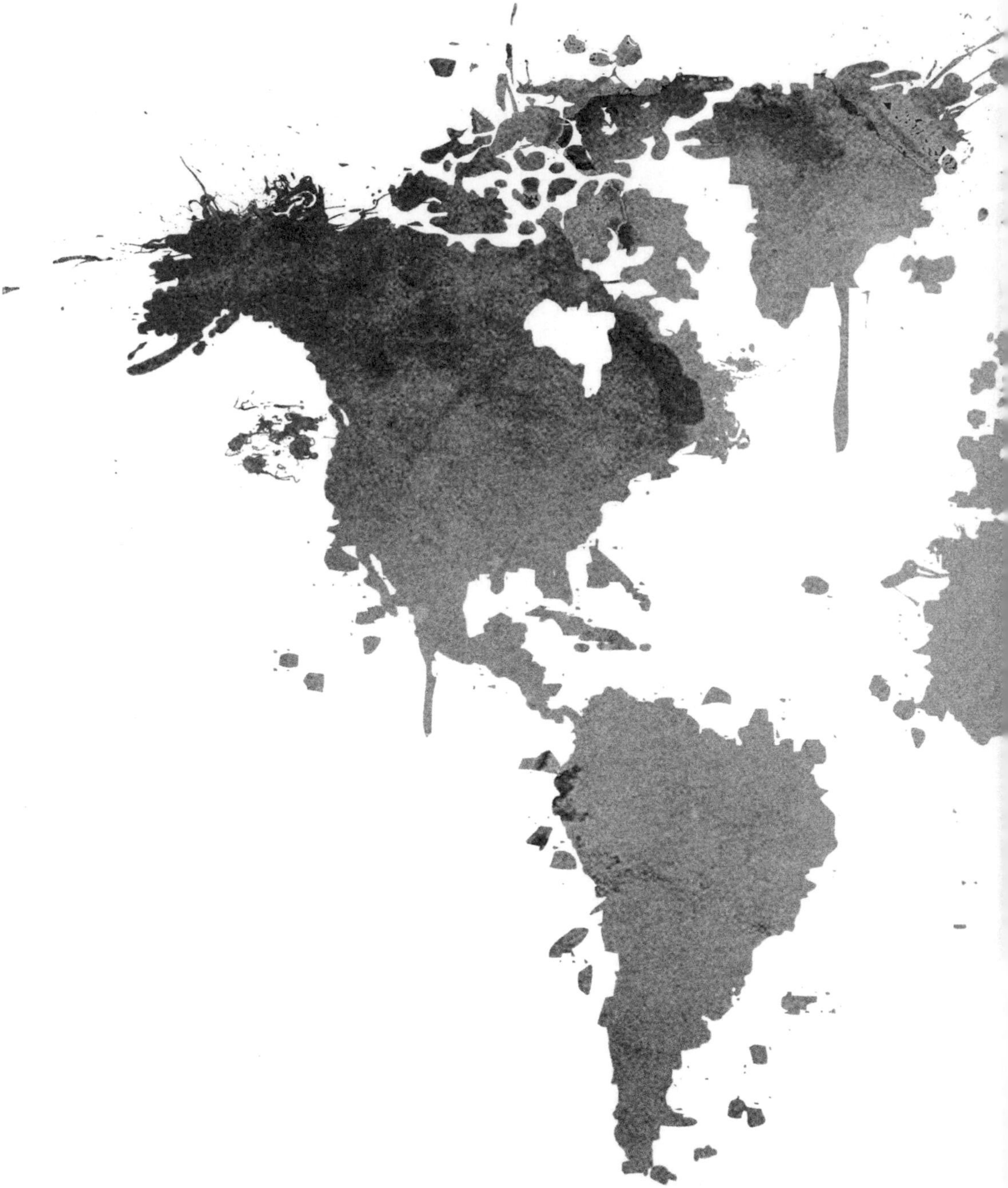

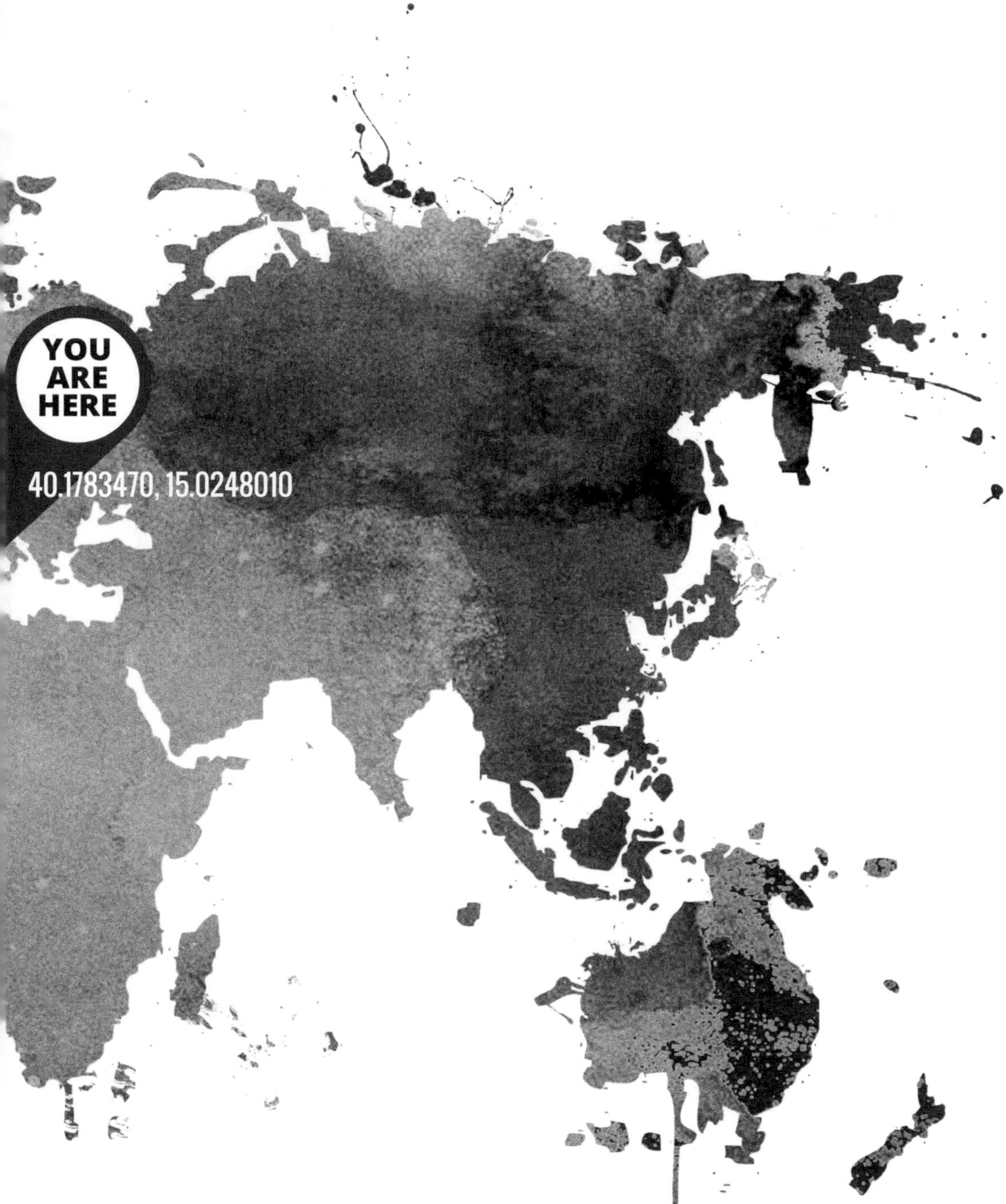
YOU ARE HERE
40.1783470, 15.0248010

Lyrics pg. 36: *Roadhouse Blues* (Morrison-Doors)

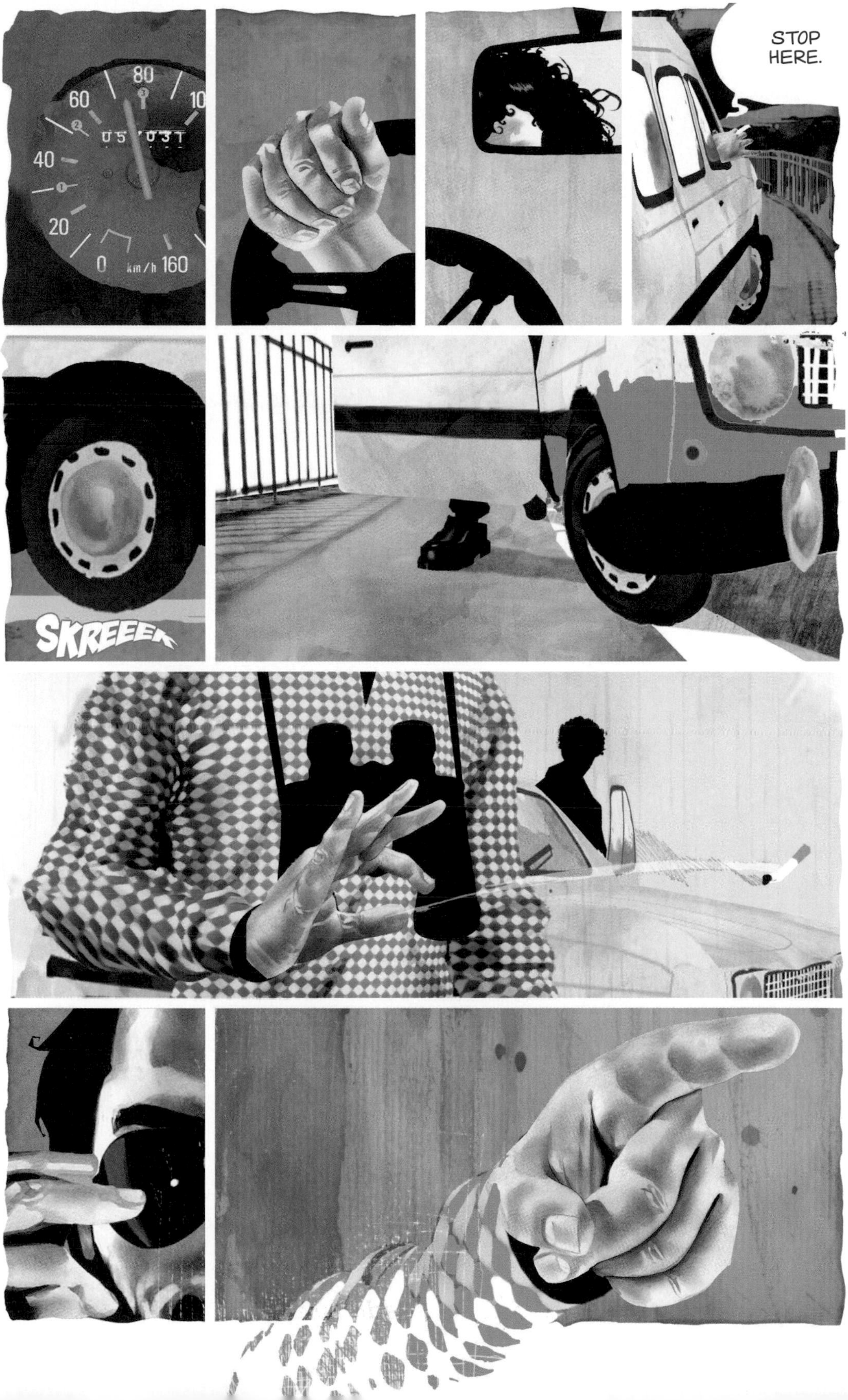

STOP HERE.
SKREEEEK

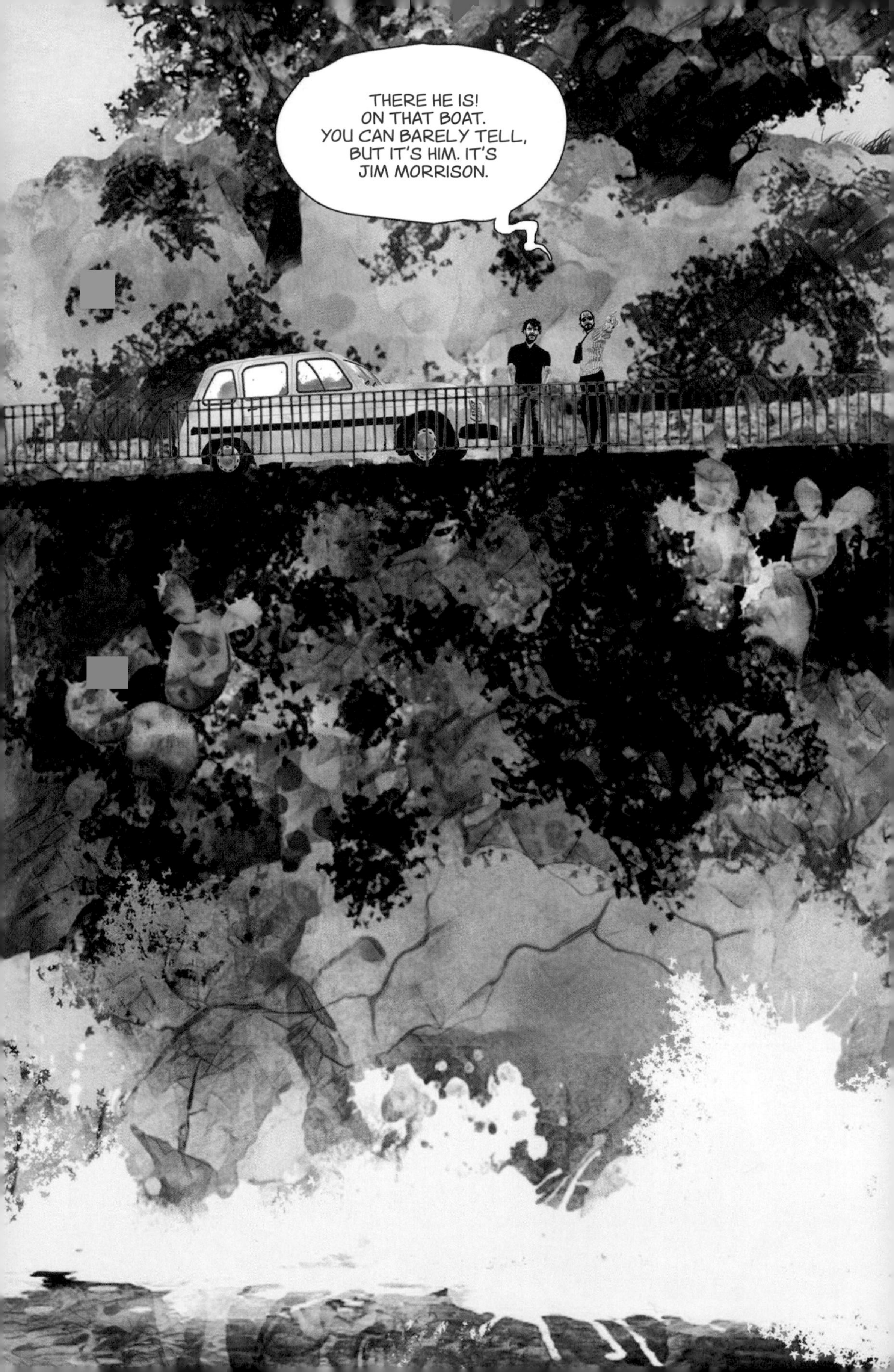
THERE HE IS! ON THAT BOAT. YOU CAN BARELY TELL, BUT IT'S HIM. IT'S JIM MORRISON.

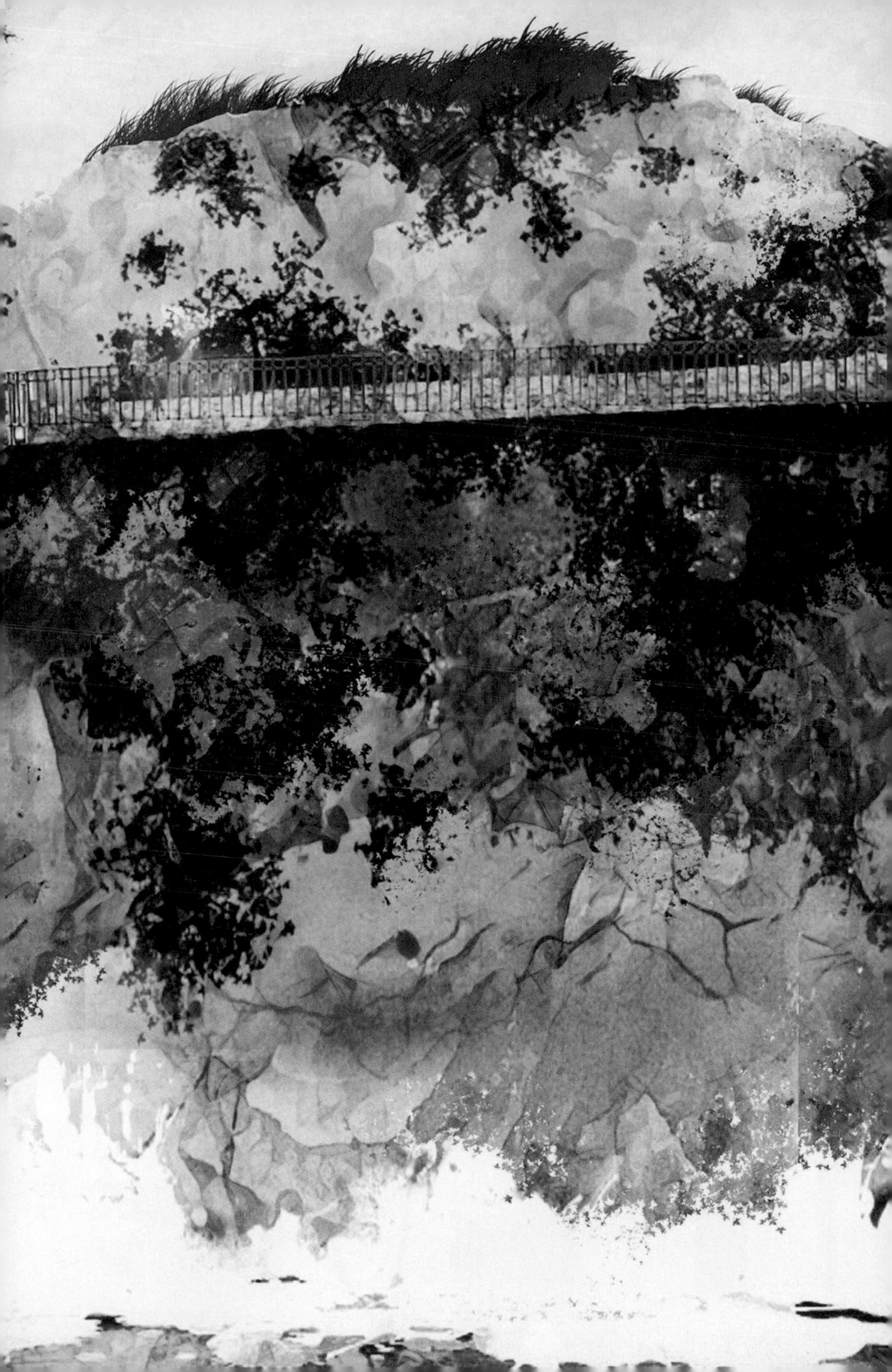

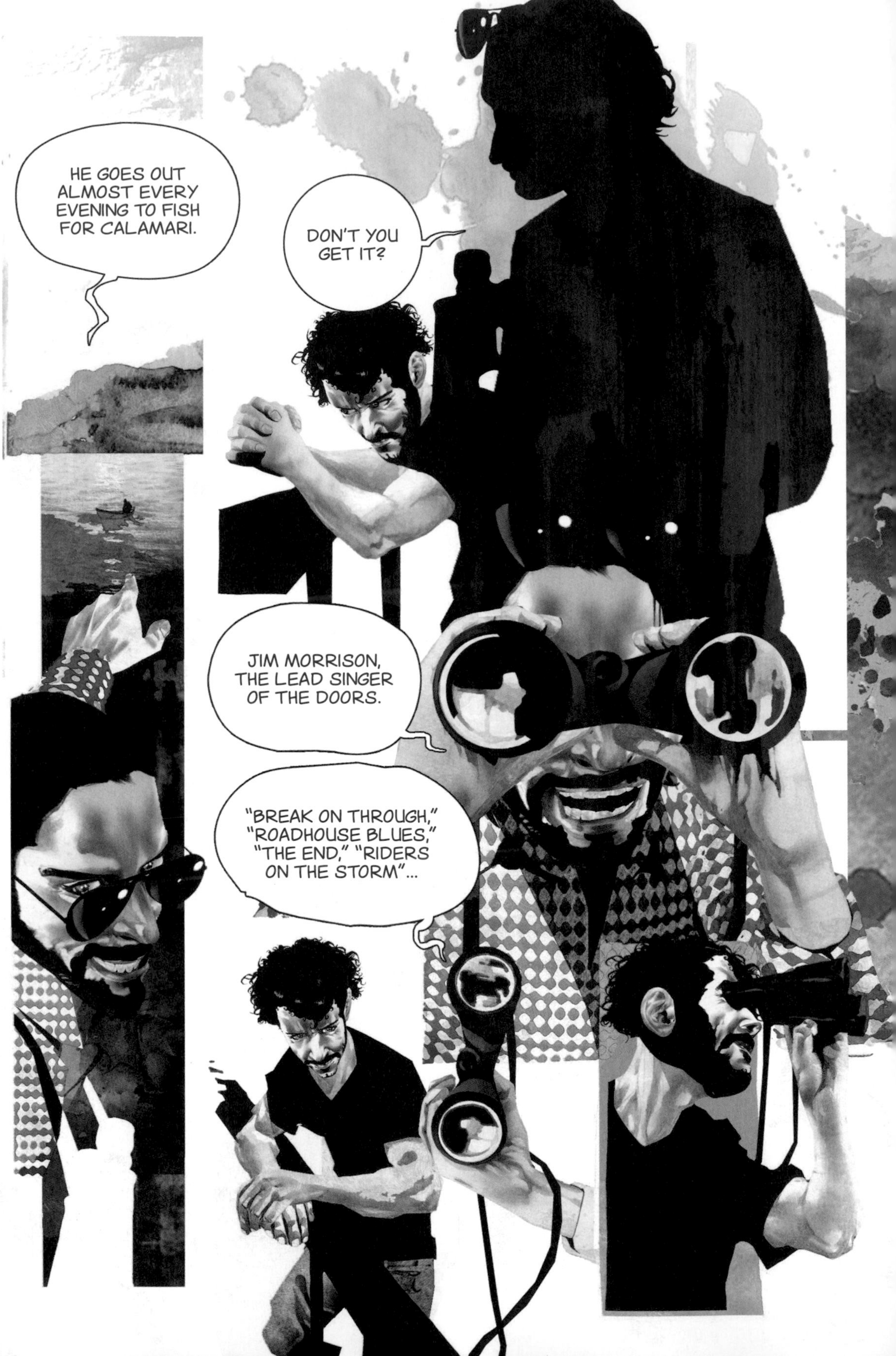
HE GOES OUT ALMOST EVERY EVENING TO FISH FOR CALAMARI.
DON'T YOU GET IT?
JIM MORRISON, THE LEAD SINGER OF THE DOORS.
"BREAK ON THROUGH," "ROADHOUSE BLUES," "THE END," "RIDERS ON THE STORM"...

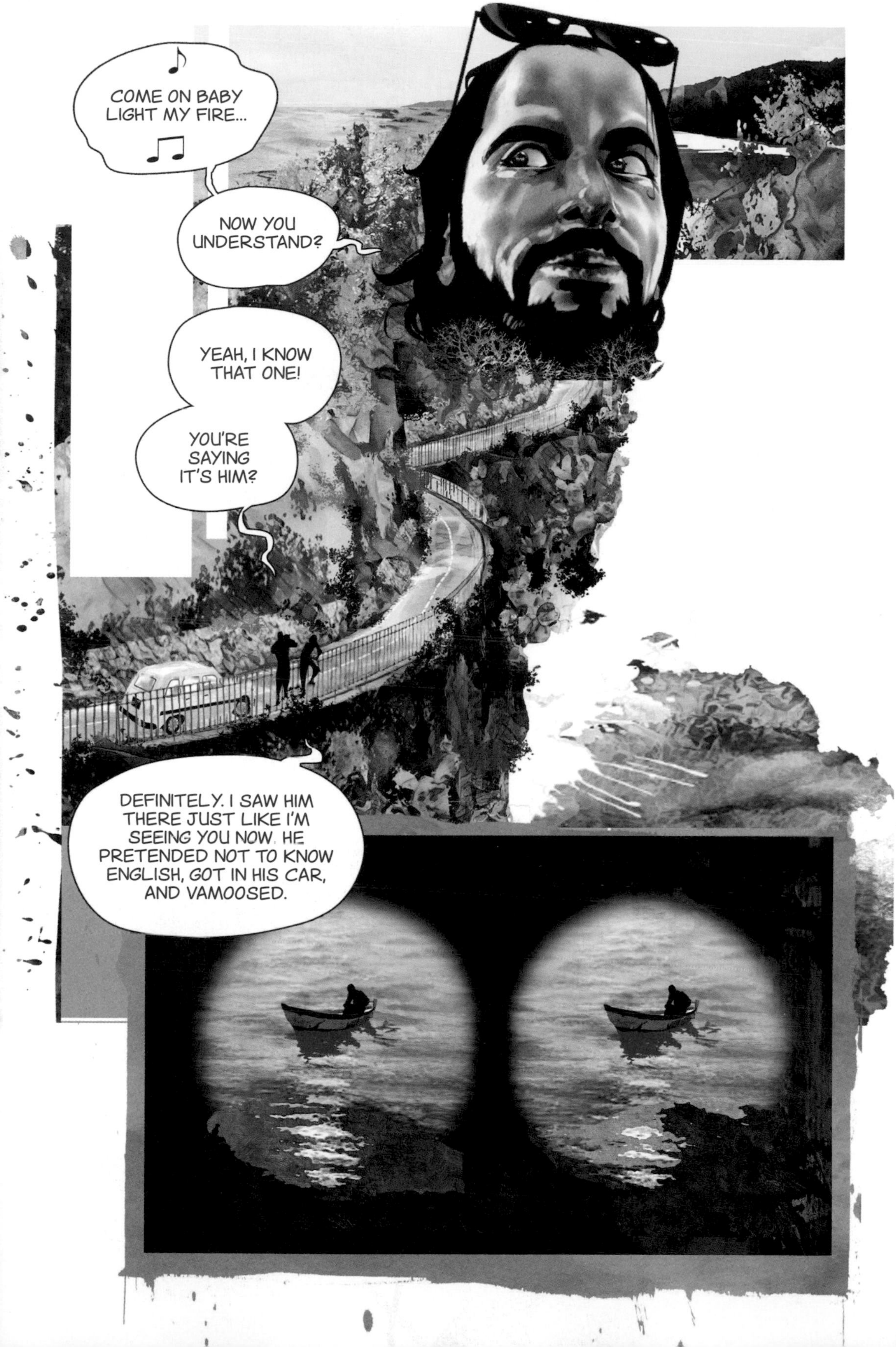
COME ON BABY LIGHT MY FIRE...
NOW YOU UNDERSTAND?
YEAH, I KNOW THAT ONE!
YOU'RE SAYING IT'S HIM?
DEFINITELY. I SAW HIM THERE JUST LIKE I'M SEEING YOU NOW. HE PRETENDED NOT TO KNOW ENGLISH, GOT IN HIS CAR, AND VAMOOSED.

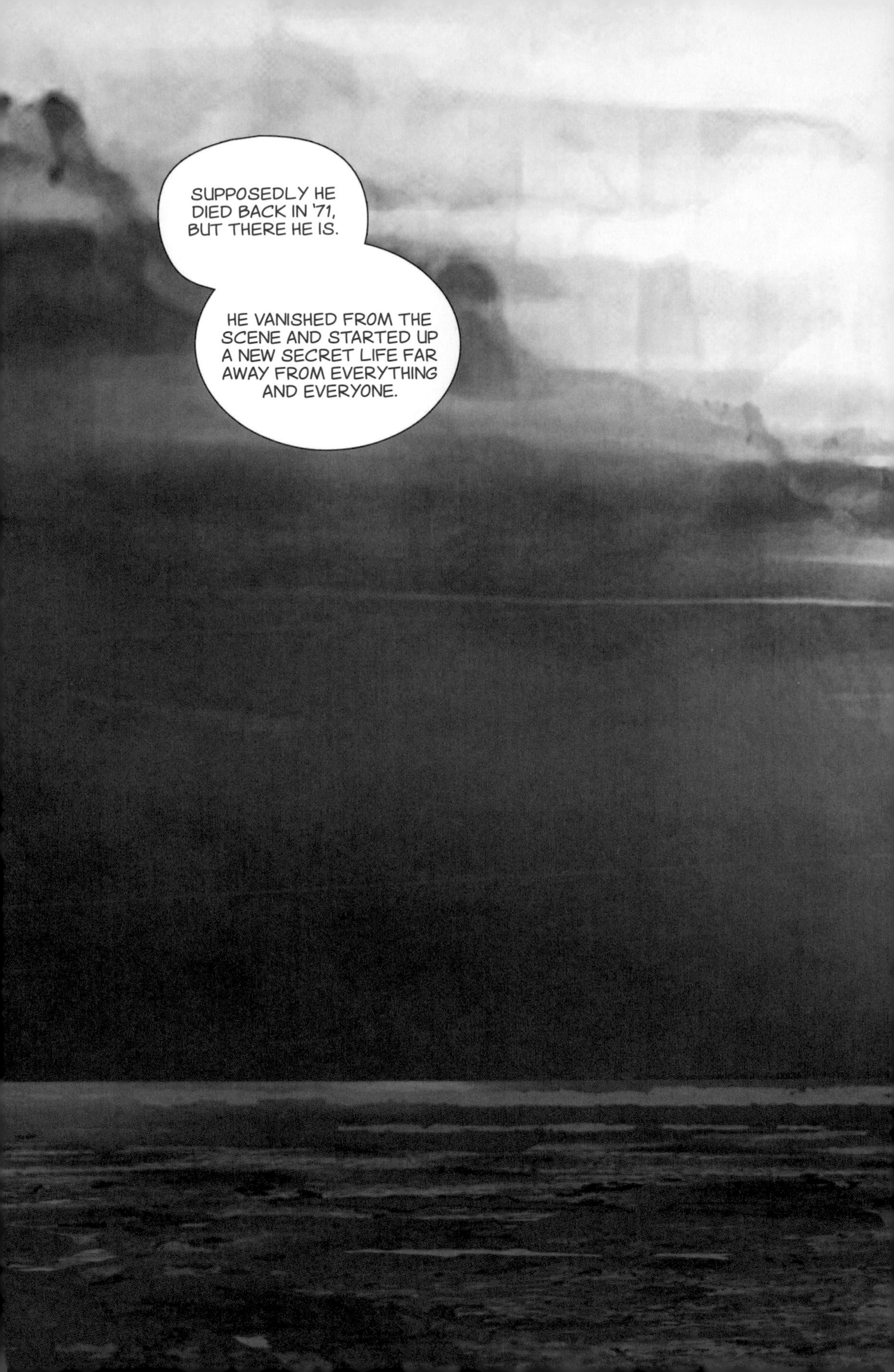
SUPPOSEDLY HE DIED BACK IN '71, BUT THERE HE IS.
HE VANISHED FROM THE SCENE AND STARTED UP A NEW SECRET LIFE FAR AWAY FROM EVERYTHING AND EVERYONE.

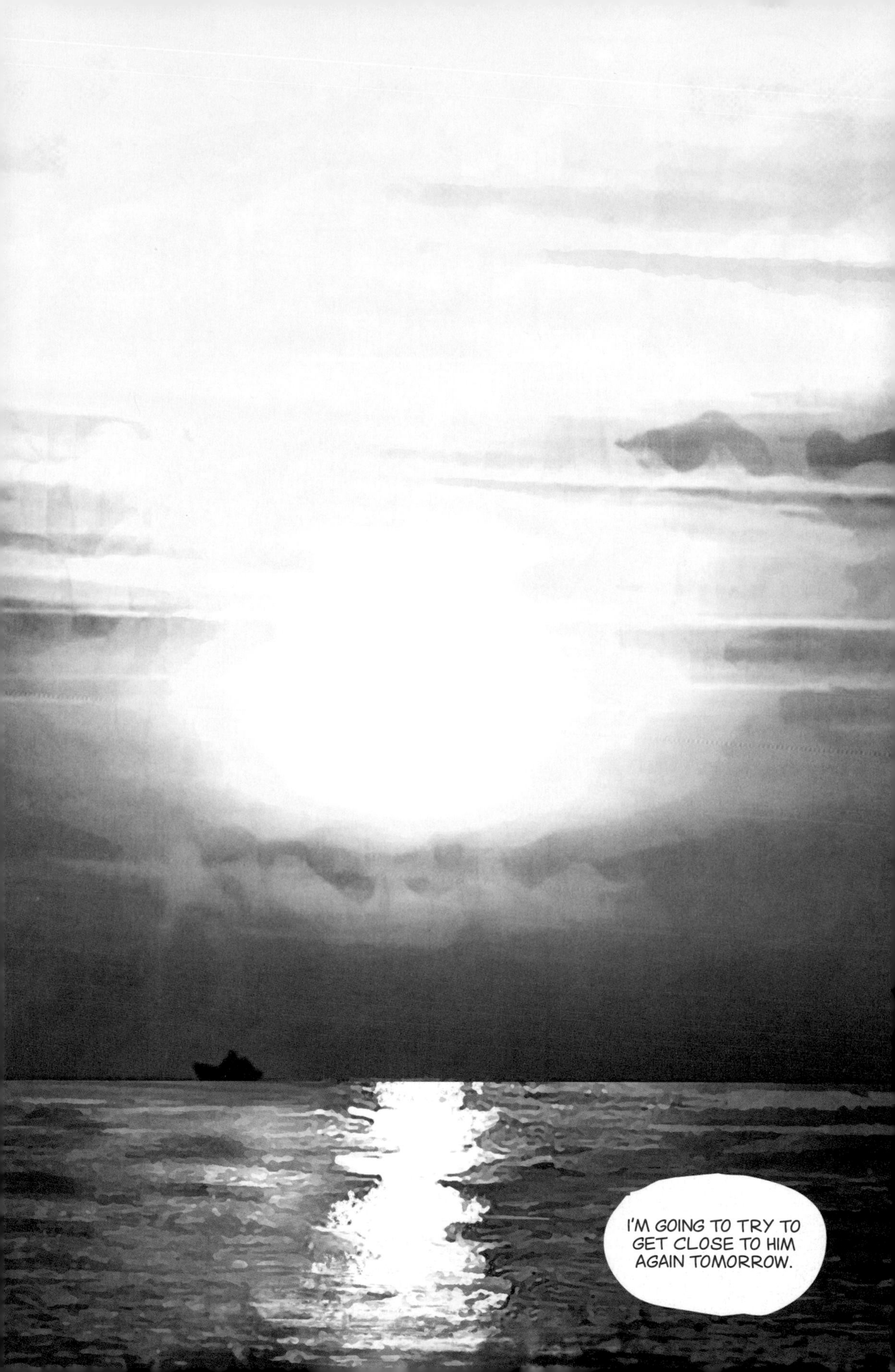
I'M GOING TO TRY TO GET CLOSE TO HIM AGAIN TOMORROW.

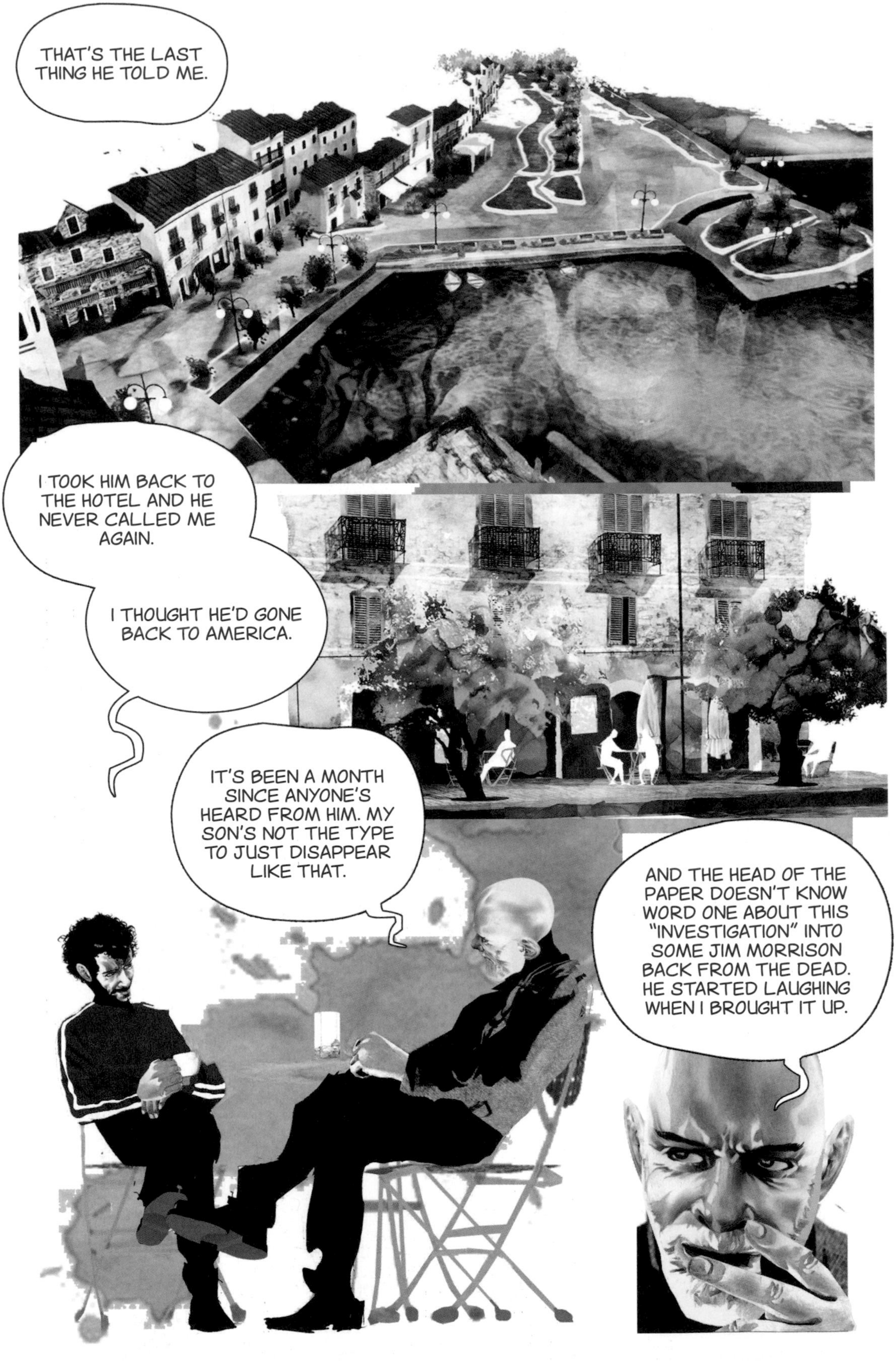
THAT'S THE LAST THING HE TOLD ME.
I TOOK HIM BACK TO THE HOTEL AND HE NEVER CALLED ME AGAIN.
I THOUGHT HE'D GONE BACK TO AMERICA.
IT'S BEEN A MONTH SINCE ANYONE'S HEARD FROM HIM. MY SON'S NOT THE TYPE TO JUST DISAPPEAR LIKE THAT.
AND THE HEAD OF THE PAPER DOESN'T KNOW WORD ONE ABOUT THIS "INVESTIGATION" INTO SOME JIM MORRISON BACK FROM THE DEAD. HE STARTED LAUGHING WHEN I BROUGHT IT UP.

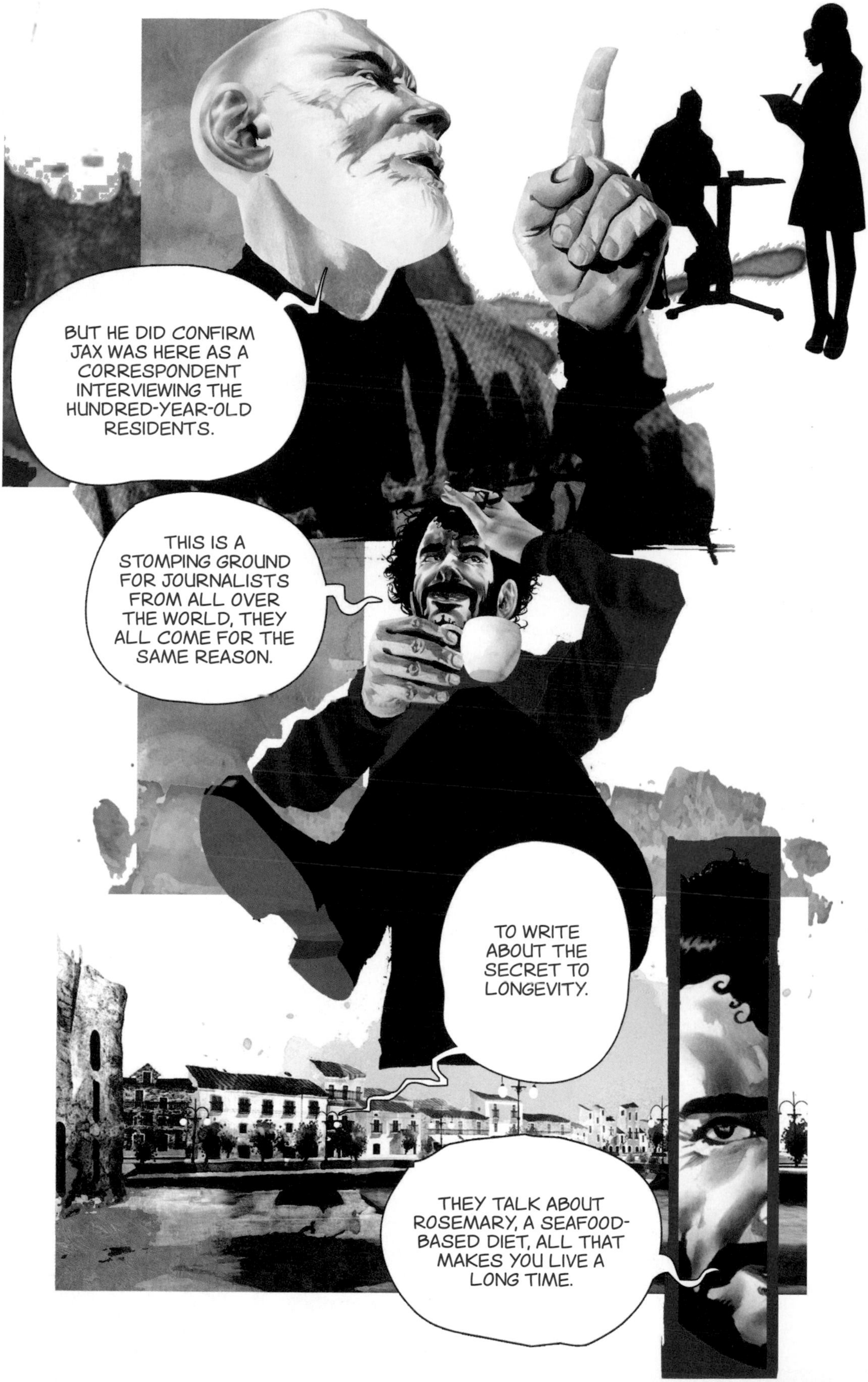
BUT HE DID CONFIRM JAX WAS HERE AS A CORRESPONDENT INTERVIEWING THE HUNDRED-YEAR-OLD RESIDENTS.
THIS IS A STOMPING GROUND FOR JOURNALISTS FROM ALL OVER THE WORLD, THEY ALL COME FOR THE SAME REASON.
TO WRITE ABOUT THE SECRET TO LONGEVITY.
THEY TALK ABOUT ROSEMARY, A SEAFOOD-BASED DIET, ALL THAT MAKES YOU LIVE A LONG TIME.

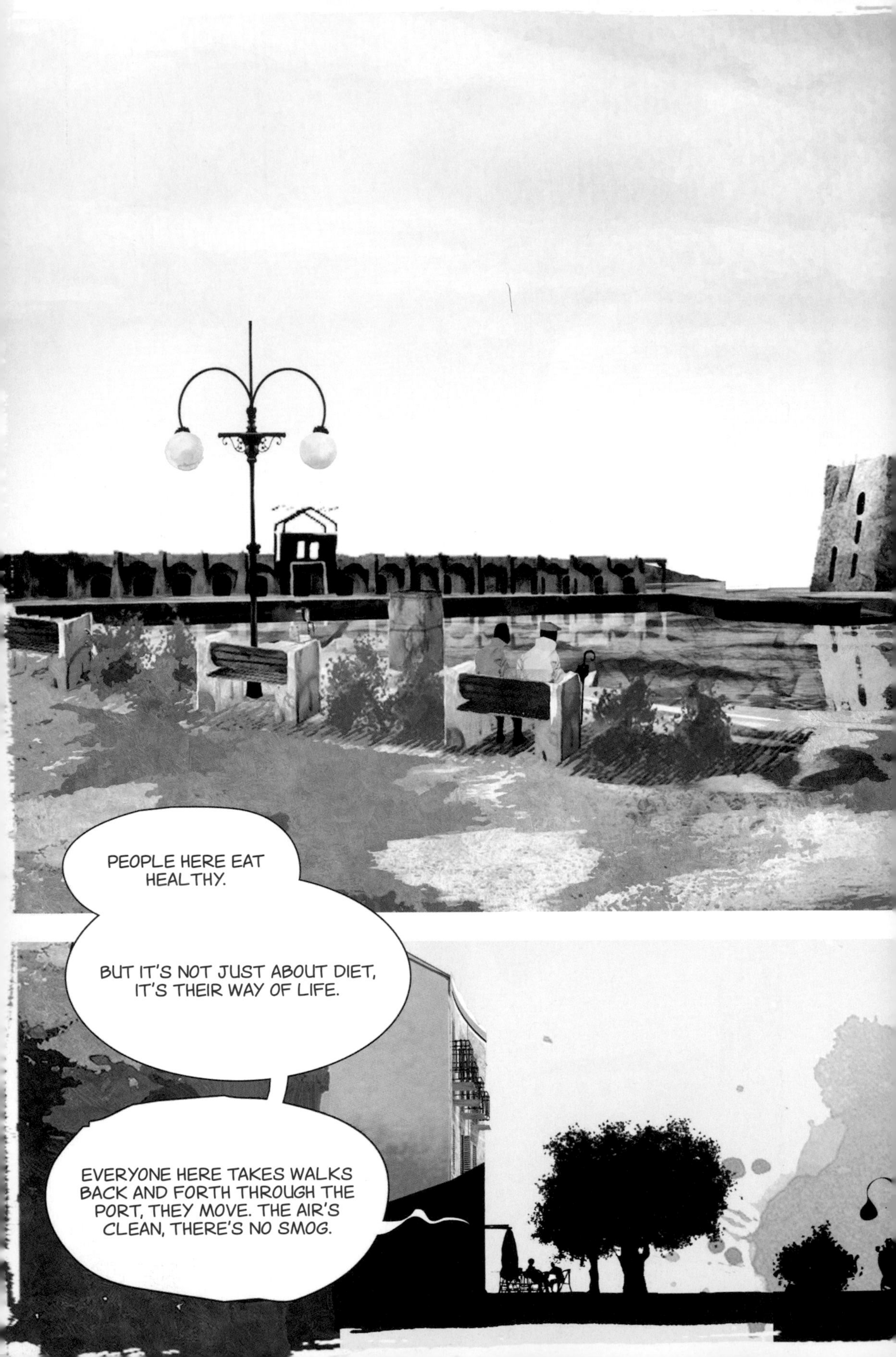
PEOPLE HERE EAT HEALTHY.
BUT IT'S NOT JUST ABOUT DIET, IT'S THEIR WAY OF LIFE.
EVERYONE HERE TAKES WALKS BACK AND FORTH THROUGH THE PORT, THEY MOVE. THE AIR'S CLEAN, THERE'S NO SMOG.

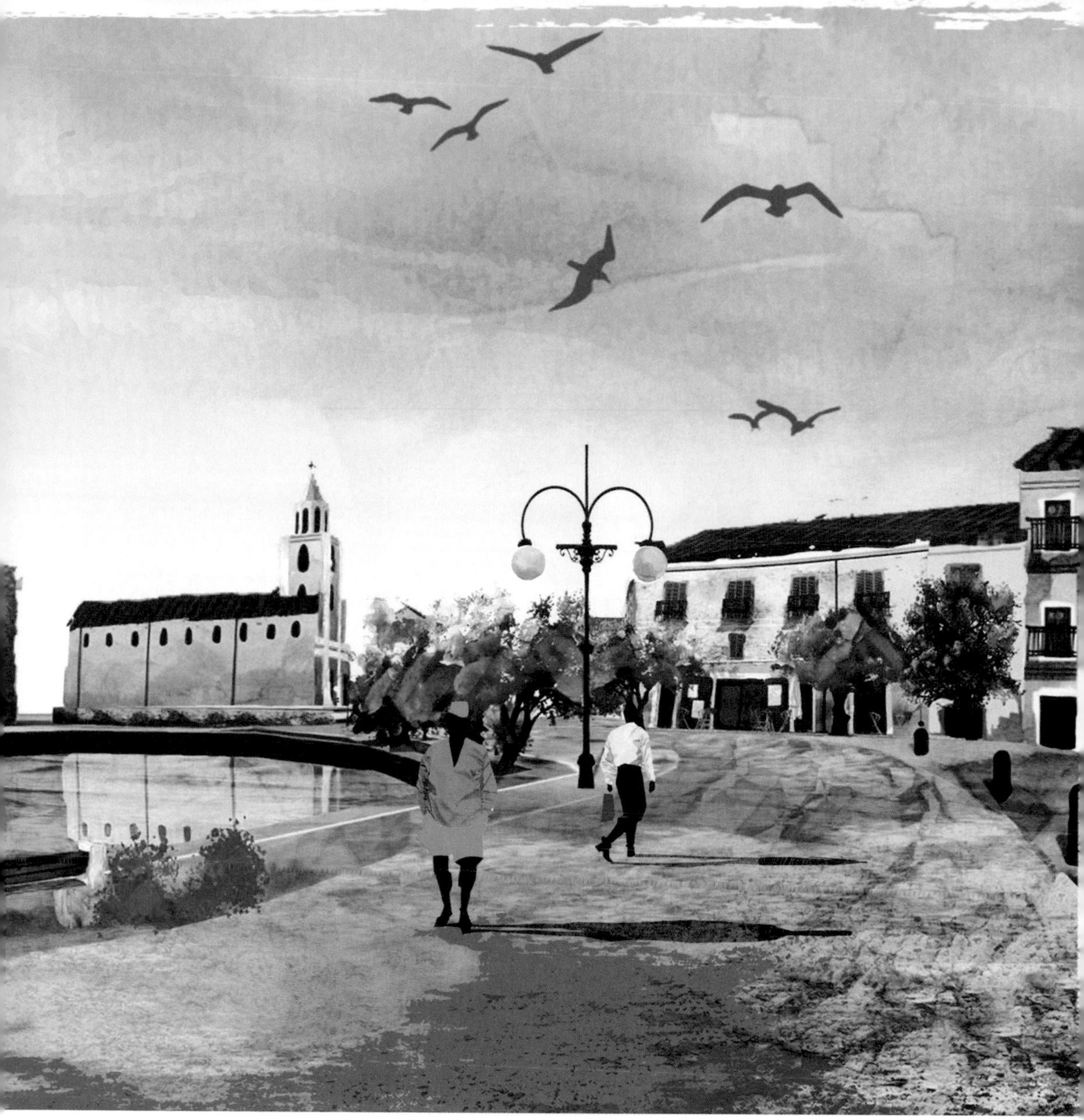

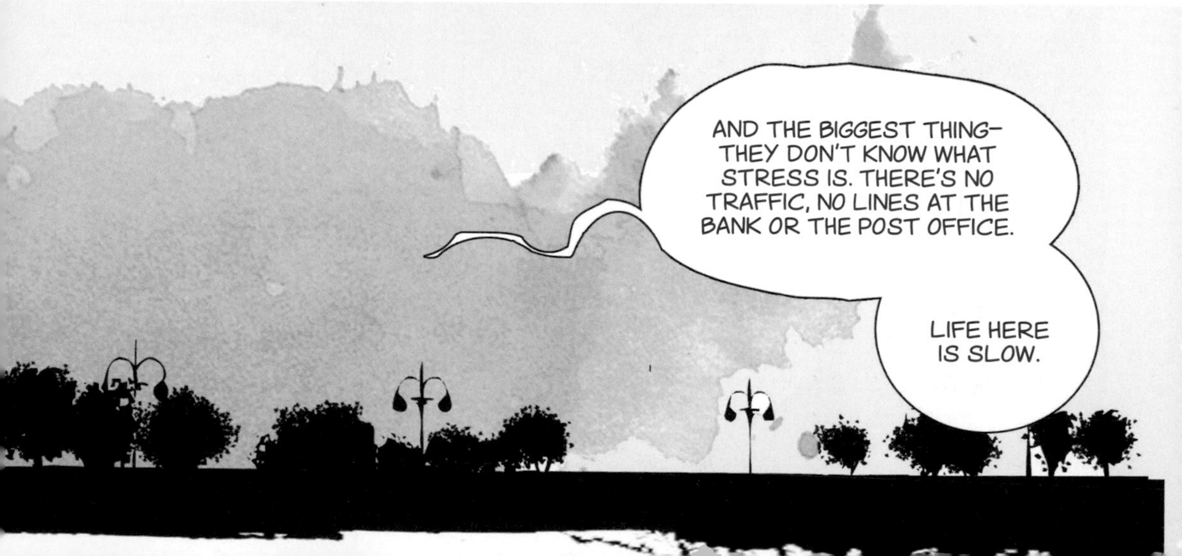
AND THE BIGGEST THING—THEY DON'T KNOW WHAT STRESS IS. THERE'S NO TRAFFIC, NO LINES AT THE BANK OR THE POST OFFICE.
LIFE HERE IS SLOW.

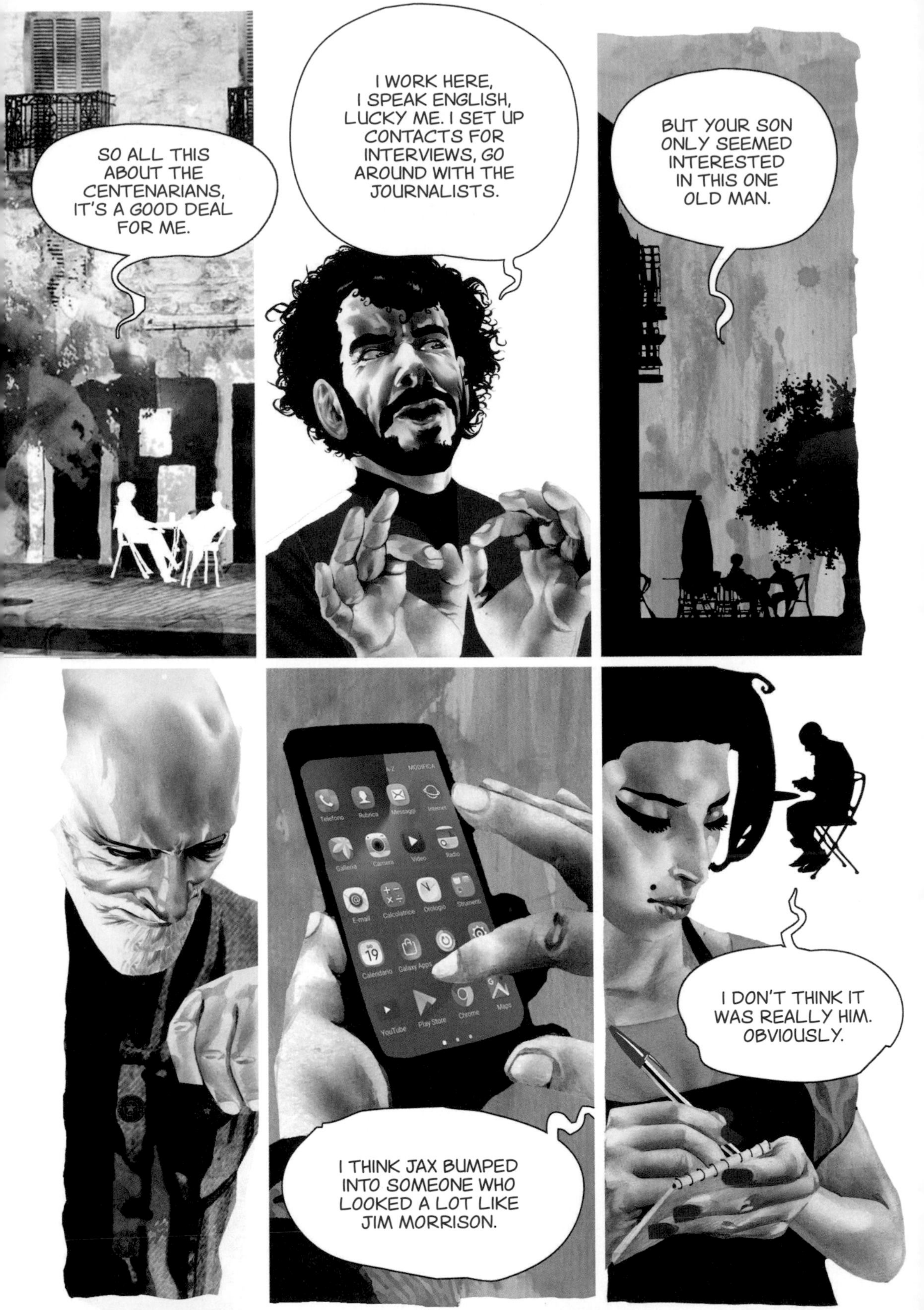
SO ALL THIS ABOUT THE CENTENARIANS, IT'S A GOOD DEAL FOR ME.
I WORK HERE, I SPEAK ENGLISH, LUCKY ME. I SET UP CONTACTS FOR INTERVIEWS, GO AROUND WITH THE JOURNALISTS.
BUT YOUR SON ONLY SEEMED INTERESTED IN THIS ONE OLD MAN.
I THINK JAX BUMPED INTO SOMEONE WHO LOOKED A LOT LIKE JIM MORRISON.
I DON'T THINK IT WAS REALLY HIM. OBVIOUSLY.

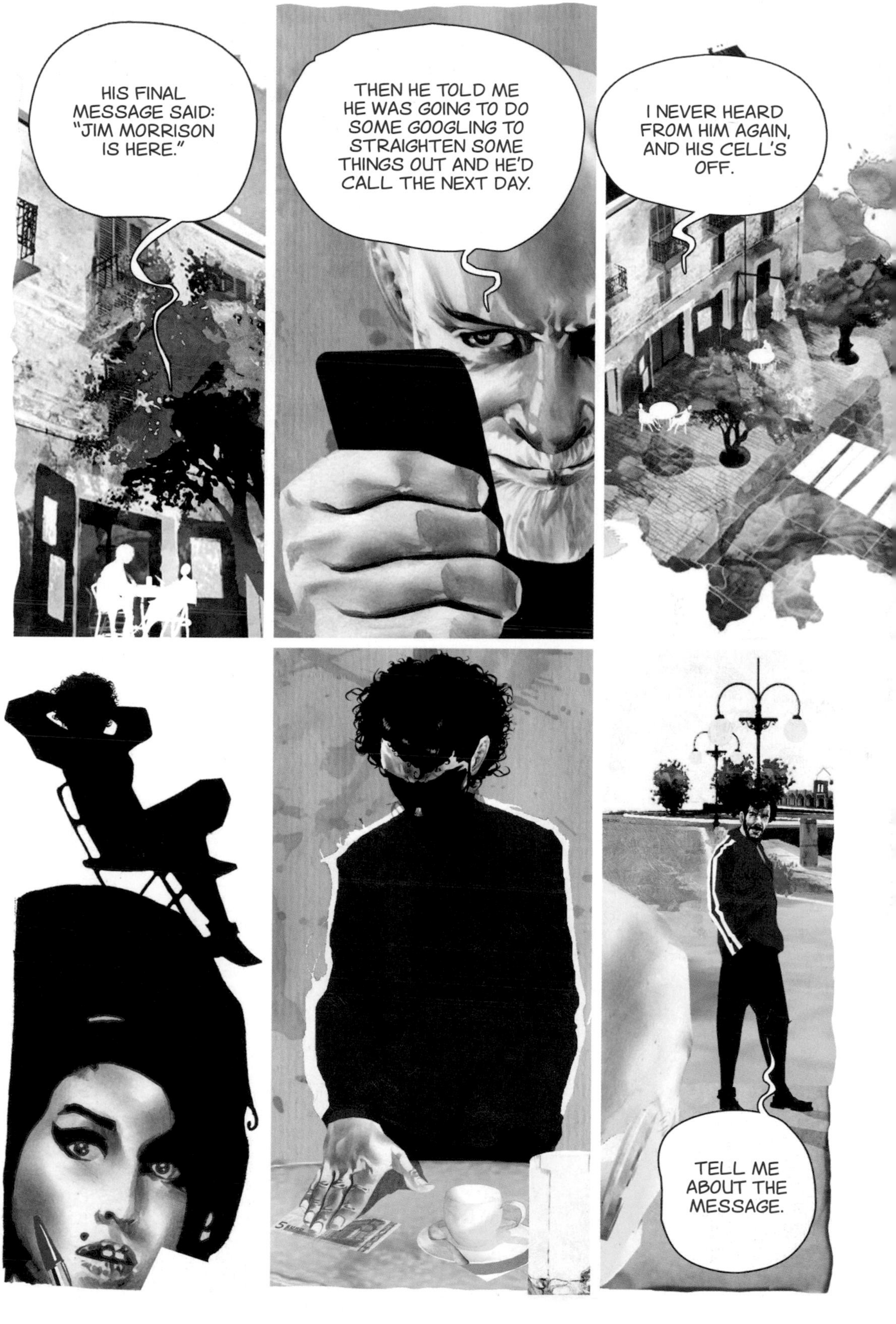
HIS FINAL MESSAGE SAID: "JIM MORRISON IS HERE."
THEN HE TOLD ME HE WAS GOING TO DO SOME GOOGLING TO STRAIGHTEN SOME THINGS OUT AND HE'D CALL THE NEXT DAY.
I NEVER HEARD FROM HIM AGAIN, AND HIS CELL'S OFF.
TELL ME ABOUT THE MESSAGE.

MESSAGE IN A SMARTPHONE
Springfield, Oregon - USA
One week earlier

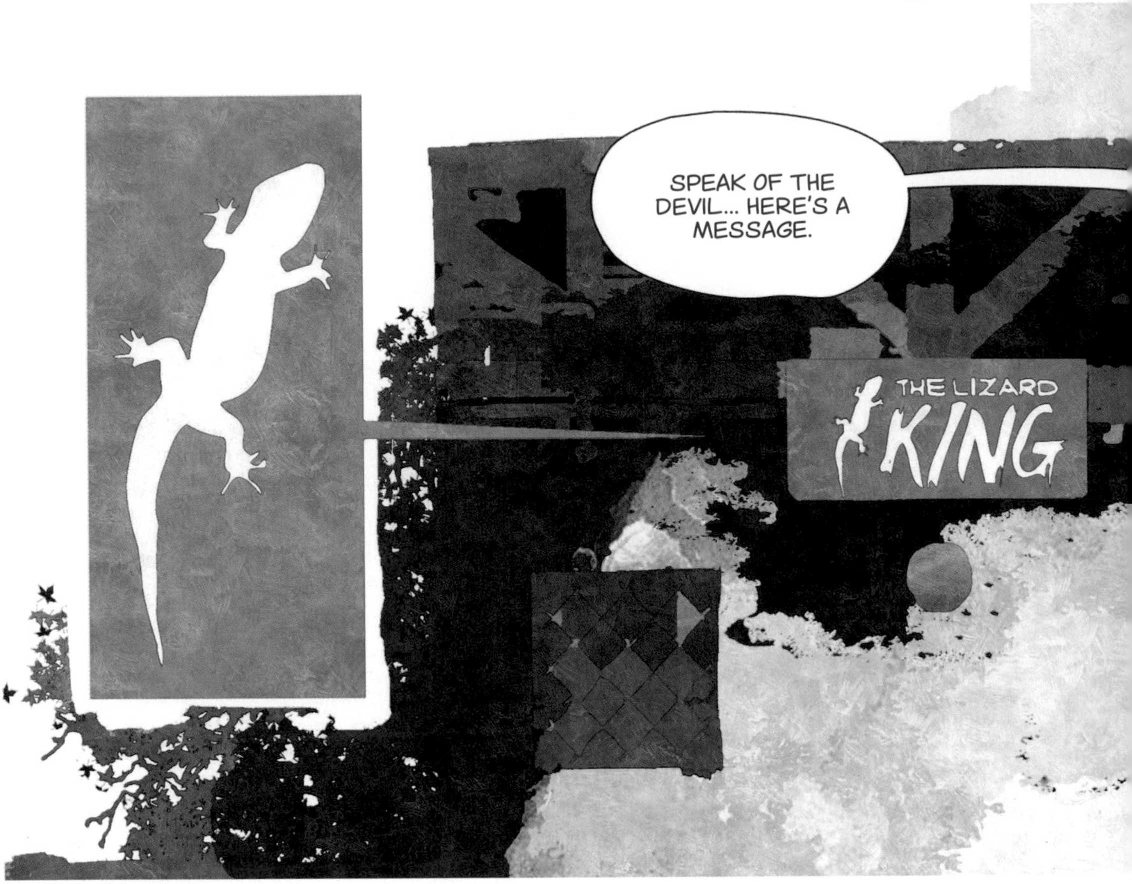
SPEAK OF THE DEVIL... HERE'S A MESSAGE.
THE LIZARD KING

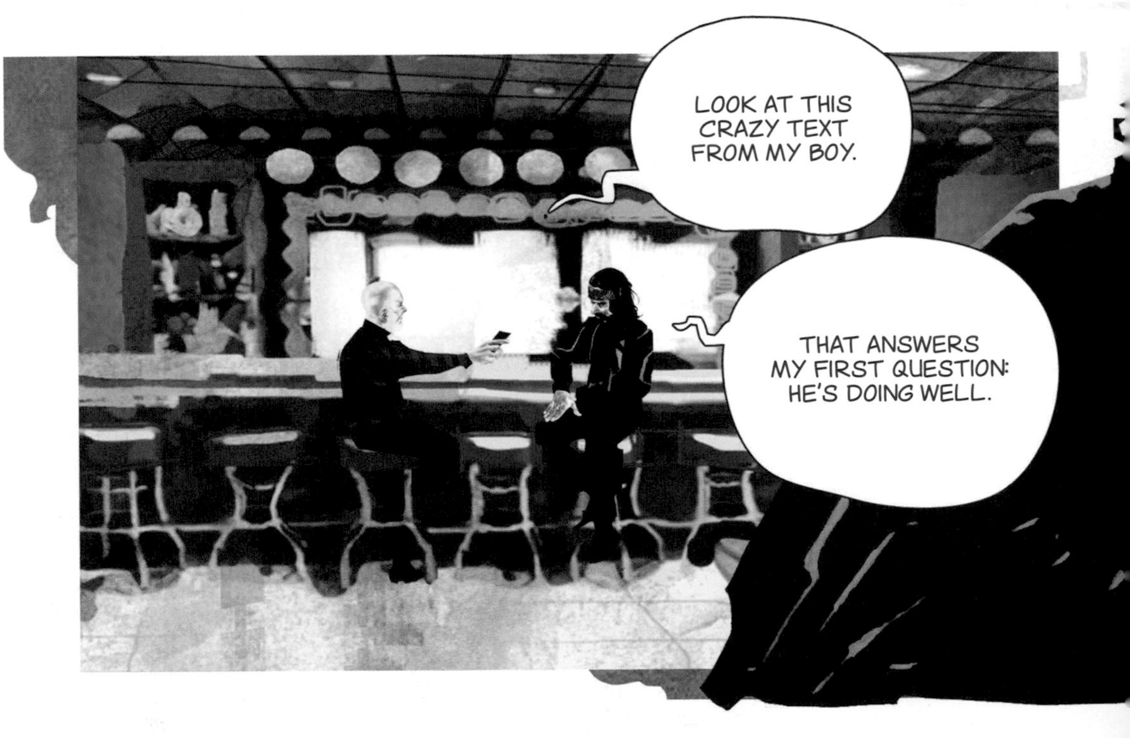
LOOK AT THIS CRAZY TEXT FROM MY BOY.
THAT ANSWERS MY FIRST QUESTION: HE'S DOING WELL.

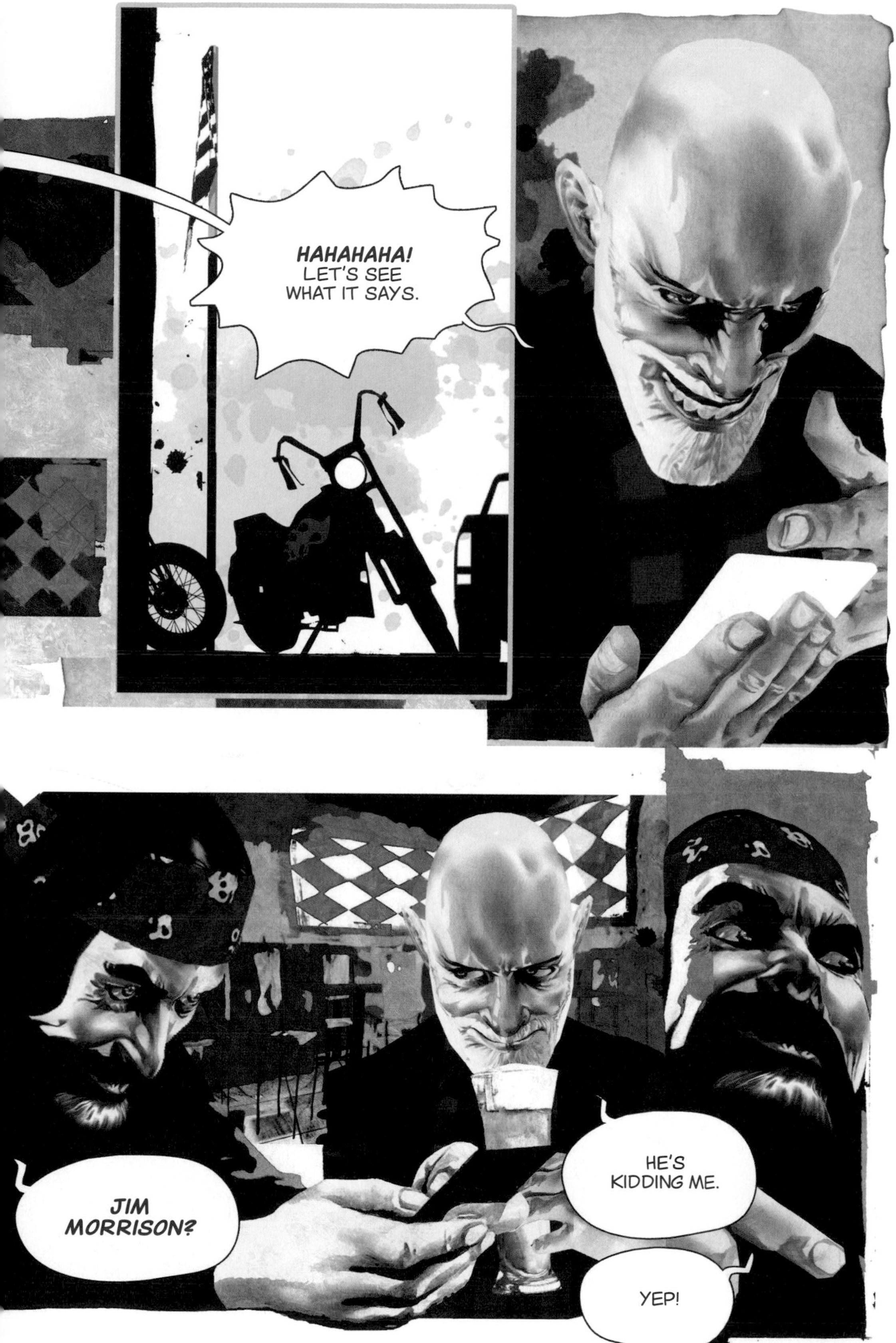
HAHAHAHA! LET'S SEE WHAT IT SAYS.
JIM MORRISON?
HE'S KIDDING ME.
YEP!

HE KNOWS
YOU WELL.

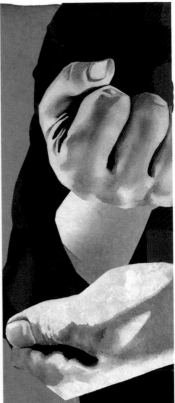

HOW IS HE?

BETTER.
I'M HOPING THIS TRIP WILL
HELP TO DISTRACT HIM.
HIS MOTHER'S DEATH WAS
A HELL OF A BLOW.

BUT IT ALSO
BROUGHT US
CLOSER.

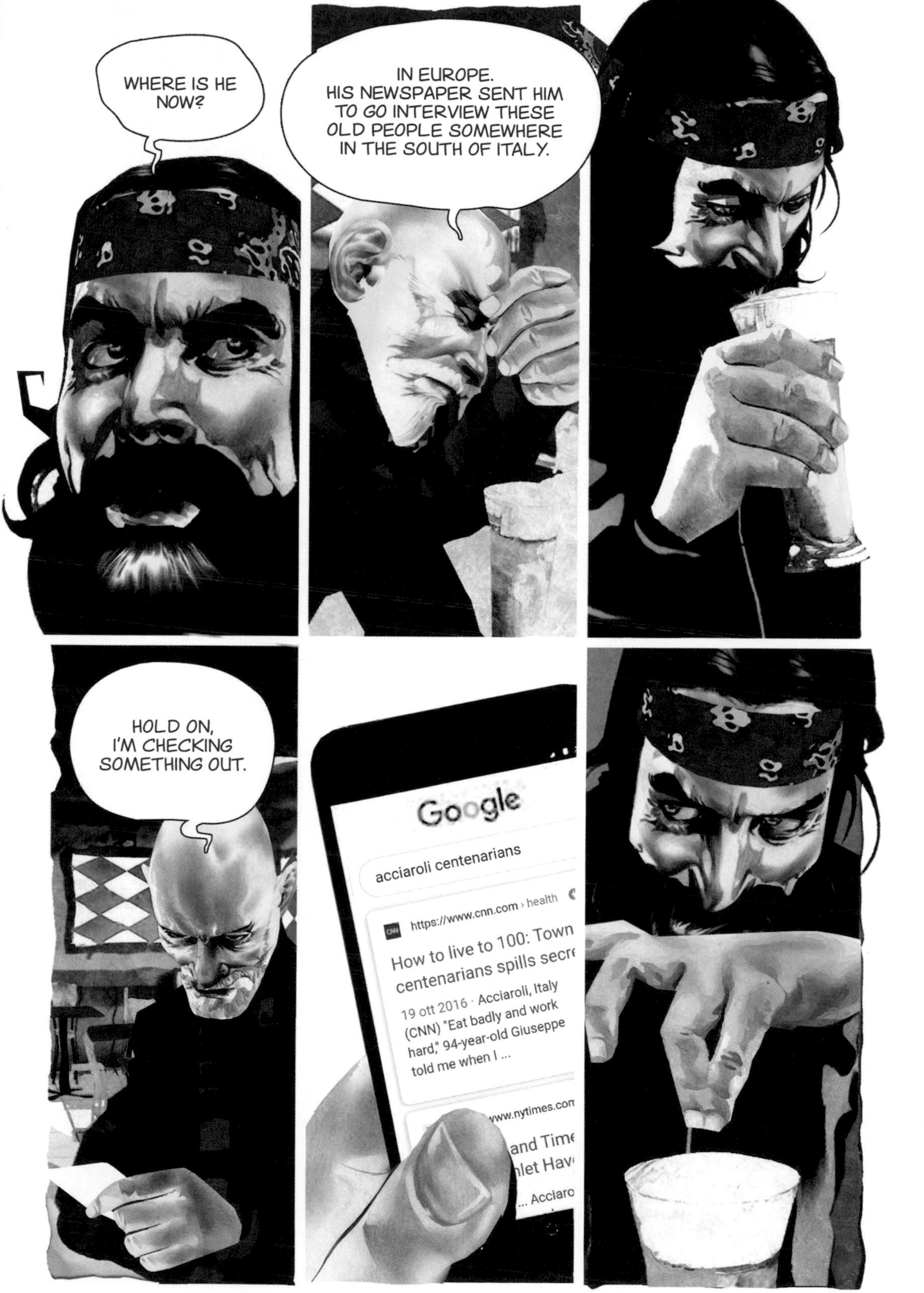
WHERE IS HE NOW?
IN EUROPE. HIS NEWSPAPER SENT HIM TO GO INTERVIEW THESE OLD PEOPLE SOMEWHERE IN THE SOUTH OF ITALY.
HOLD ON, I'M CHECKING SOMETHING OUT.
Google
acciaroli centenarians
https://www.cnn.com › health
How to live to 100: Town
centenarians spills secre
19 ott 2016 · Acciaroli, Italy (CNN) "Eat badly and work hard," 94-year-old Giuseppe told me when I ...
www.nytimes.com

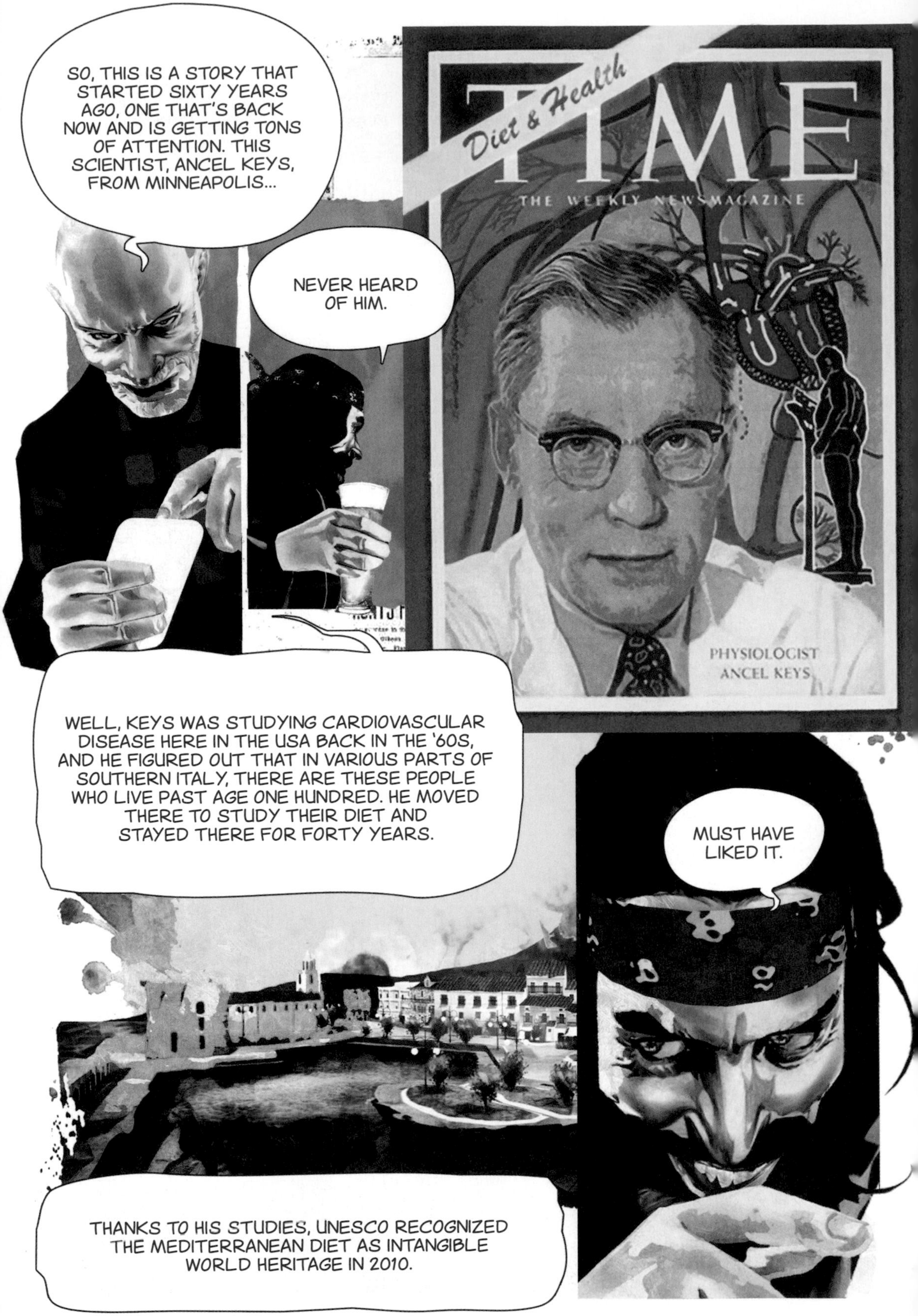
SO, THIS IS A STORY THAT STARTED SIXTY YEARS AGO, ONE THAT'S BACK NOW AND IS GETTING TONS OF ATTENTION. THIS SCIENTIST, ANCEL KEYS, FROM MINNEAPOLIS...
NEVER HEARD OF HIM.
Diet & Health
TIME
THE WEEKLY NEWSMAGAZINE
PHYSIOLOGIST ANCEL KEYS
WELL, KEYS WAS STUDYING CARDIOVASCULAR DISEASE HERE IN THE USA BACK IN THE '60S, AND HE FIGURED OUT THAT IN VARIOUS PARTS OF SOUTHERN ITALY, THERE ARE THESE PEOPLE WHO LIVE PAST AGE ONE HUNDRED. HE MOVED THERE TO STUDY THEIR DIET AND STAYED THERE FOR FORTY YEARS.
MUST HAVE LIKED IT.
THANKS TO HIS STUDIES, UNESCO RECOGNIZED THE MEDITERRANEAN DIET AS INTANGIBLE WORLD HERITAGE IN 2010.

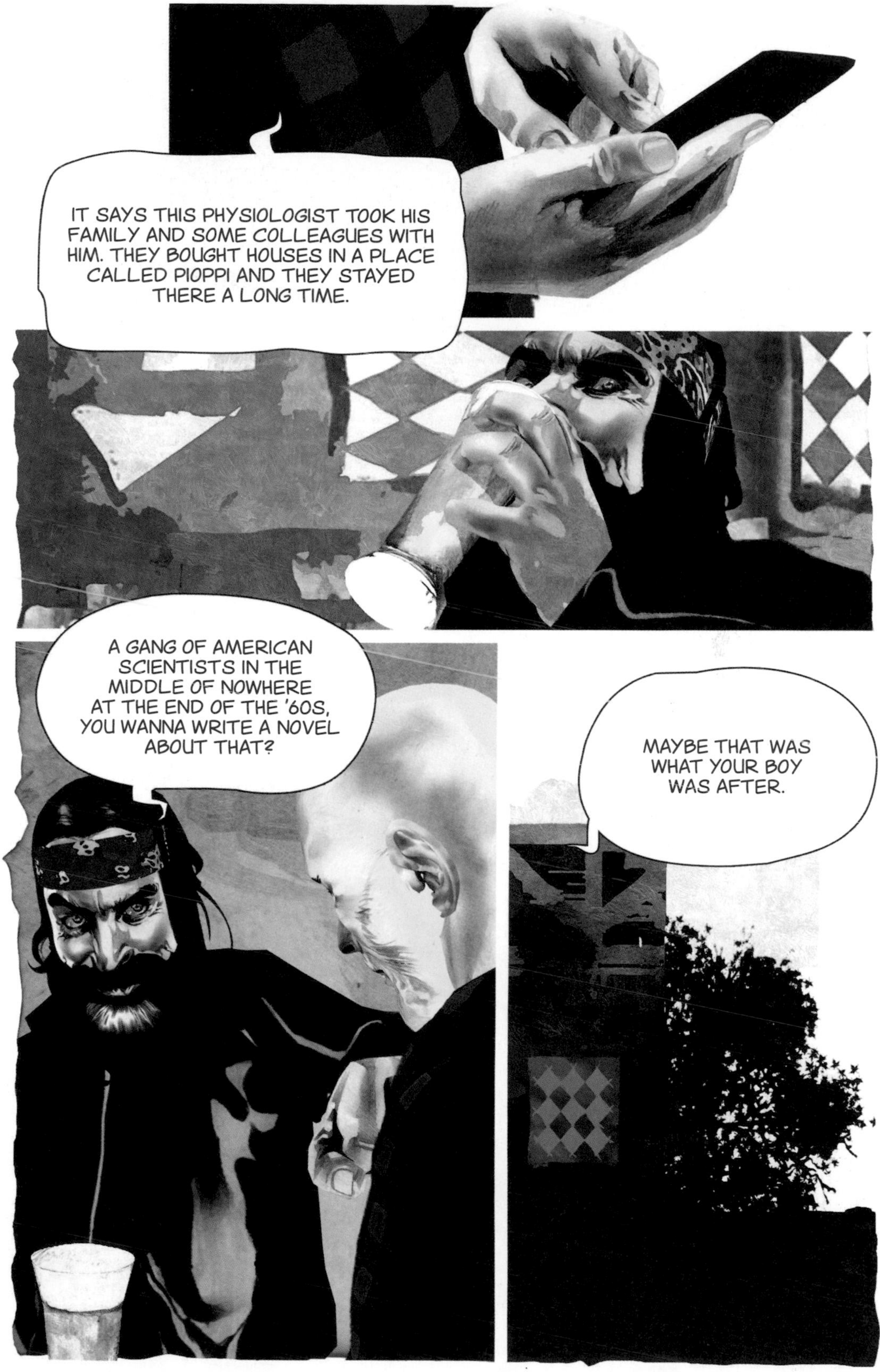
IT SAYS THIS PHYSIOLOGIST TOOK HIS FAMILY AND SOME COLLEAGUES WITH HIM. THEY BOUGHT HOUSES IN A PLACE CALLED PIOPPI AND THEY STAYED THERE A LONG TIME.
A GANG OF AMERICAN SCIENTISTS IN THE MIDDLE OF NOWHERE AT THE END OF THE '60S, YOU WANNA WRITE A NOVEL ABOUT THAT?
MAYBE THAT WAS WHAT YOUR BOY WAS AFTER.

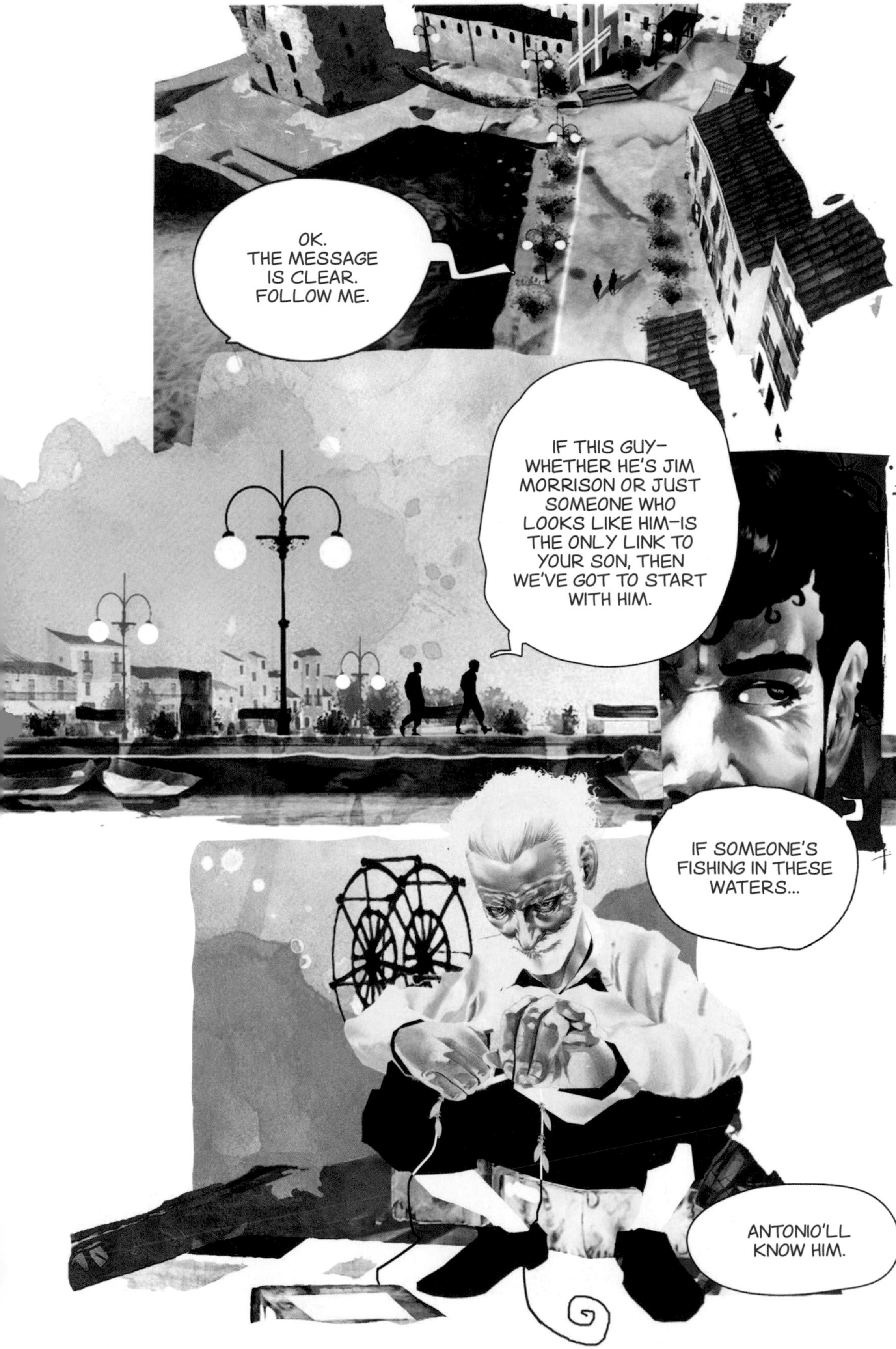
OK. THE MESSAGE IS CLEAR. FOLLOW ME.
IF THIS GUY— WHETHER HE'S JIM MORRISON OR JUST SOMEONE WHO LOOKS LIKE HIM—IS THE ONLY LINK TO YOUR SON, THEN WE'VE GOT TO START WITH HIM.
IF SOMEONE'S FISHING IN THESE WATERS...
ANTONIO'LL KNOW HIM.

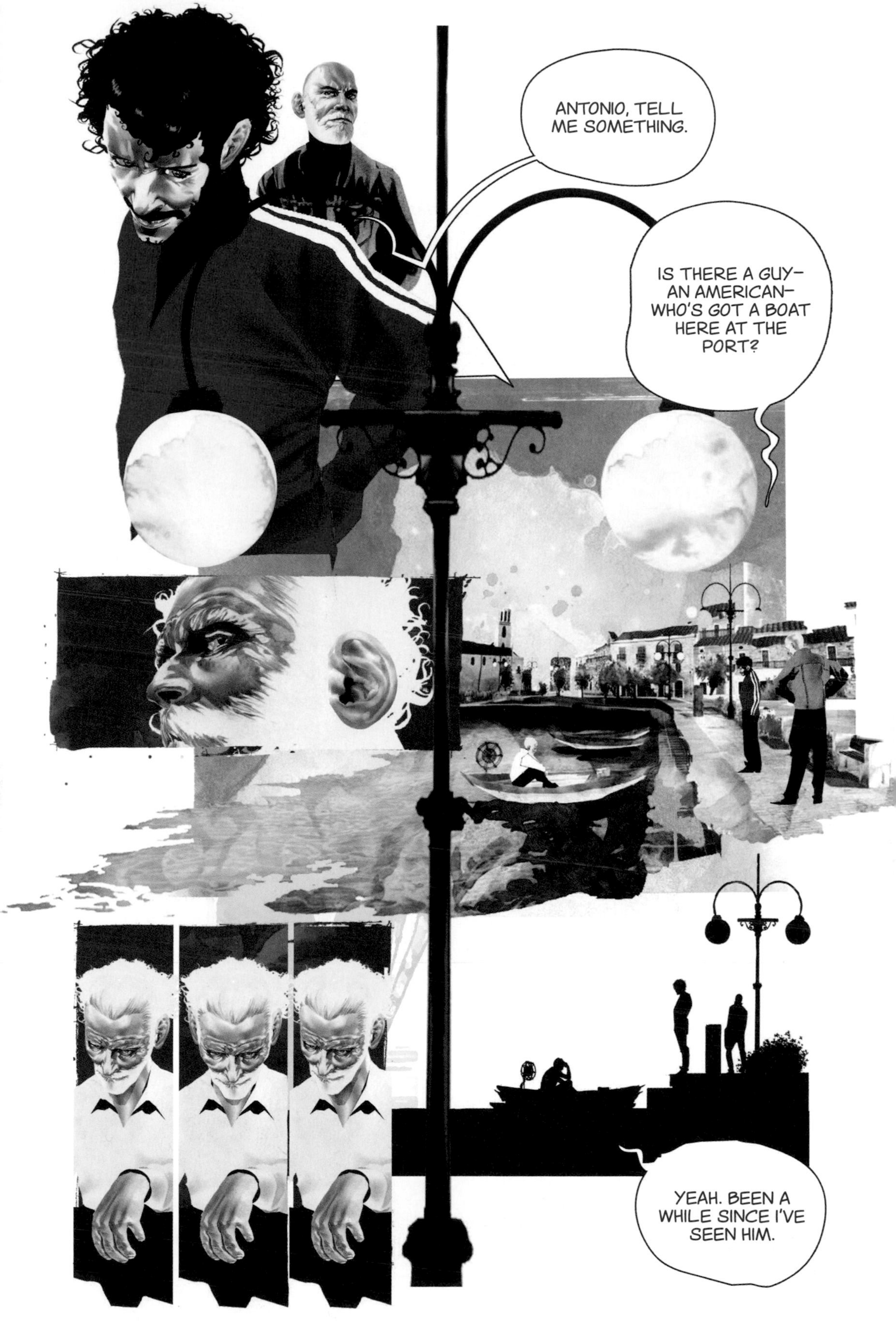
ANTONIO, TELL ME SOMETHING.
IS THERE A GUY— AN AMERICAN— WHO'S GOT A BOAT HERE AT THE PORT?
YEAH. BEEN A WHILE SINCE I'VE SEEN HIM.

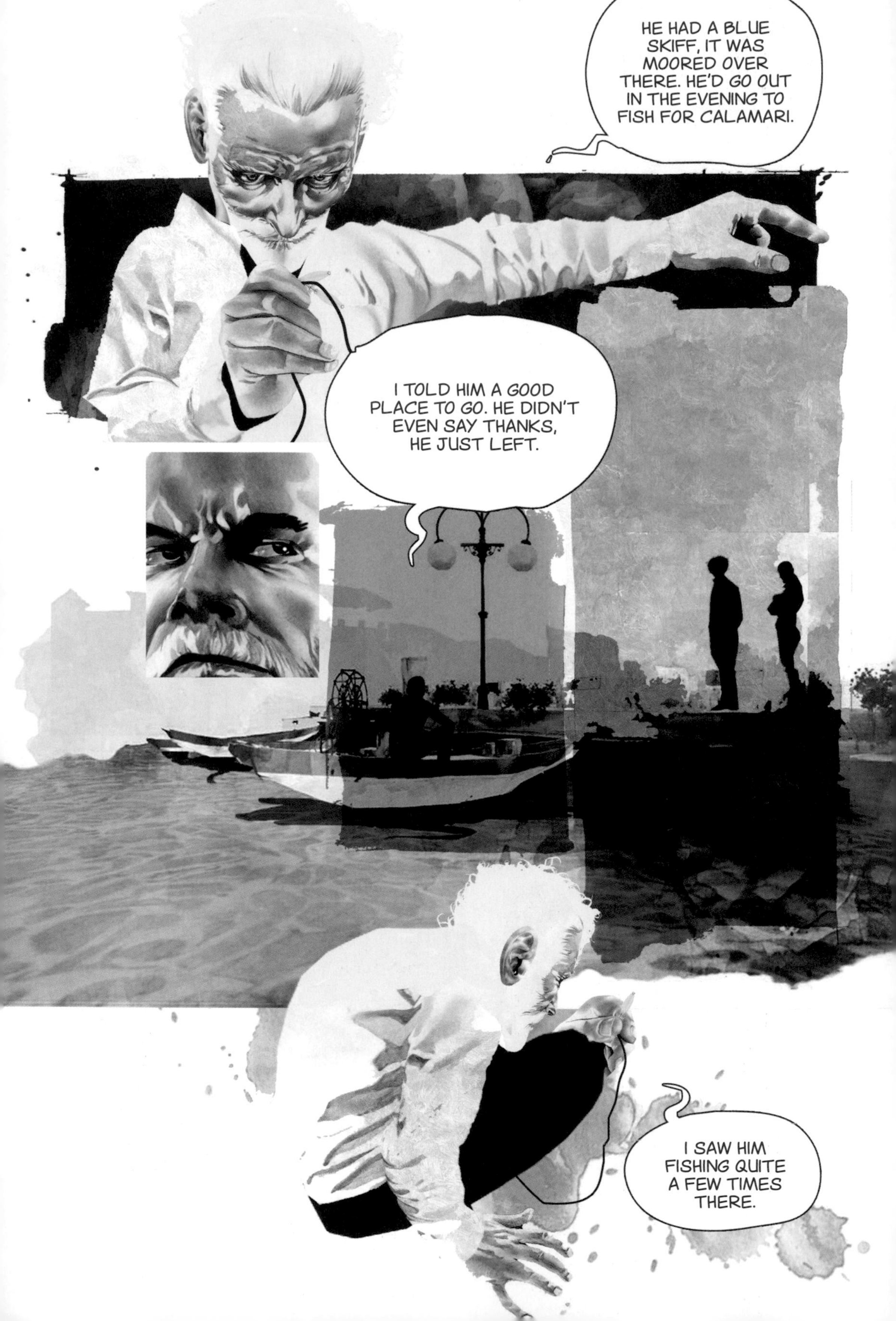
HE HAD A BLUE SKIFF, IT WAS MOORED OVER THERE. HE'D GO OUT IN THE EVENING TO FISH FOR CALAMARI.
I TOLD HIM A GOOD PLACE TO GO. HE DIDN'T EVEN SAY THANKS, HE JUST LEFT.
I SAW HIM FISHING QUITE A FEW TIMES THERE.

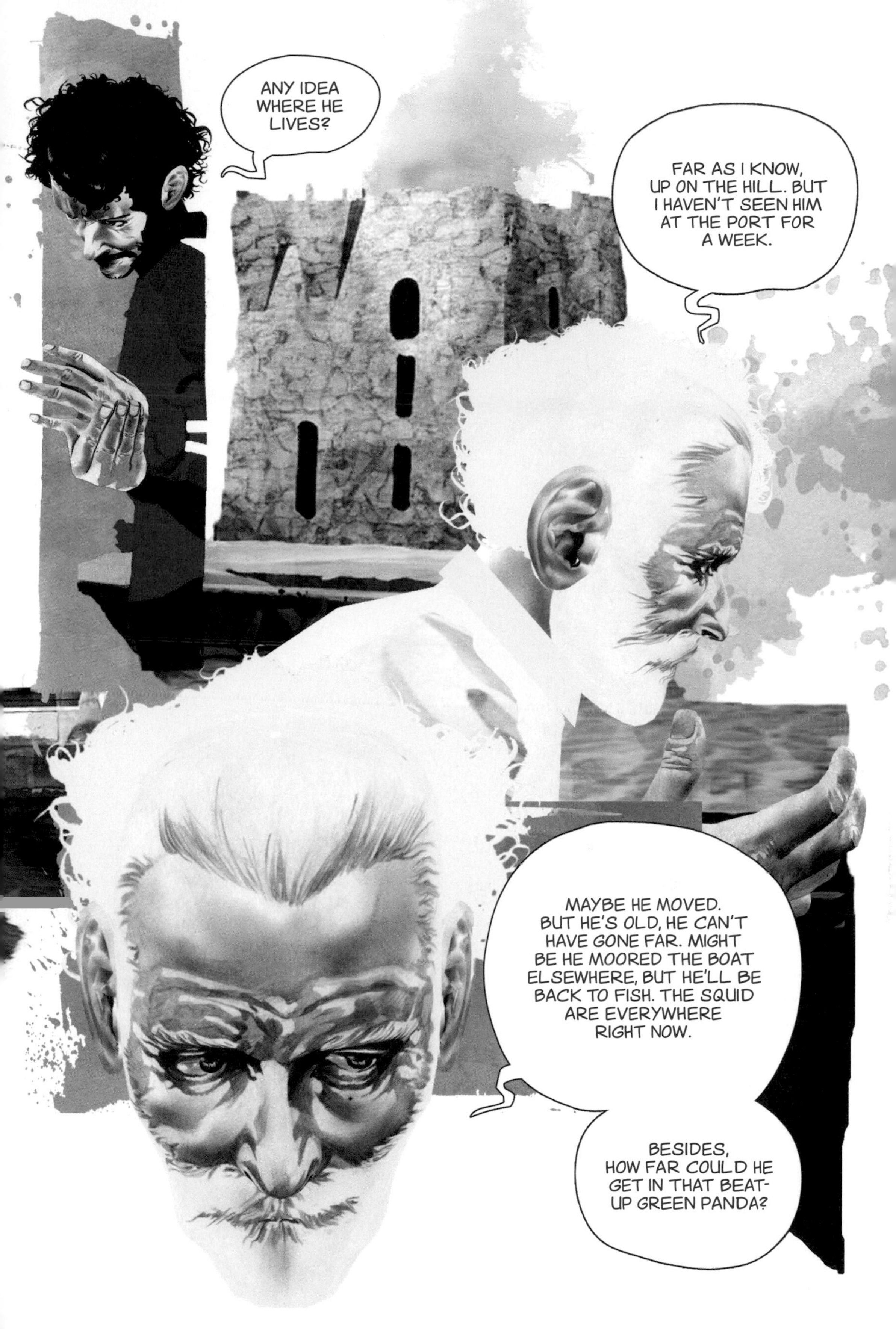
ANY IDEA WHERE HE LIVES?
FAR AS I KNOW, UP ON THE HILL. BUT I HAVEN'T SEEN HIM AT THE PORT FOR A WEEK.
MAYBE HE MOVED. BUT HE'S OLD, HE CAN'T HAVE GONE FAR. MIGHT BE HE MOORED THE BOAT ELSEWHERE, BUT HE'LL BE BACK TO FISH. THE SQUID ARE EVERYWHERE RIGHT NOW.
BESIDES, HOW FAR COULD HE GET IN THAT BEAT-UP GREEN PANDA?

GREEN CARS
LOOK BETTER IN THE SHADE
One week earlier

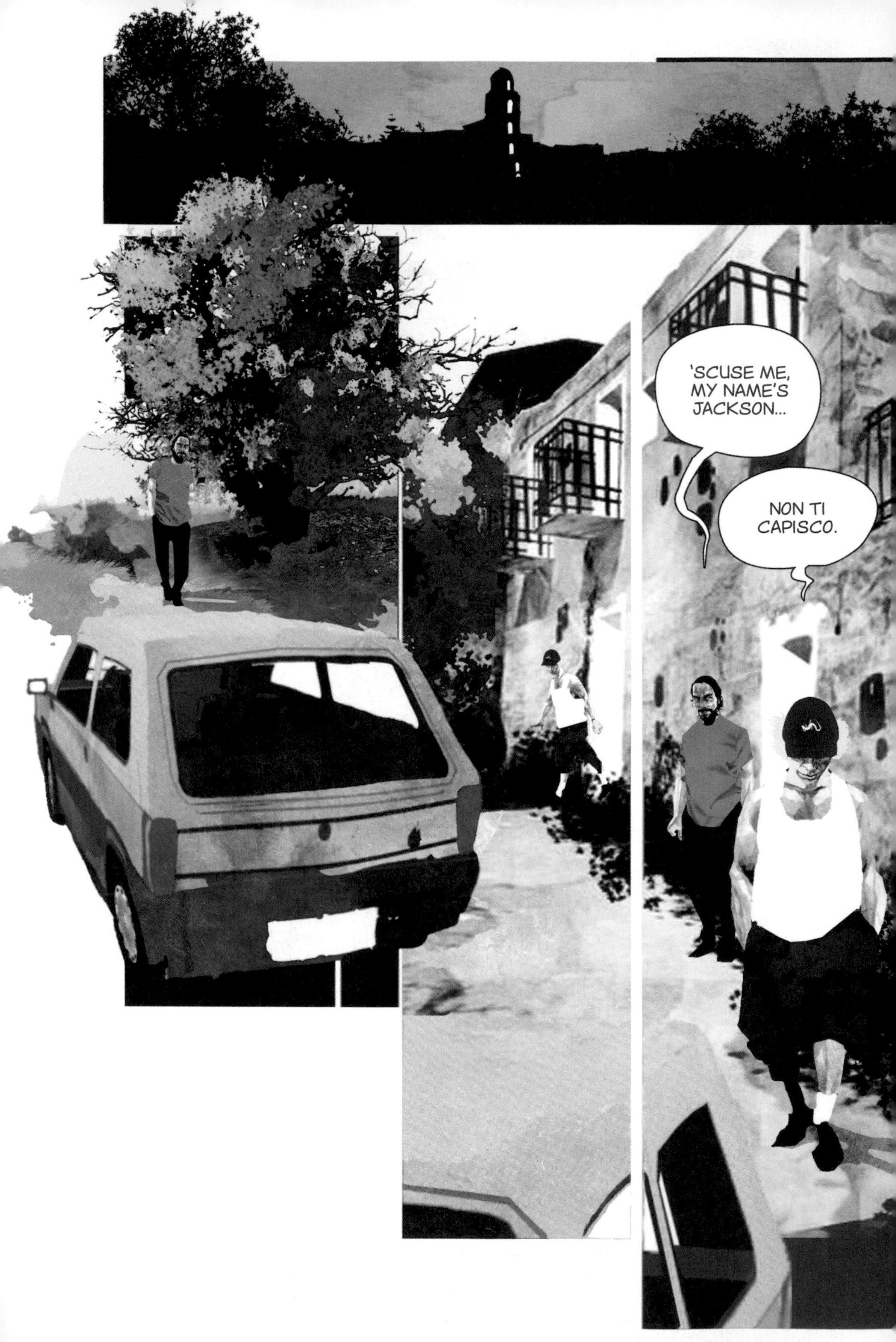
'SCUSE ME, MY NAME'S JACKSON...
NON TI CAPISCO.

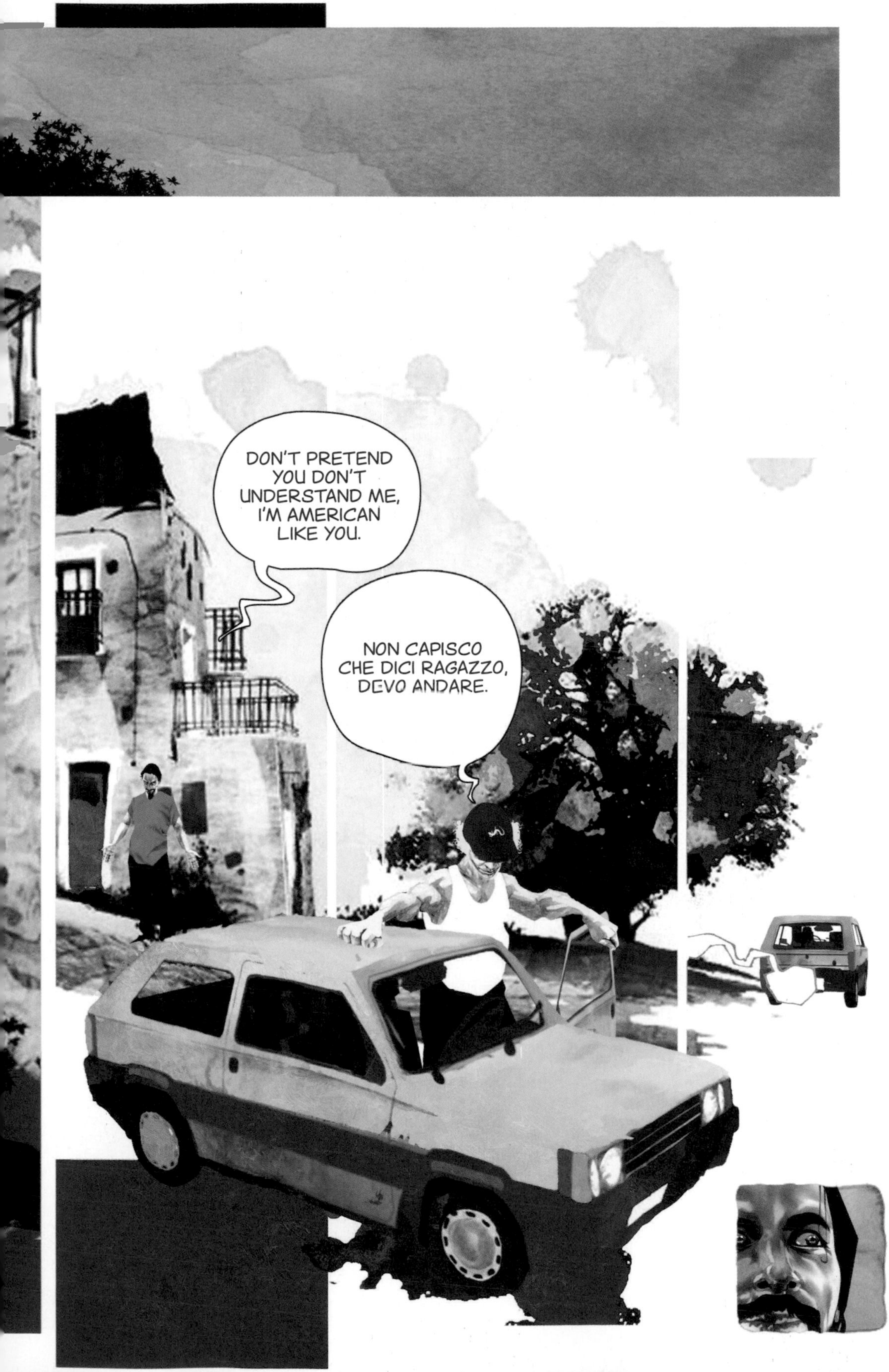
DON'T PRETEND YOU DON'T UNDERSTAND ME, I'M AMERICAN LIKE YOU.
NON CAPISCO CHE DICI RAGAZZO, DEVO ANDARE.

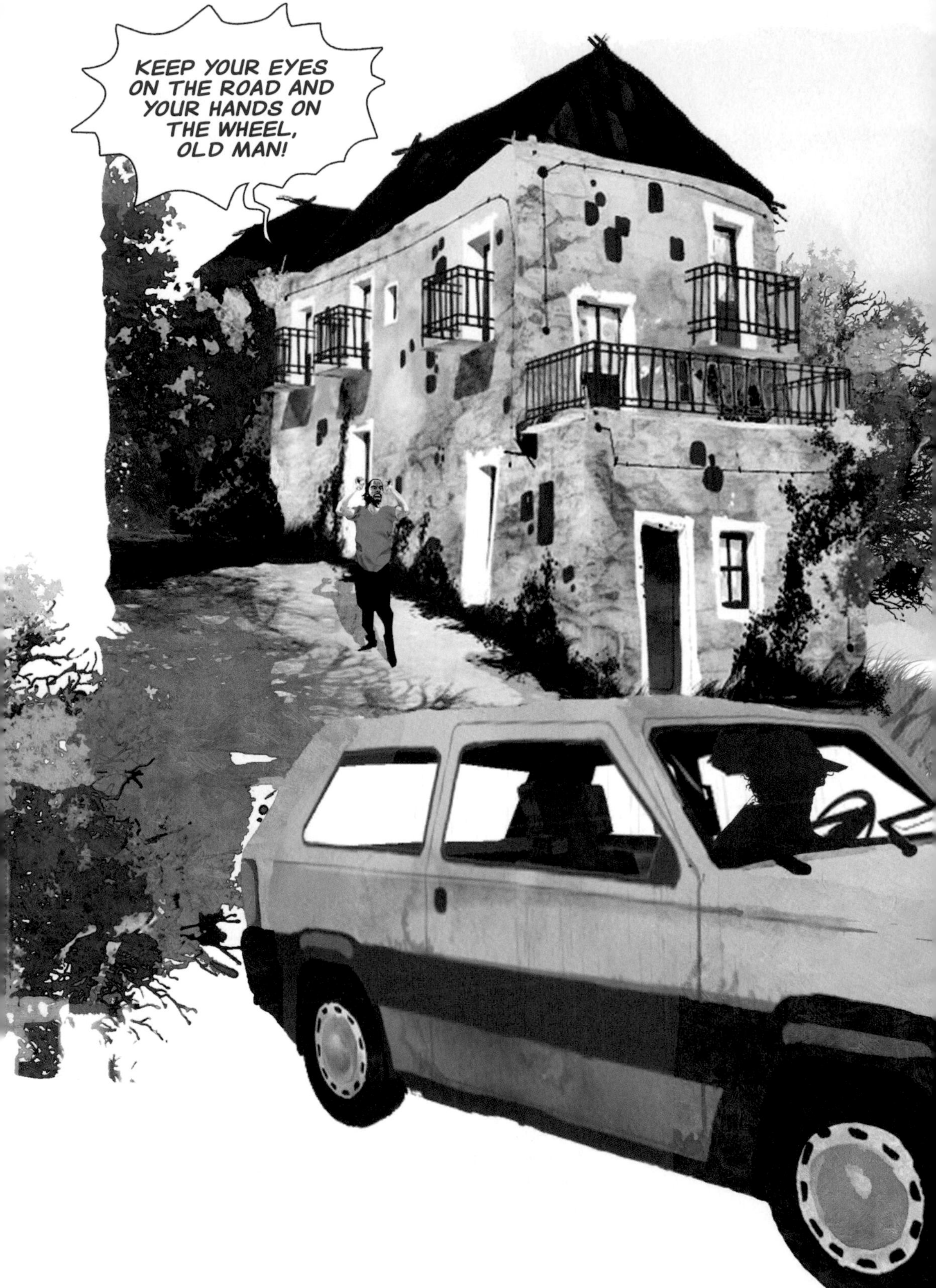
KEEP YOUR EYES ON THE ROAD AND YOUR HANDS ON THE WHEEL, OLD MAN!

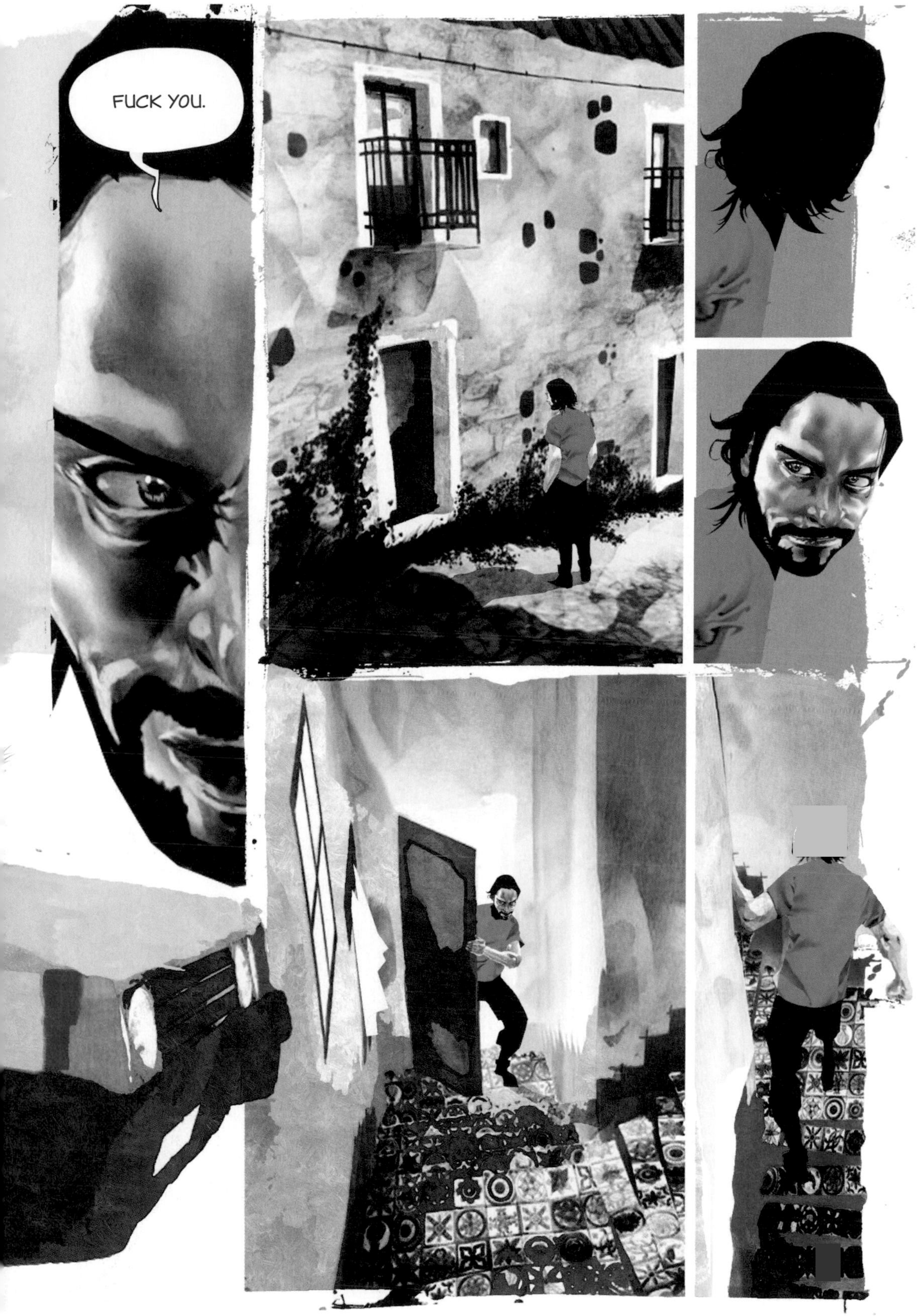
FUCK YOU.

EDIPO

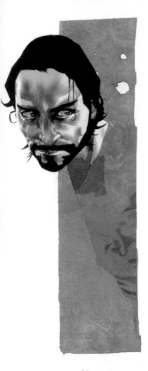

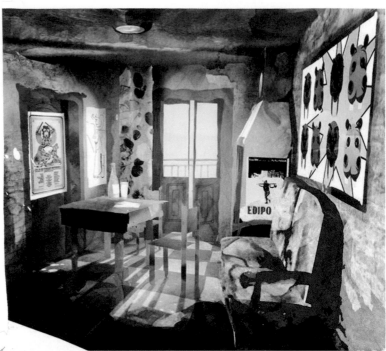

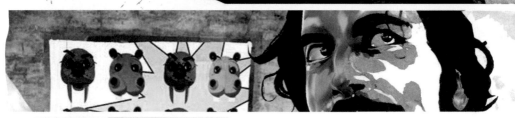

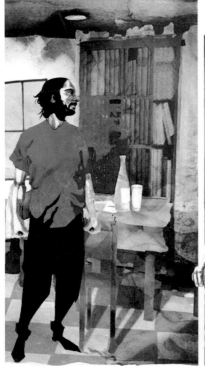

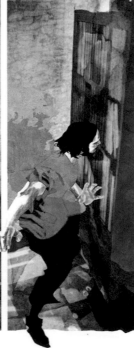

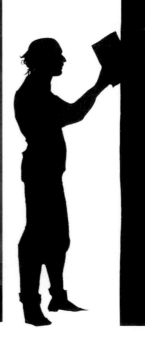

ALDOUS HUXLEY
2
The Doors of Perception
Heaven and Hell
WILLIAM BURROUGHS
THE NAKED LUNCH
Rimbaud
Complete Works, Selected Letters
Translation, Introduction and Notes by
The Complete Poetry & Prose of William Blake
David V. Erdman
Harold Bloom
FRIEDRICH NIETZSCHE
THE BIRTH OF TRAGEDY
&
GENEALOGY OF MORALS
A CONEY ISLAND OF THE MIND
POEMS BY LAWRENCE FERLINGHETTI
MON, NOVEMBER

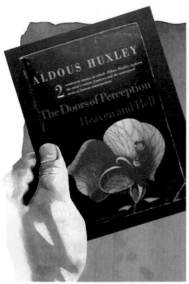

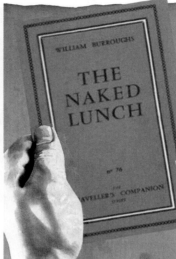

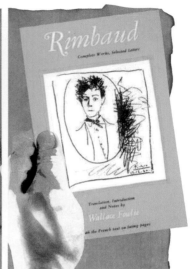

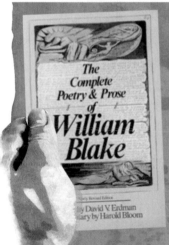

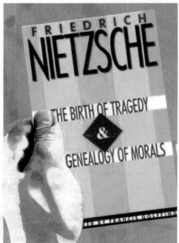

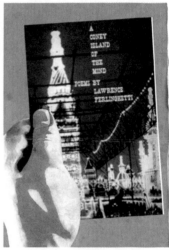

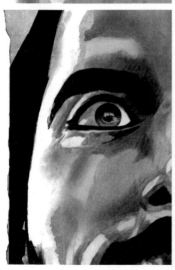

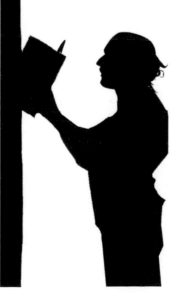

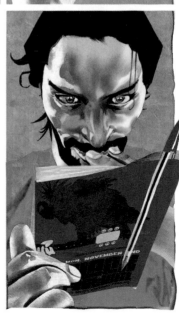

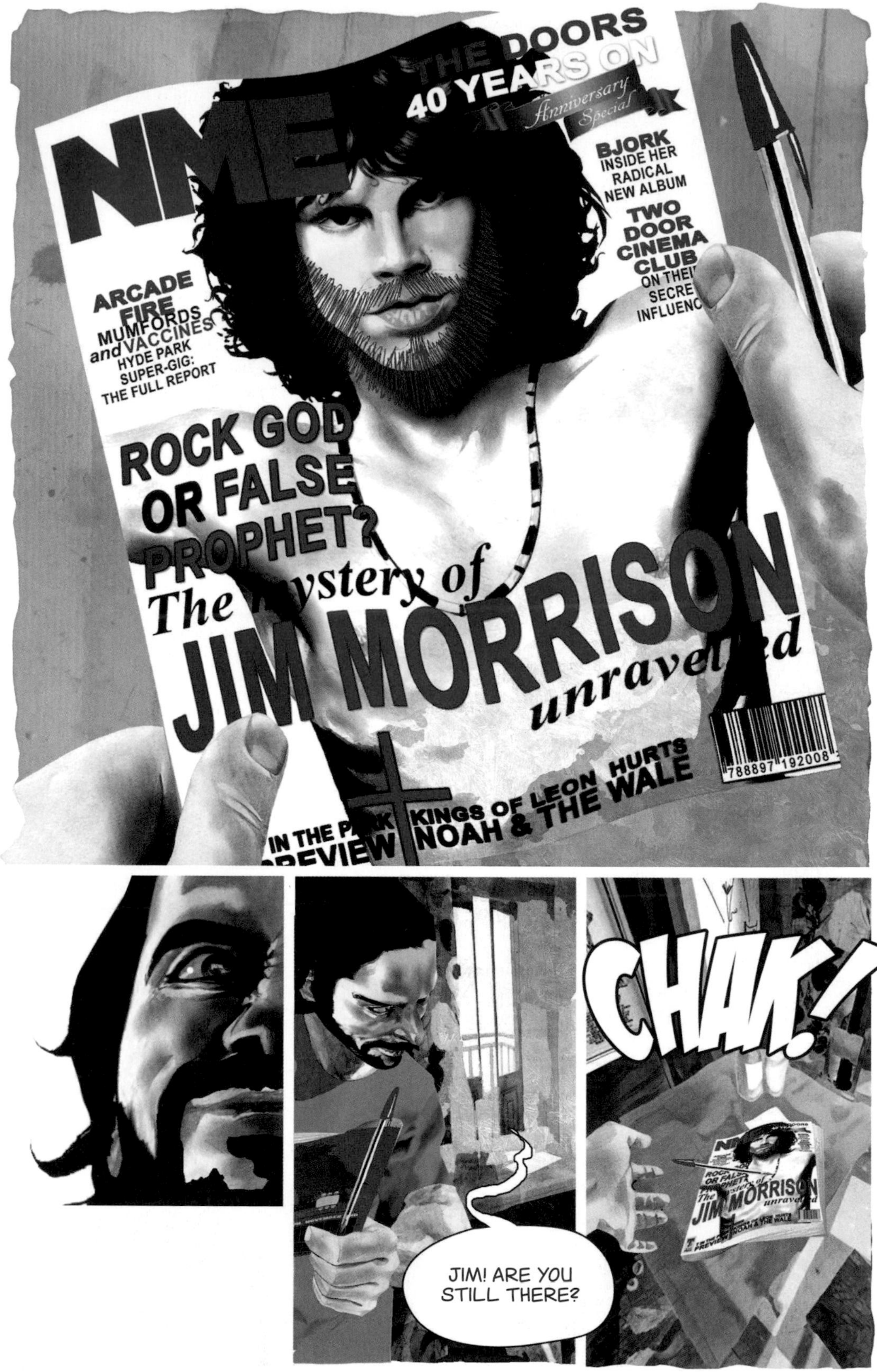

THE DOORS
40 YEARS ON
Anniversary Special
NME
BJORK
INSIDE HER
RADICAL
NEW ALBUM
TWO
DOOR
CINEMA
CLUB
ARCADE
FIRE
MUMFORDS
and VACCINES
HYDE PARK
SUPER-GIG:
THE FULL REPORT
ROCK GOD
OR FALSE
PROPHET?
The Mystery of
JIM MORRISON
unravelled
KINGS OF LEON HURTS
IN THE PARK
PREVIEW
NOAH & THE WALE
788897 192008
CHAK!
JIM! ARE YOU
STILL THERE?

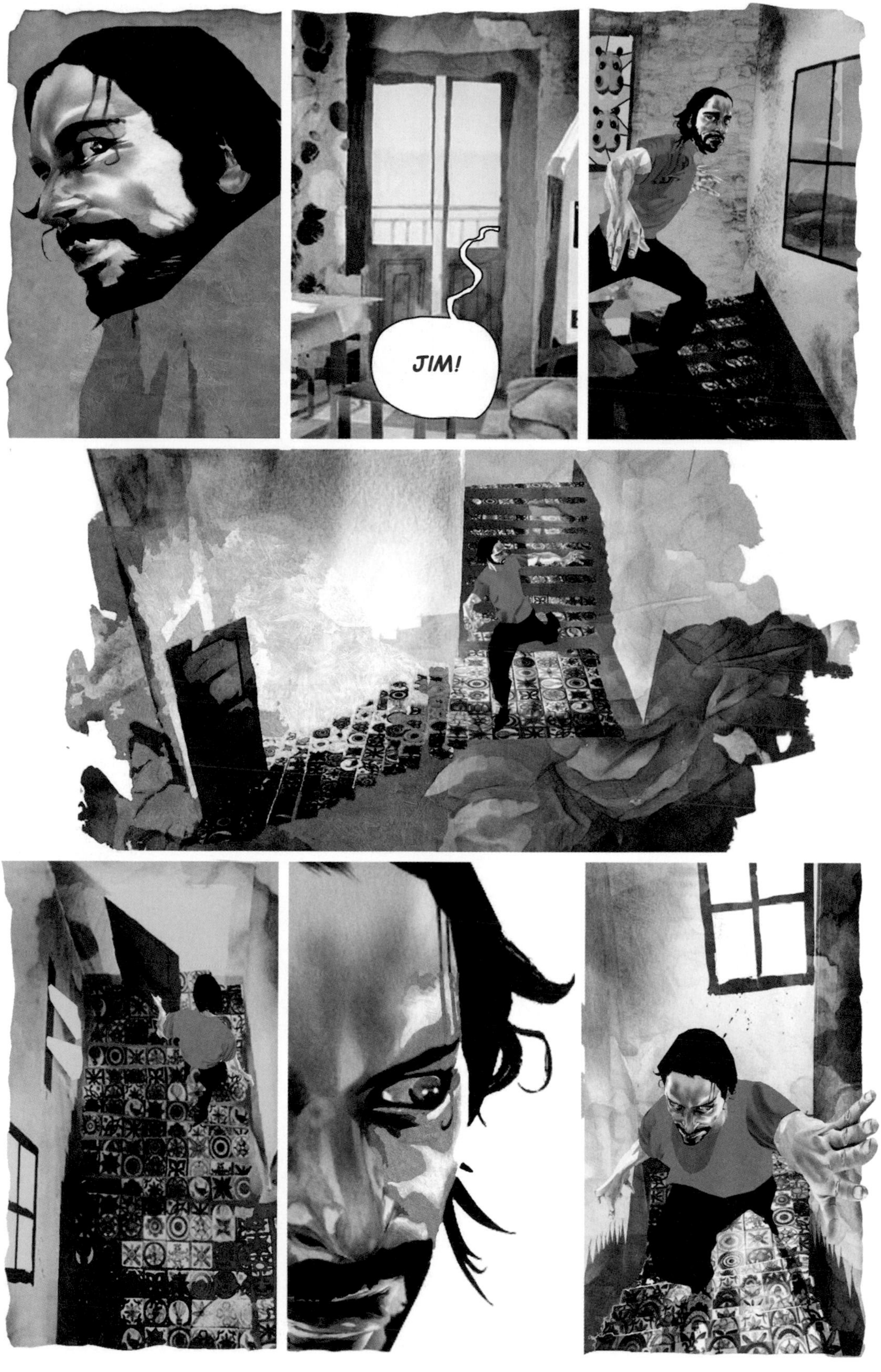
JIM!

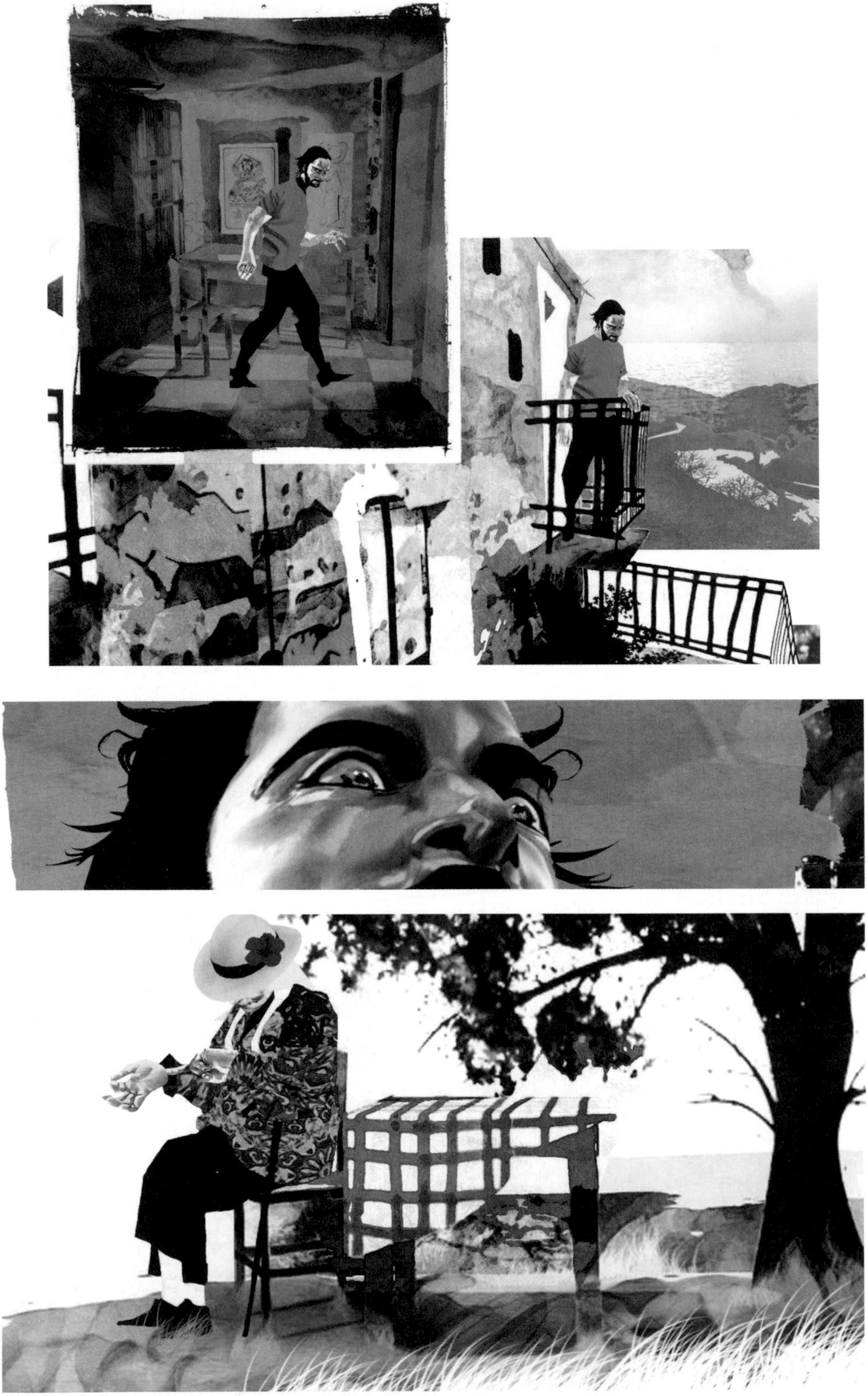

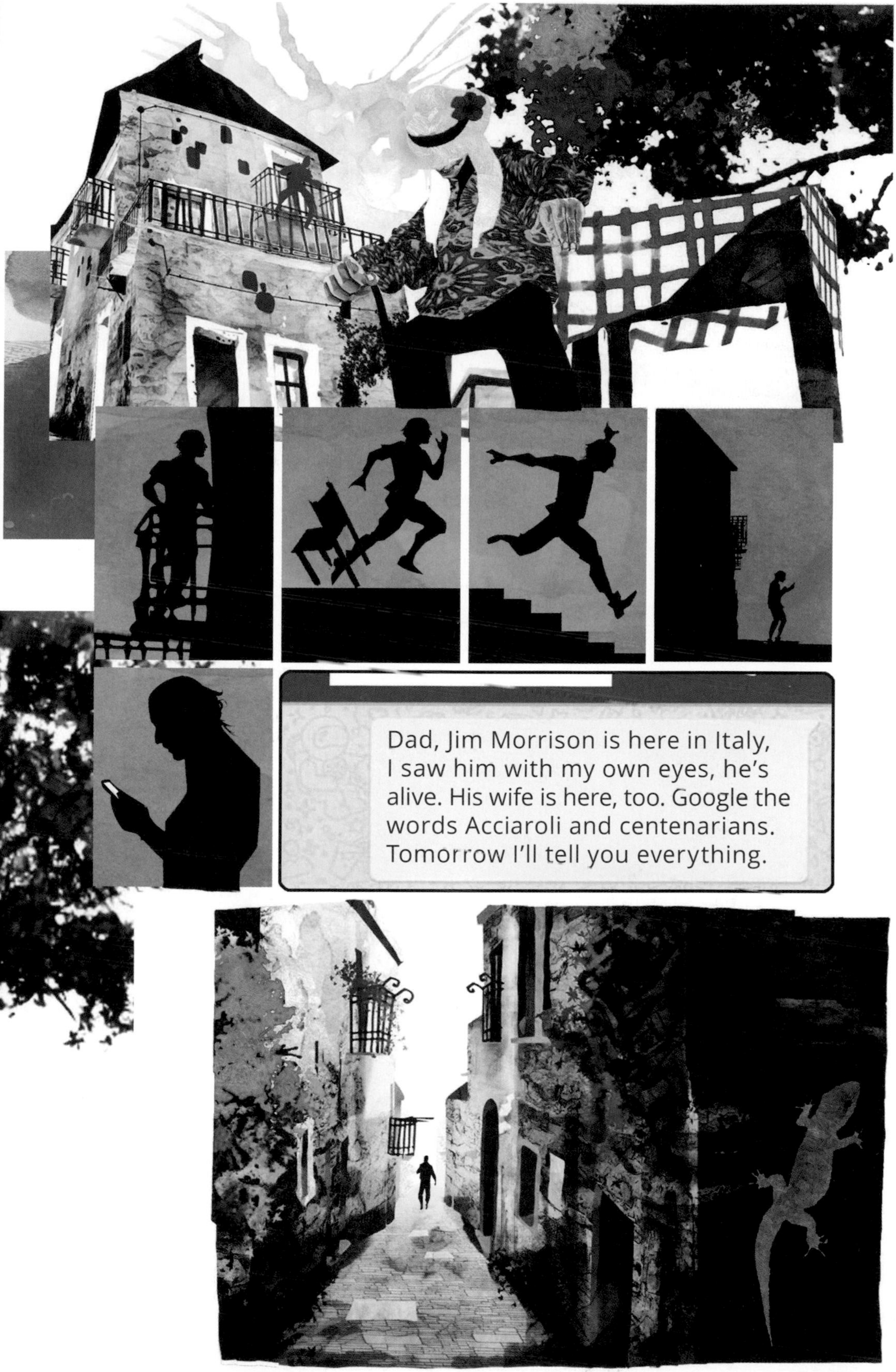
Dad, Jim Morrison is here in Italy,
I saw him with my own eyes, he's
alive. His wife is here, too. Google the
words Acciaroli and centenarians.
Tomorrow I'll tell you everything.

WHERE THE SEAS HAVE NO NAME
Jax, where are you now?

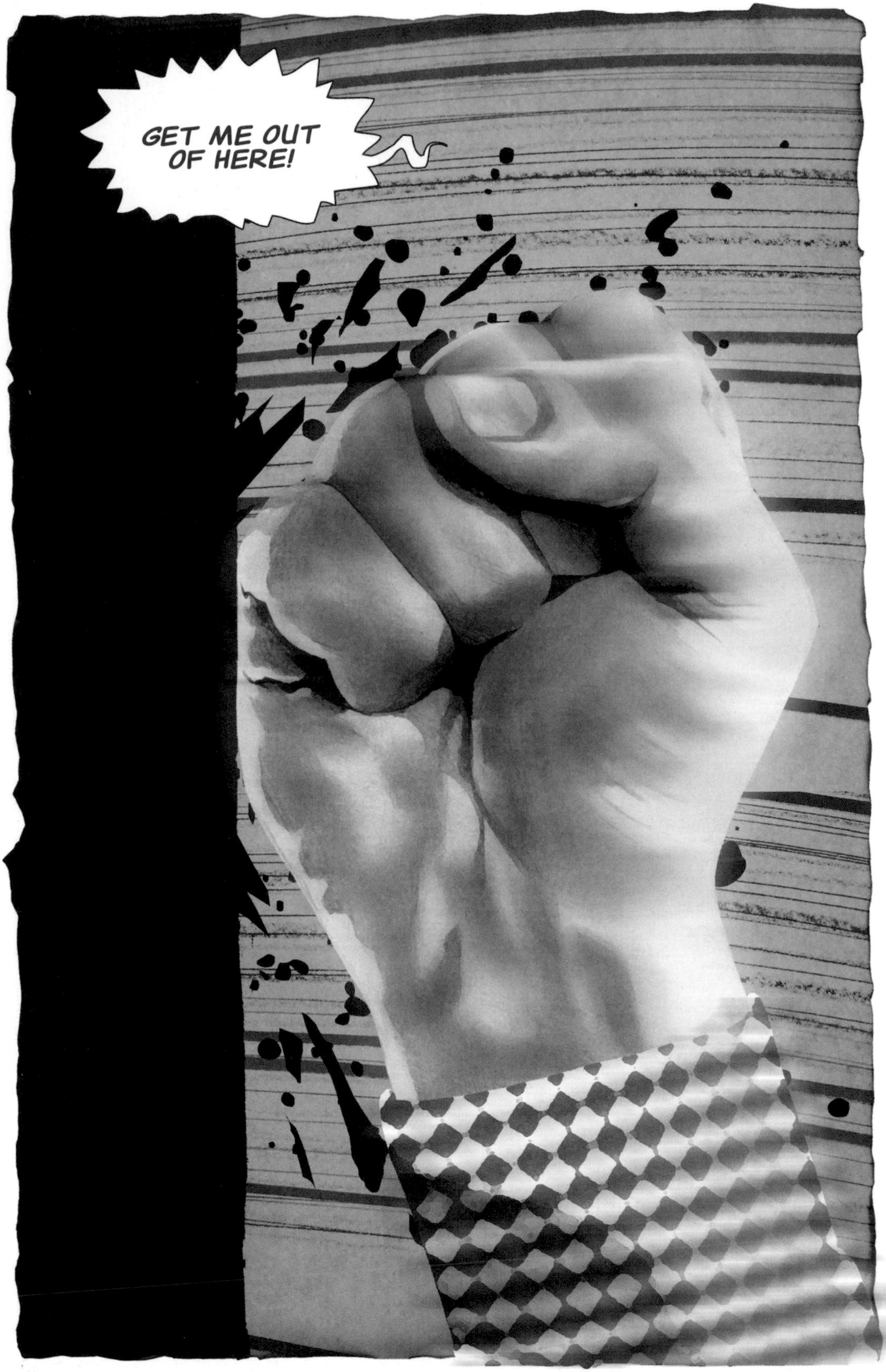
GET ME OUT OF HERE!

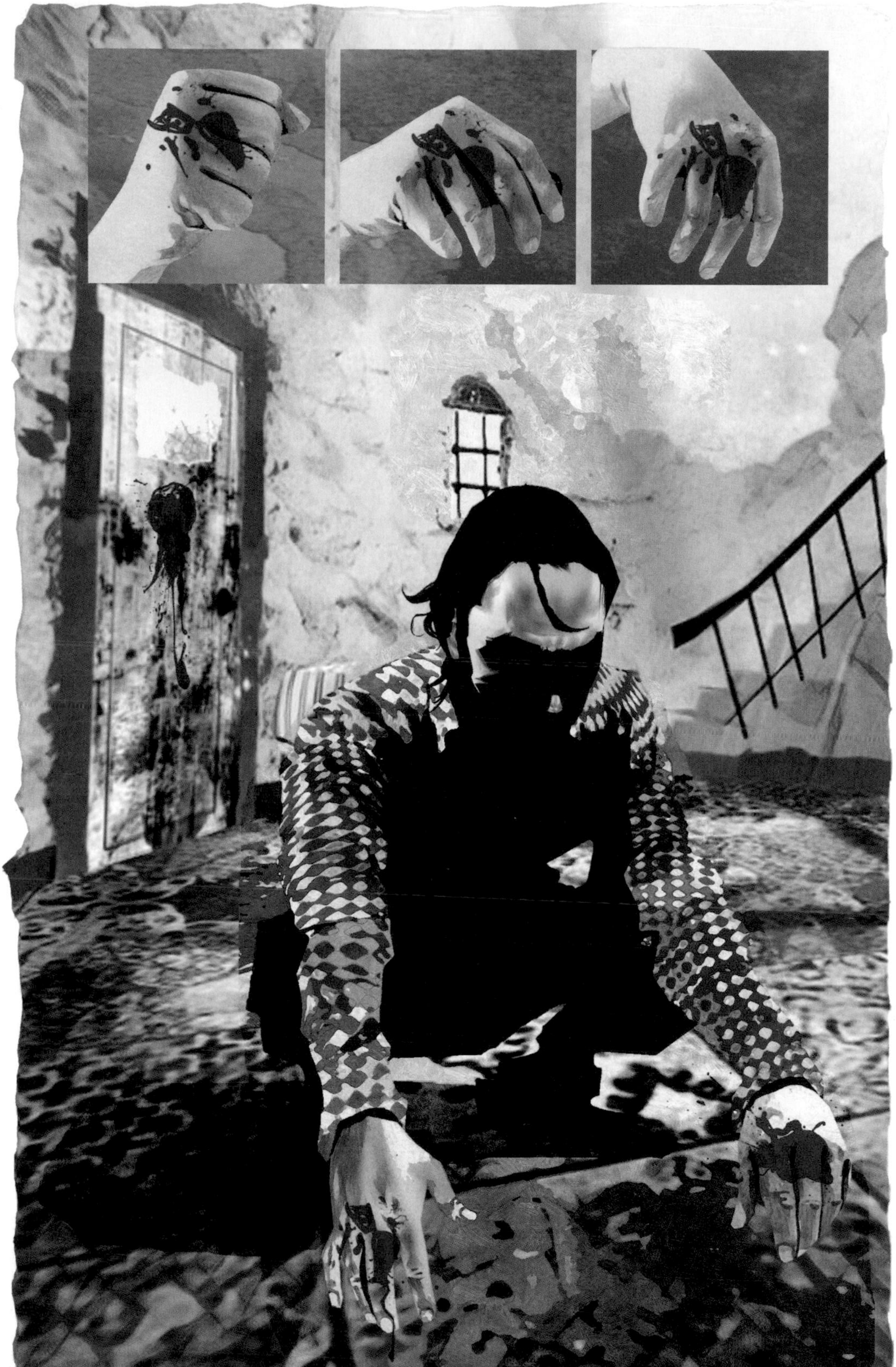

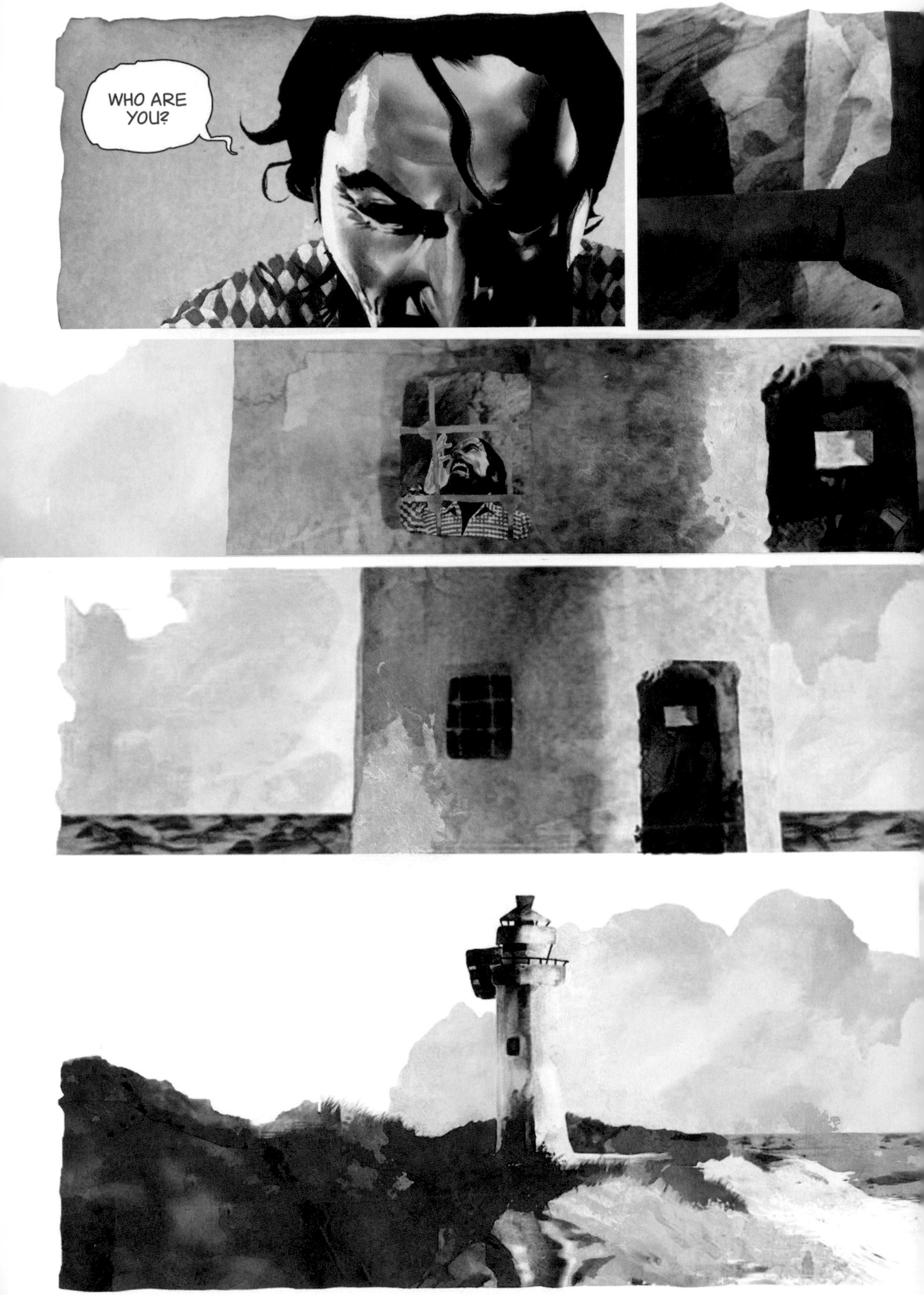
WHO ARE YOU?

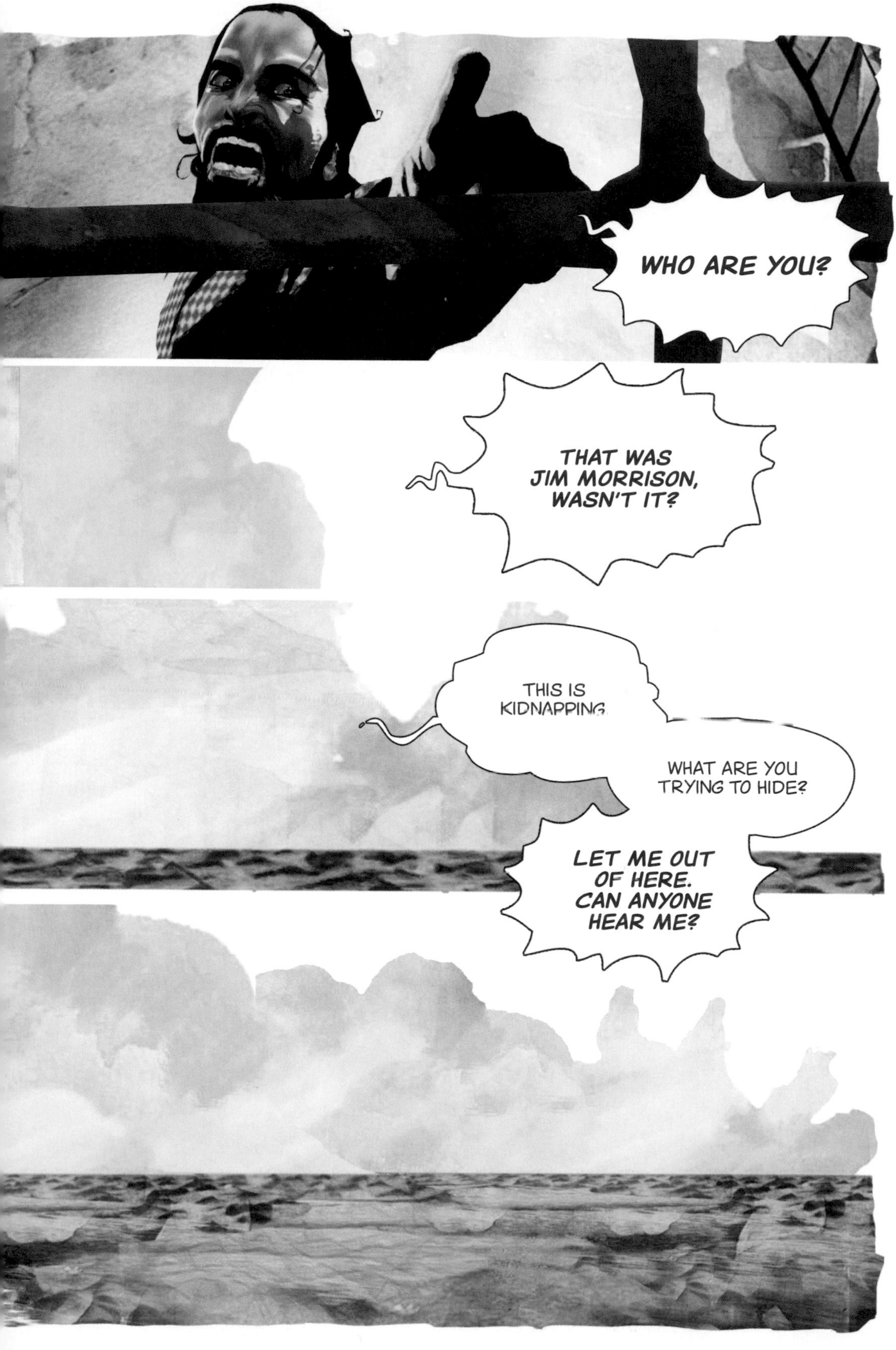
WHO ARE YOU?
THAT WAS JIM MORRISON, WASN'T IT?
THIS IS KIDNAPPING.
WHAT ARE YOU TRYING TO HIDE?
LET ME OUT OF HERE. CAN ANYONE HEAR ME?

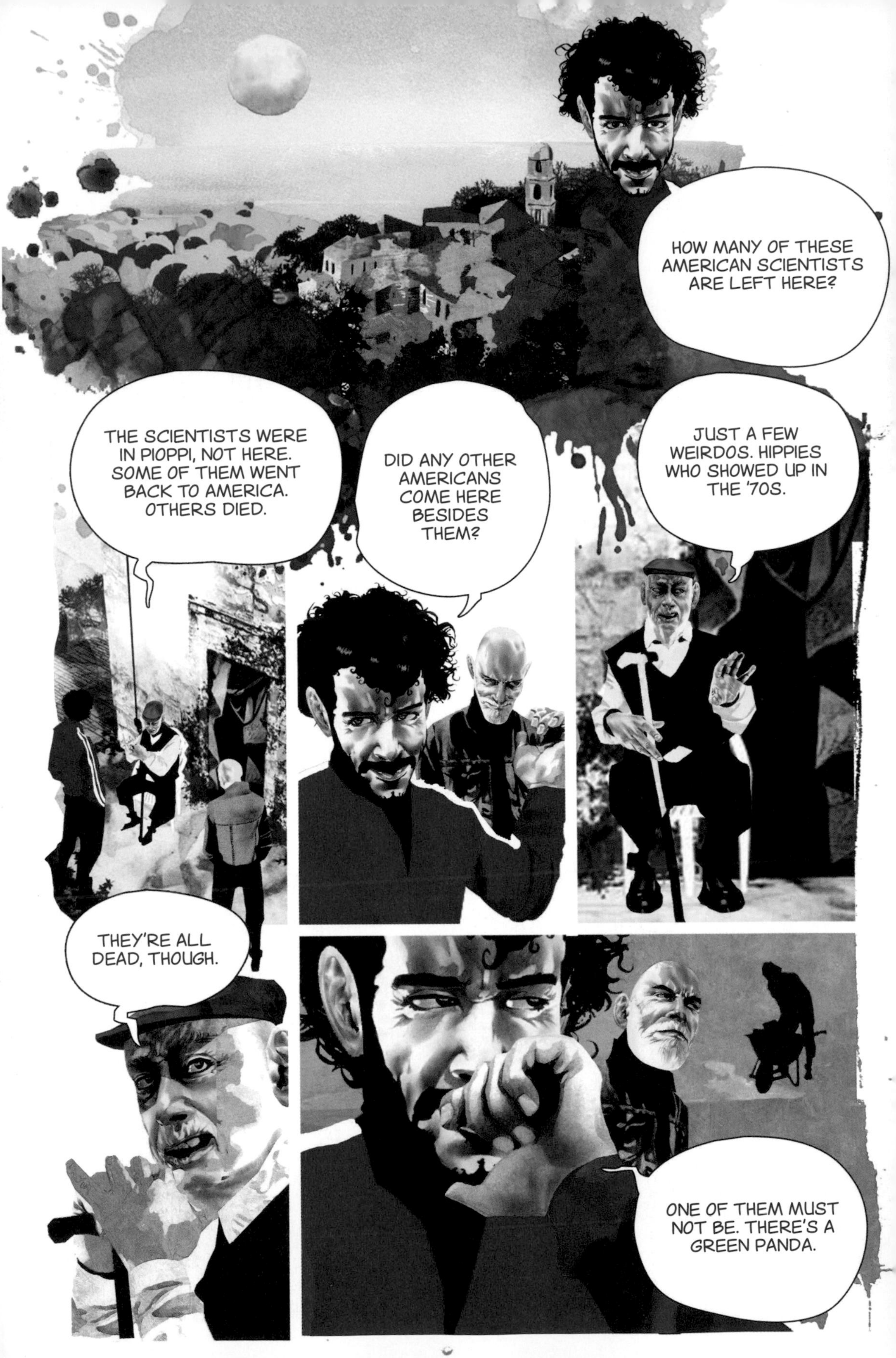
HOW MANY OF THESE AMERICAN SCIENTISTS ARE LEFT HERE?
THE SCIENTISTS WERE IN PIOPPI, NOT HERE. SOME OF THEM WENT BACK TO AMERICA. OTHERS DIED.
DID ANY OTHER AMERICANS COME HERE BESIDES THEM?
JUST A FEW WEIRDOS. HIPPIES WHO SHOWED UP IN THE '70S.
THEY'RE ALL DEAD, THOUGH.
ONE OF THEM MUST NOT BE. THERE'S A GREEN PANDA.

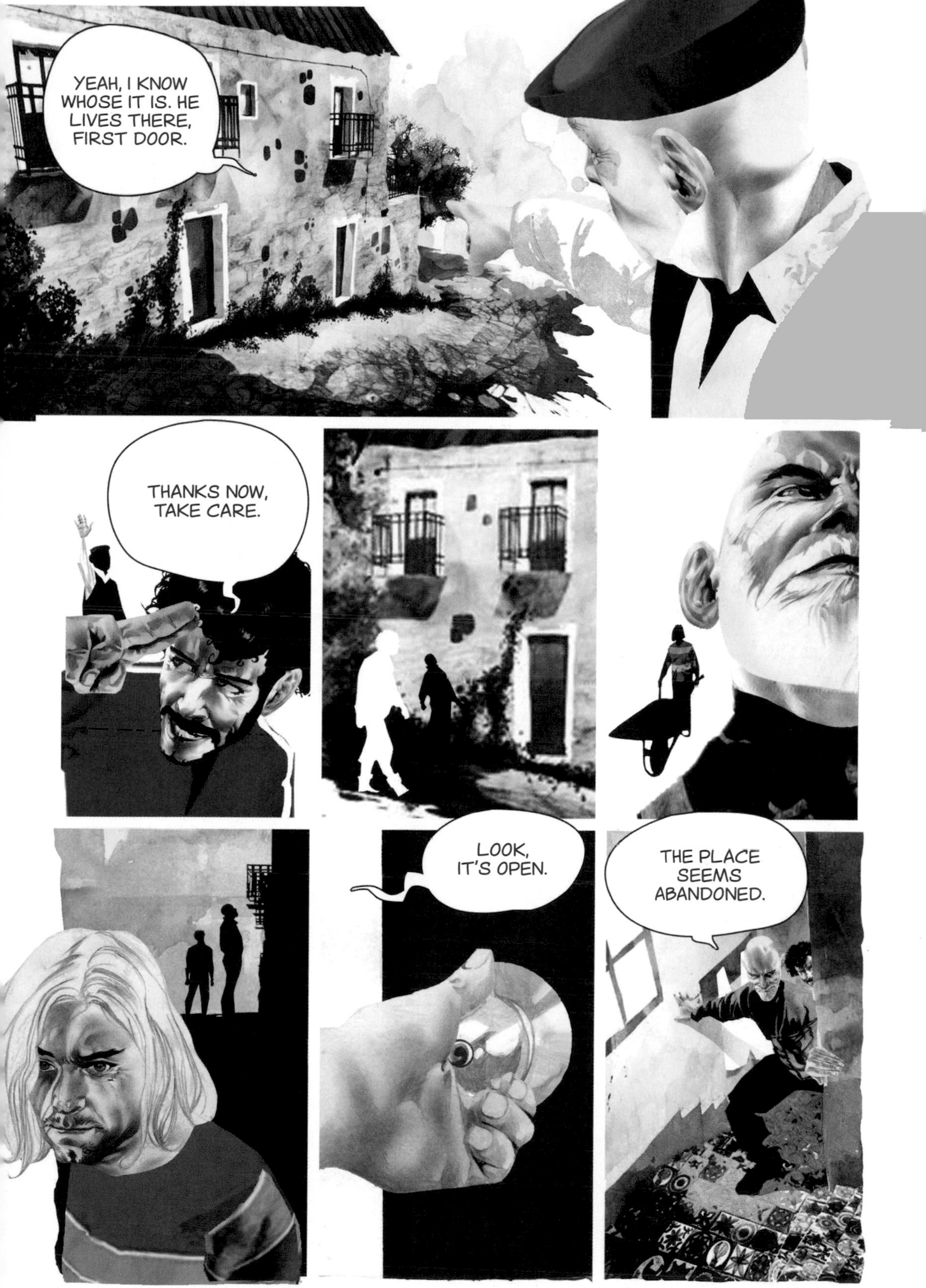
YEAH, I KNOW WHOSE IT IS. HE LIVES THERE, FIRST DOOR.
THANKS NOW, TAKE CARE.
LOOK, IT'S OPEN.
THE PLACE SEEMS ABANDONED.

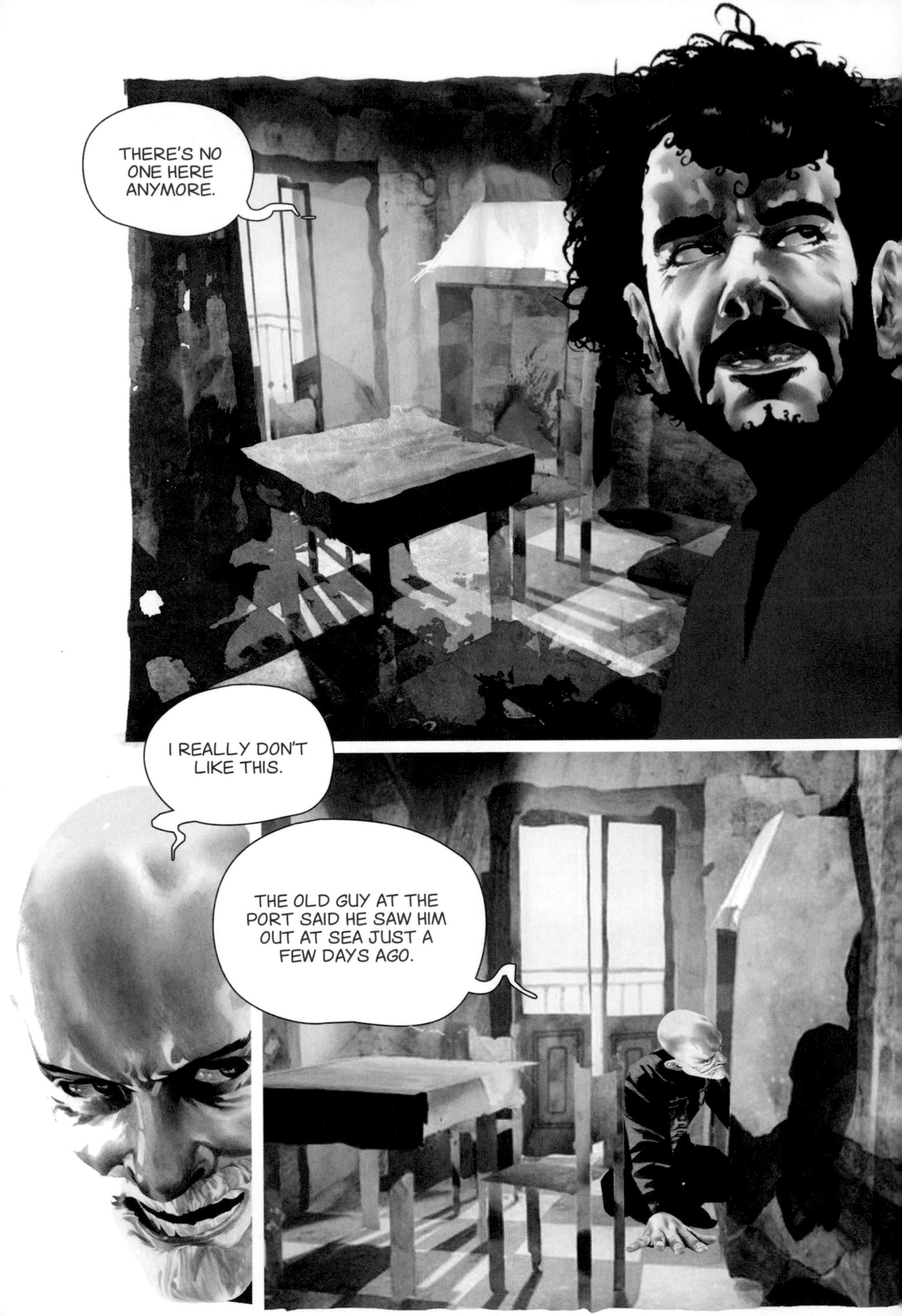
THERE'S NO ONE HERE ANYMORE.
I REALLY DON'T LIKE THIS.
THE OLD GUY AT THE PORT SAID HE SAW HIM OUT AT SEA JUST A FEW DAYS AGO.

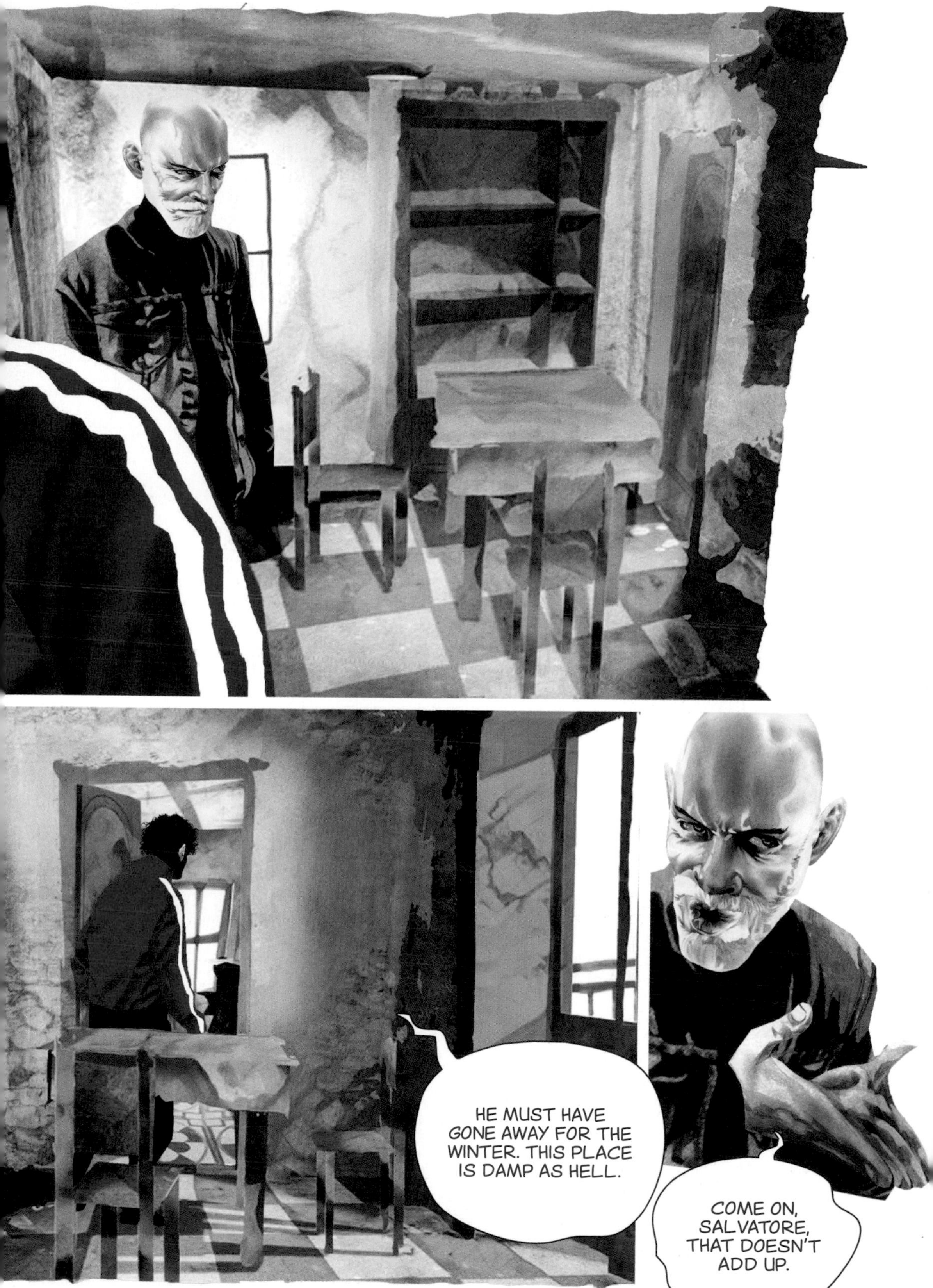
HE MUST HAVE GONE AWAY FOR THE WINTER. THIS PLACE IS DAMP AS HELL.
COME ON, SALVATORE, THAT DOESN'T ADD UP.

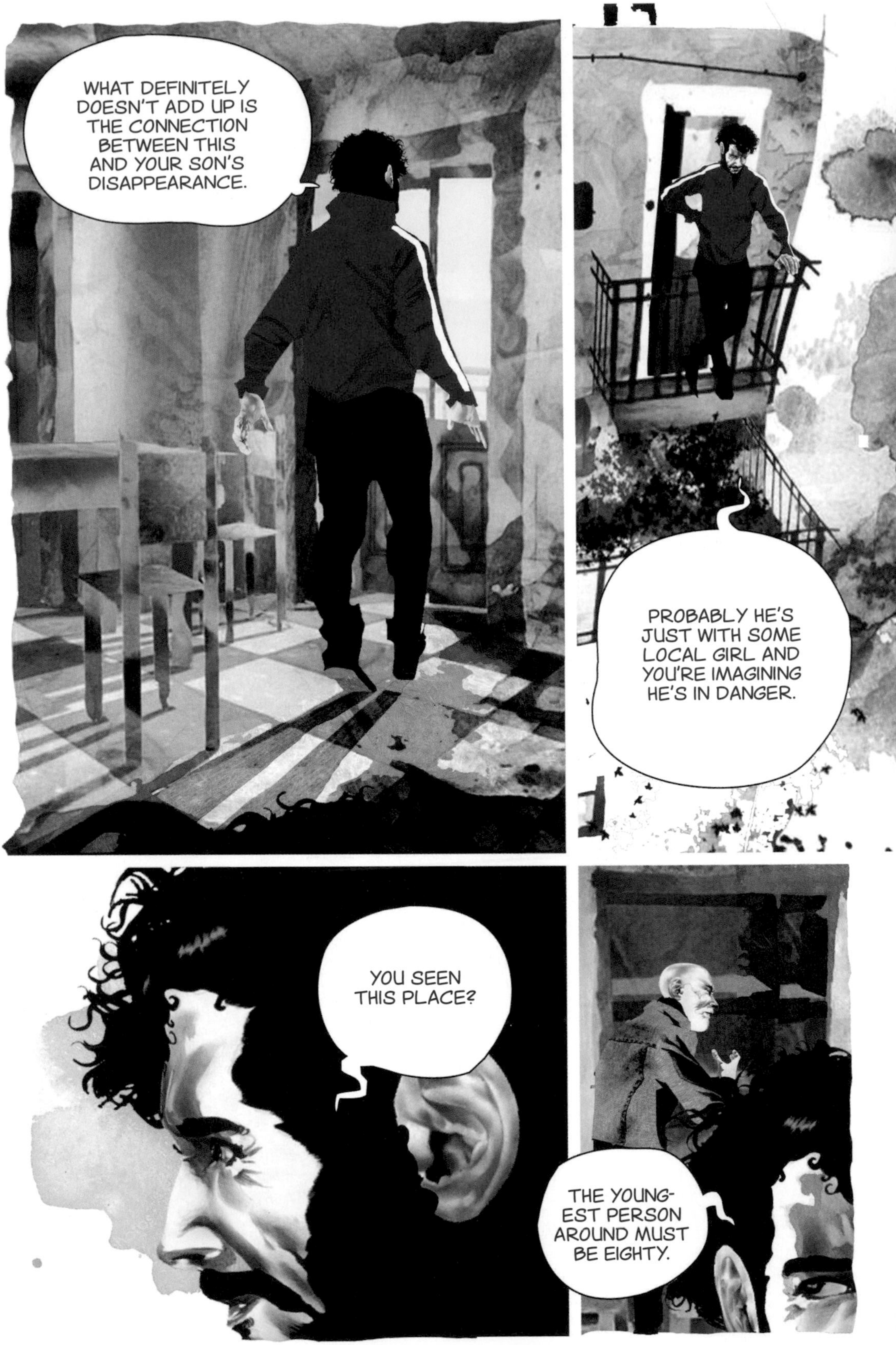
WHAT DEFINITELY DOESN'T ADD UP IS THE CONNECTION BETWEEN THIS AND YOUR SON'S DISAPPEARANCE.
PROBABLY HE'S JUST WITH SOME LOCAL GIRL AND YOU'RE IMAGINING HE'S IN DANGER.
YOU SEEN THIS PLACE?
THE YOUNG-EST PERSON AROUND MUST BE EIGHTY.

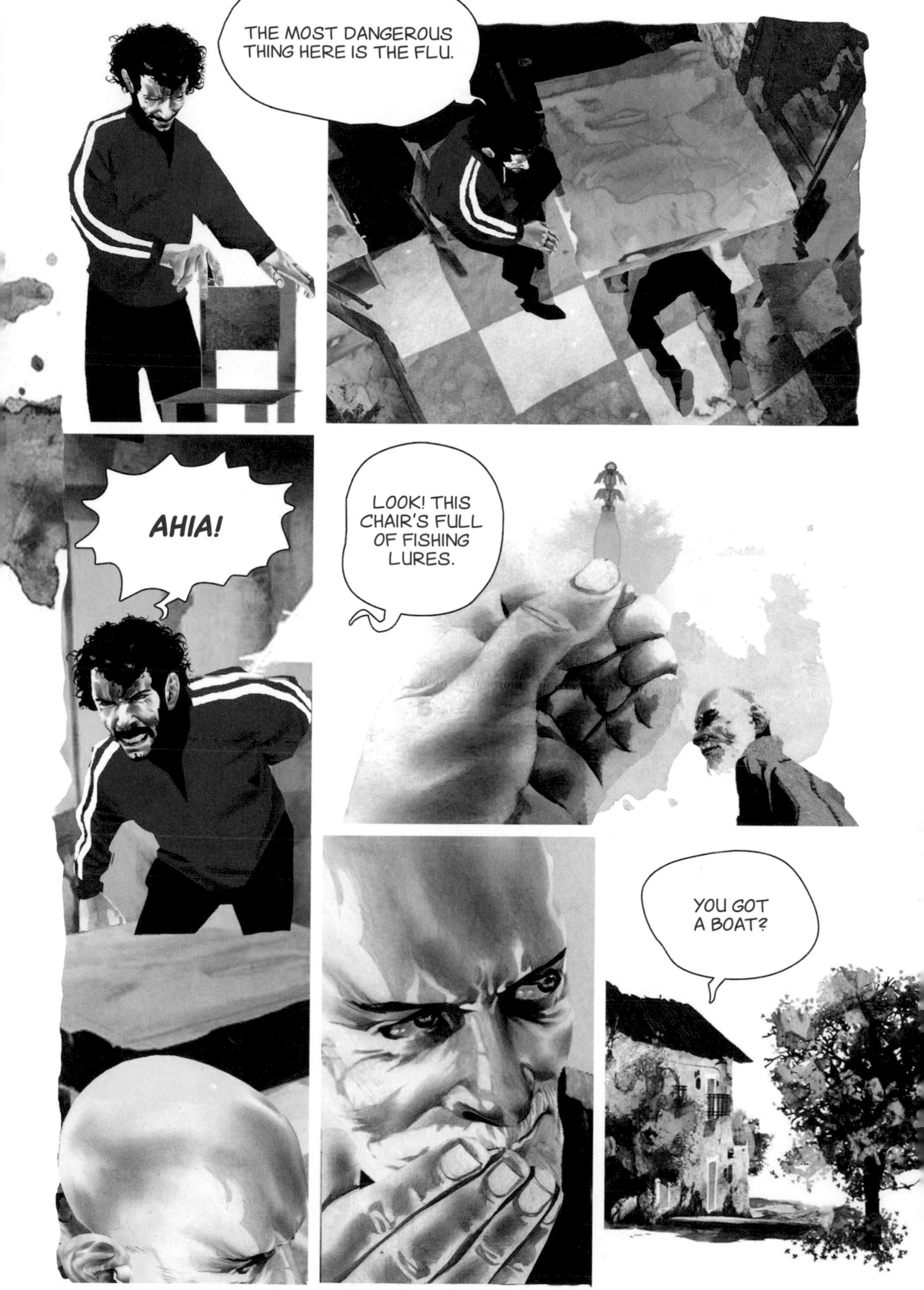
THE MOST DANGEROUS THING HERE IS THE FLU.
AHIA!
LOOK! THIS CHAIR'S FULL OF FISHING LURES.
YOU GOT A BOAT?

DON'T STAND SO CLOSE TO JIM

The mystery of the lead singer of The Doors and the 27 Club

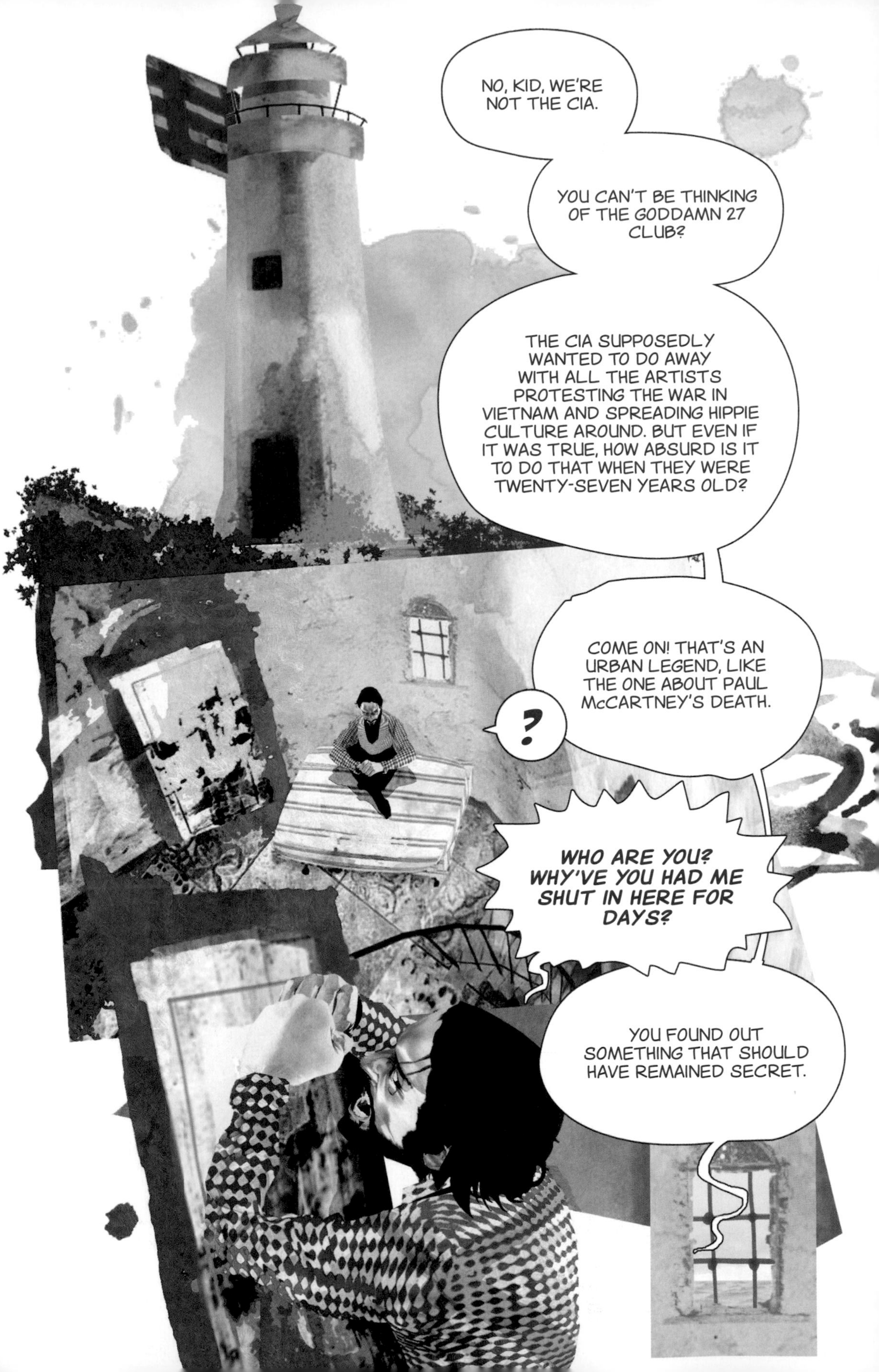
NO, KID, WE'RE NOT THE CIA.
YOU CAN'T BE THINKING OF THE GODDAMN 27 CLUB?
THE CIA SUPPOSEDLY WANTED TO DO AWAY WITH ALL THE ARTISTS PROTESTING THE WAR IN VIETNAM AND SPREADING HIPPIE CULTURE AROUND. BUT EVEN IF IT WAS TRUE, HOW ABSURD IS IT TO DO THAT WHEN THEY WERE TWENTY-SEVEN YEARS OLD?
COME ON! THAT'S AN URBAN LEGEND, LIKE THE ONE ABOUT PAUL McCARTNEY'S DEATH.
?
WHO ARE YOU? WHY'VE YOU HAD ME SHUT IN HERE FOR DAYS?
YOU FOUND OUT SOMETHING THAT SHOULD HAVE REMAINED SECRET.

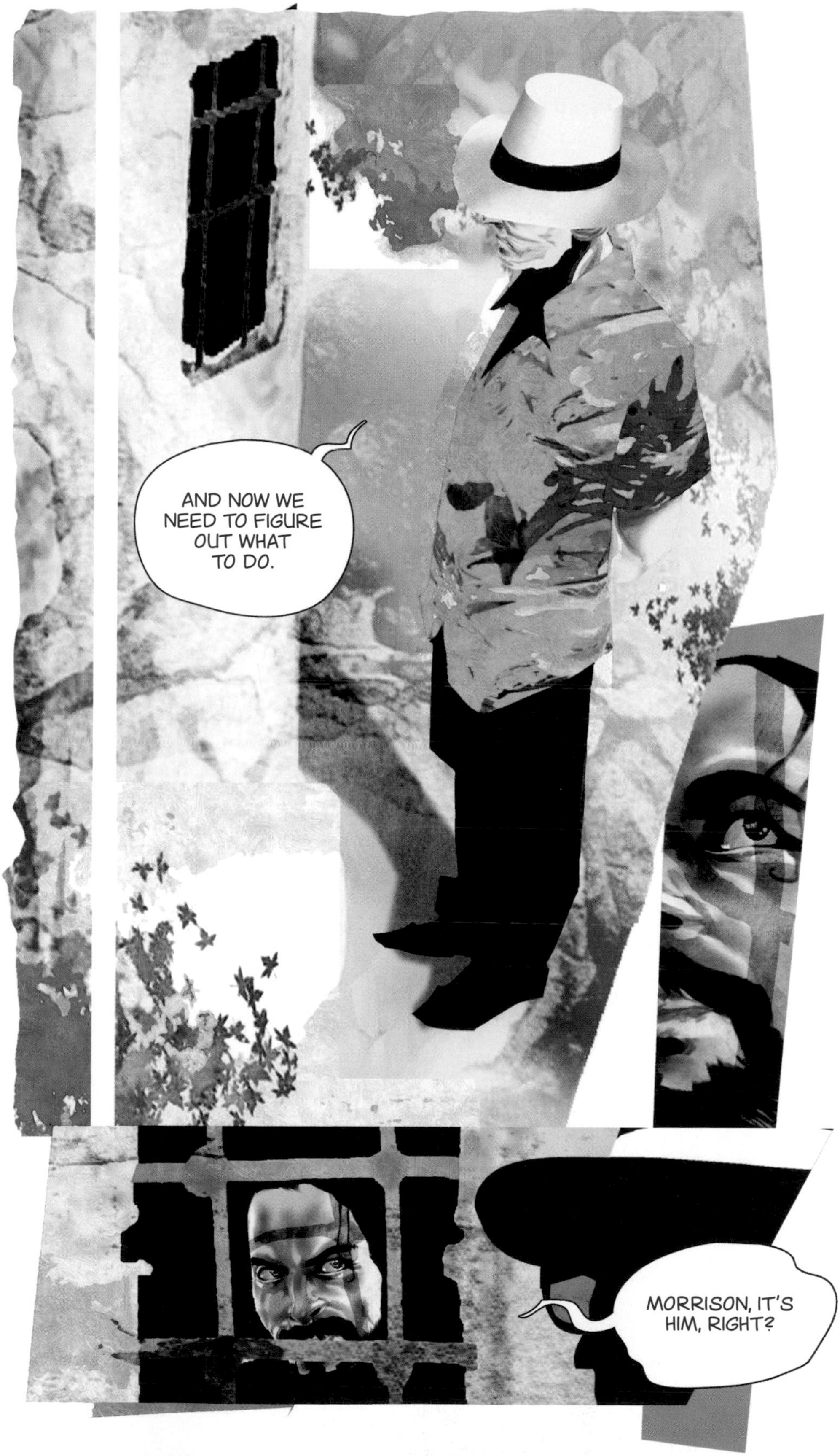
AND NOW WE NEED TO FIGURE OUT WHAT TO DO.
MORRISON, IT'S HIM, RIGHT?

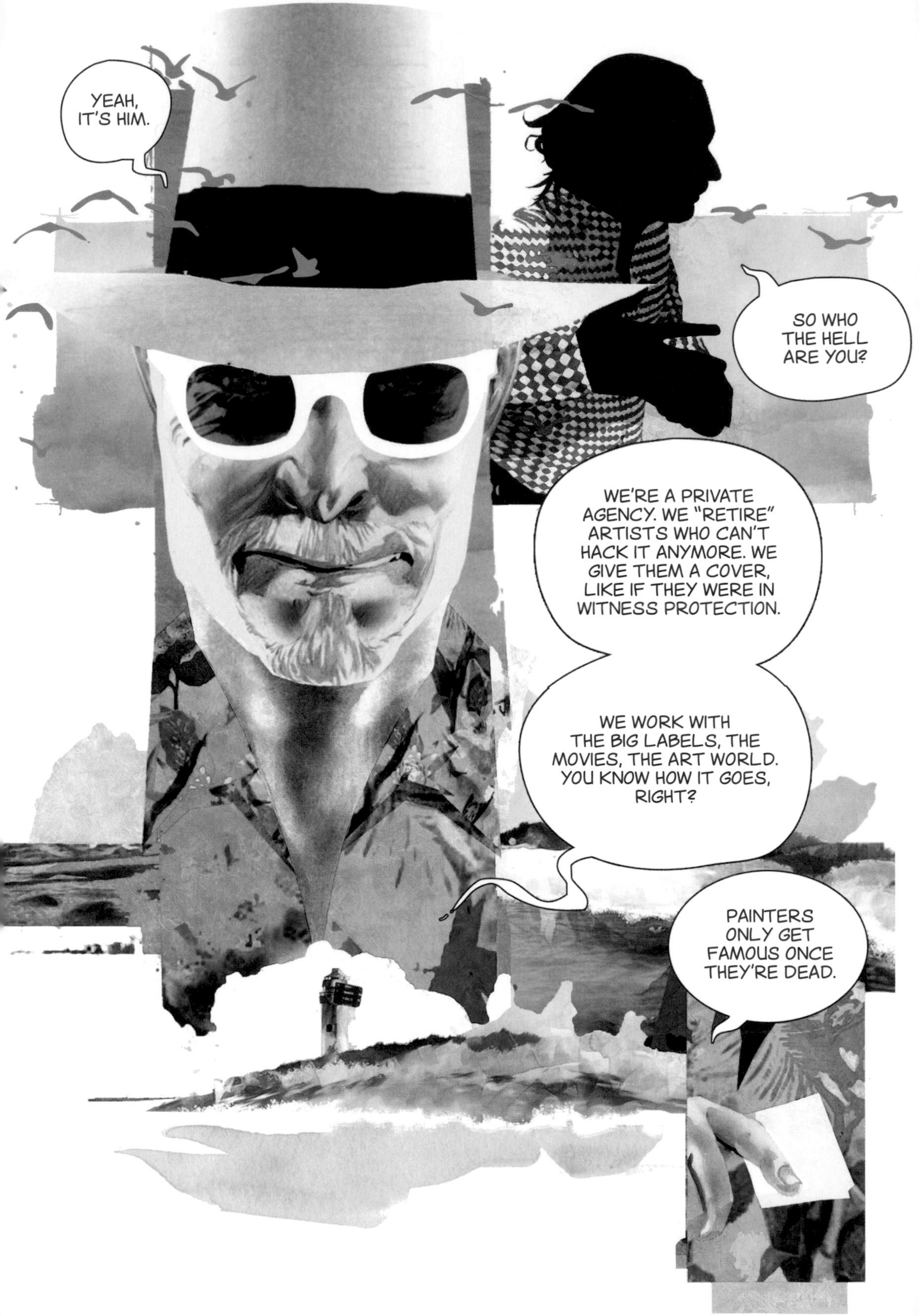
YEAH, IT'S HIM.
SO WHO THE HELL ARE YOU?
WE'RE A PRIVATE AGENCY. WE "RETIRE" ARTISTS WHO CAN'T HACK IT ANYMORE. WE GIVE THEM A COVER, LIKE IF THEY WERE IN WITNESS PROTECTION.
WE WORK WITH THE BIG LABELS, THE MOVIES, THE ART WORLD. YOU KNOW HOW IT GOES, RIGHT?
PAINTERS ONLY GET FAMOUS ONCE THEY'RE DEAD.

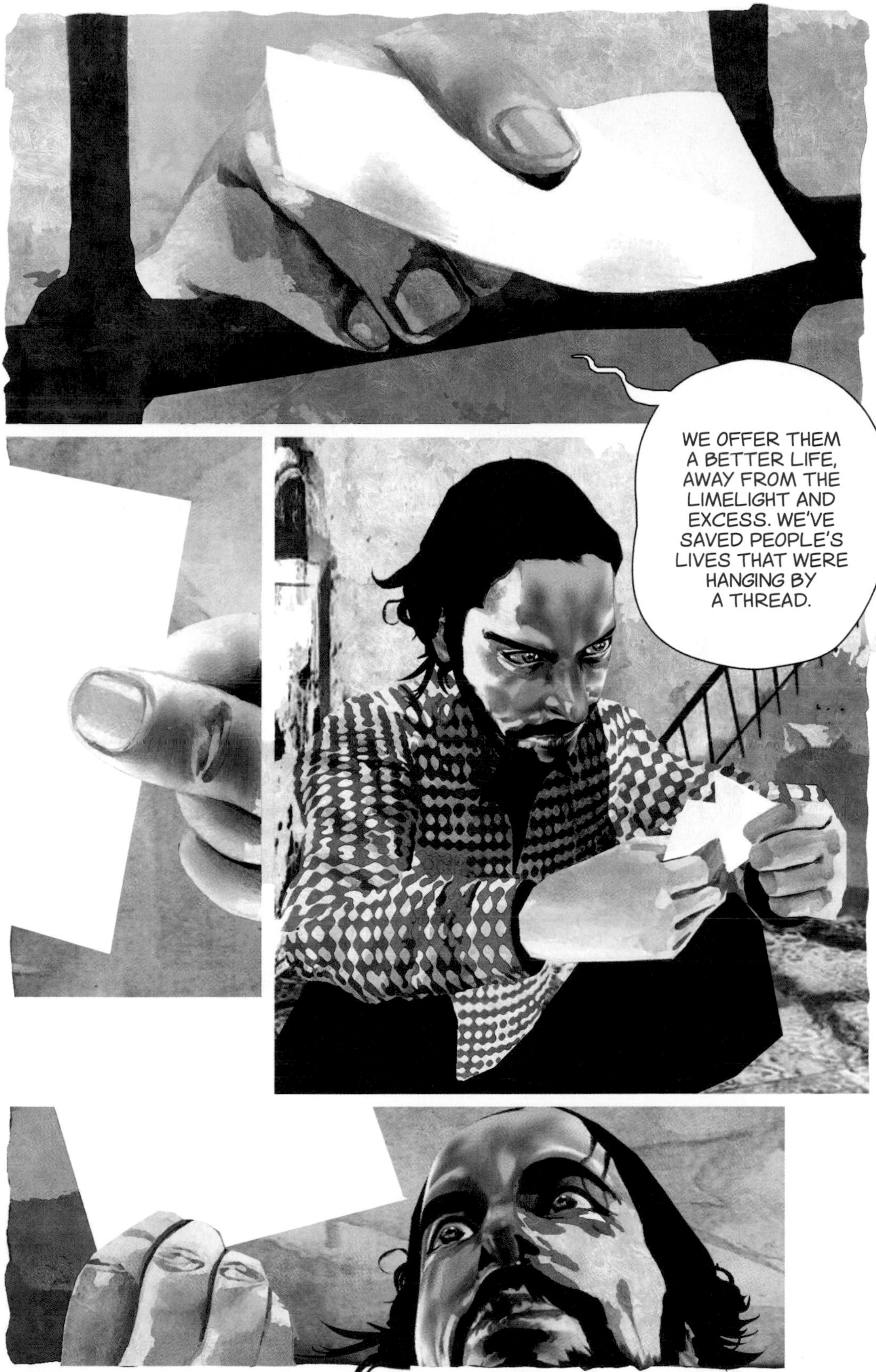
WE OFFER THEM A BETTER LIFE, AWAY FROM THE LIMELIGHT AND EXCESS. WE'VE SAVED PEOPLE'S LIVES THAT WERE HANGING BY A THREAD.

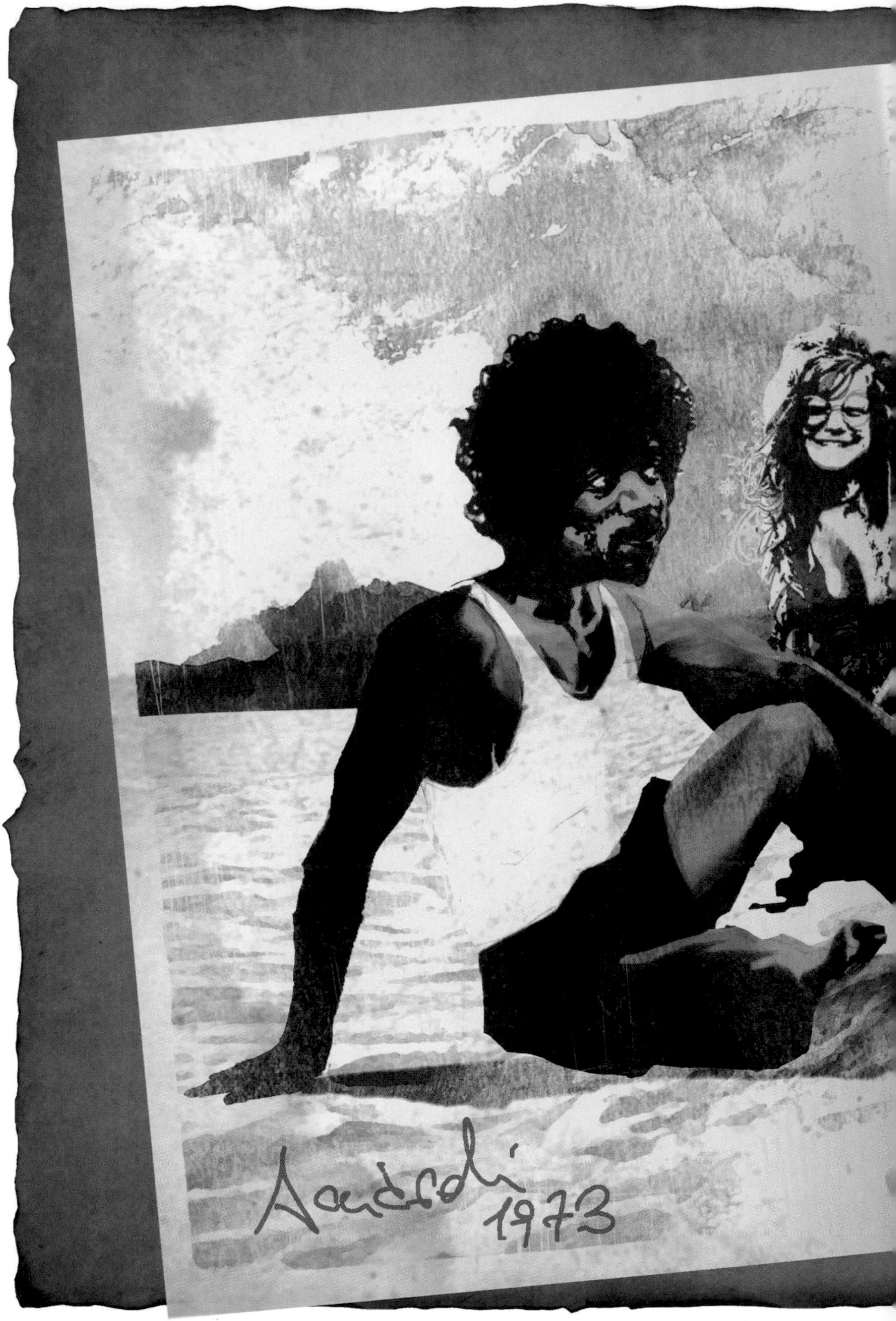
1973

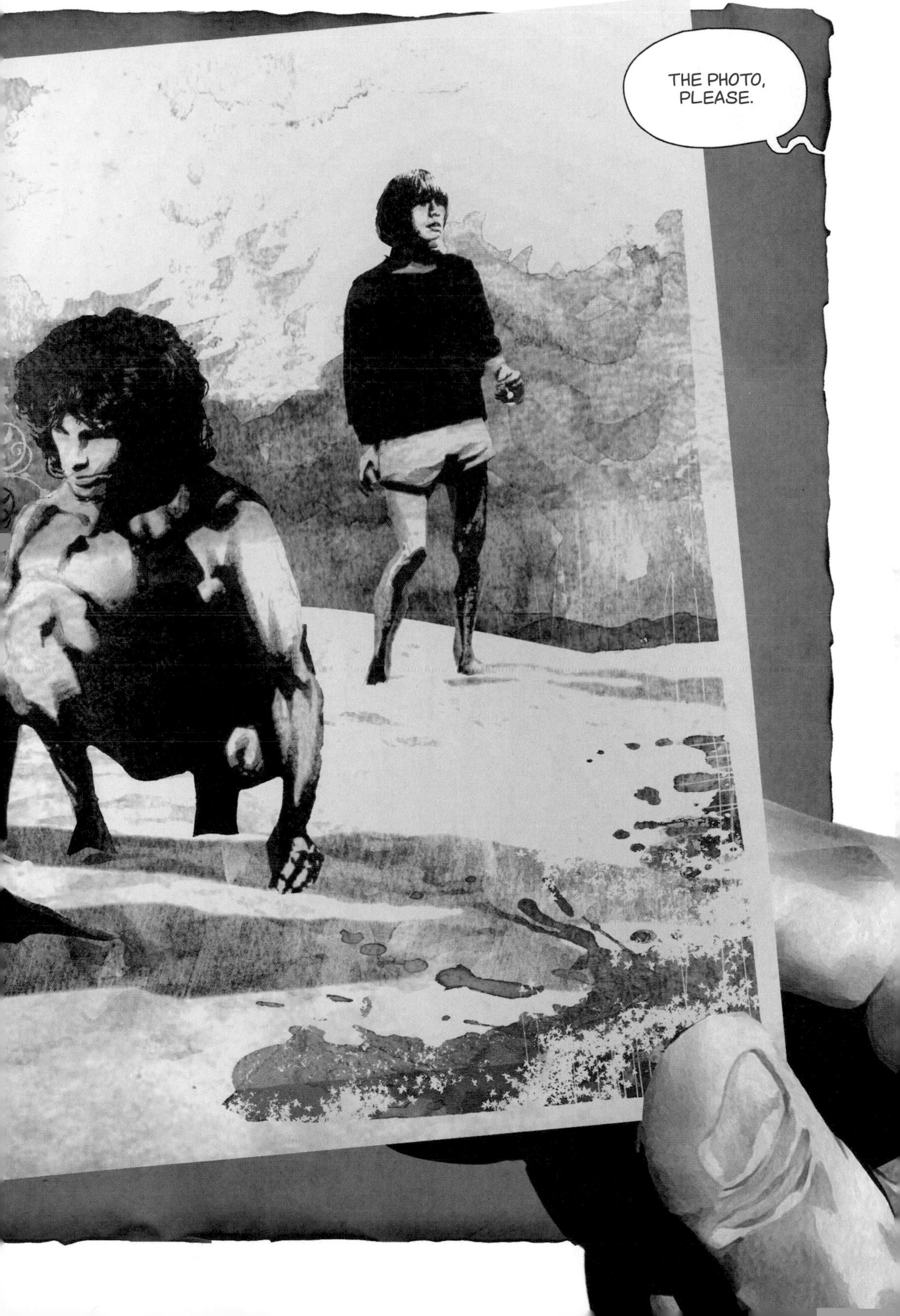
THE PHOTO, PLEASE.

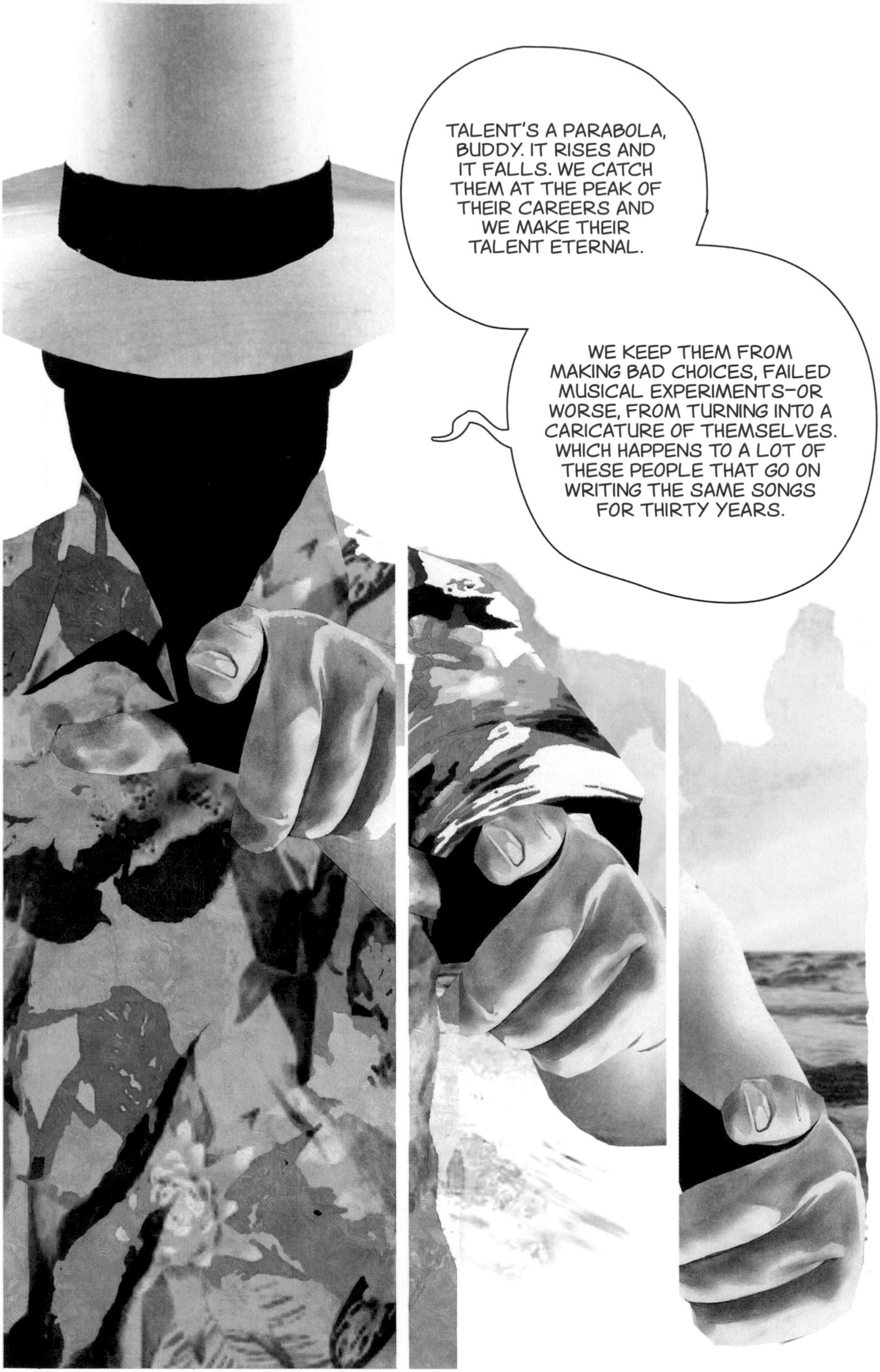

TALENT'S A PARABOLA, BUDDY. IT RISES AND IT FALLS. WE CATCH THEM AT THE PEAK OF THEIR CAREERS AND WE MAKE THEIR TALENT ETERNAL.
WE KEEP THEM FROM MAKING BAD CHOICES, FAILED MUSICAL EXPERIMENTS–OR WORSE, FROM TURNING INTO A CARICATURE OF THEMSELVES. WHICH HAPPENS TO A LOT OF THESE PEOPLE THAT GO ON WRITING THE SAME SONGS FOR THIRTY YEARS.

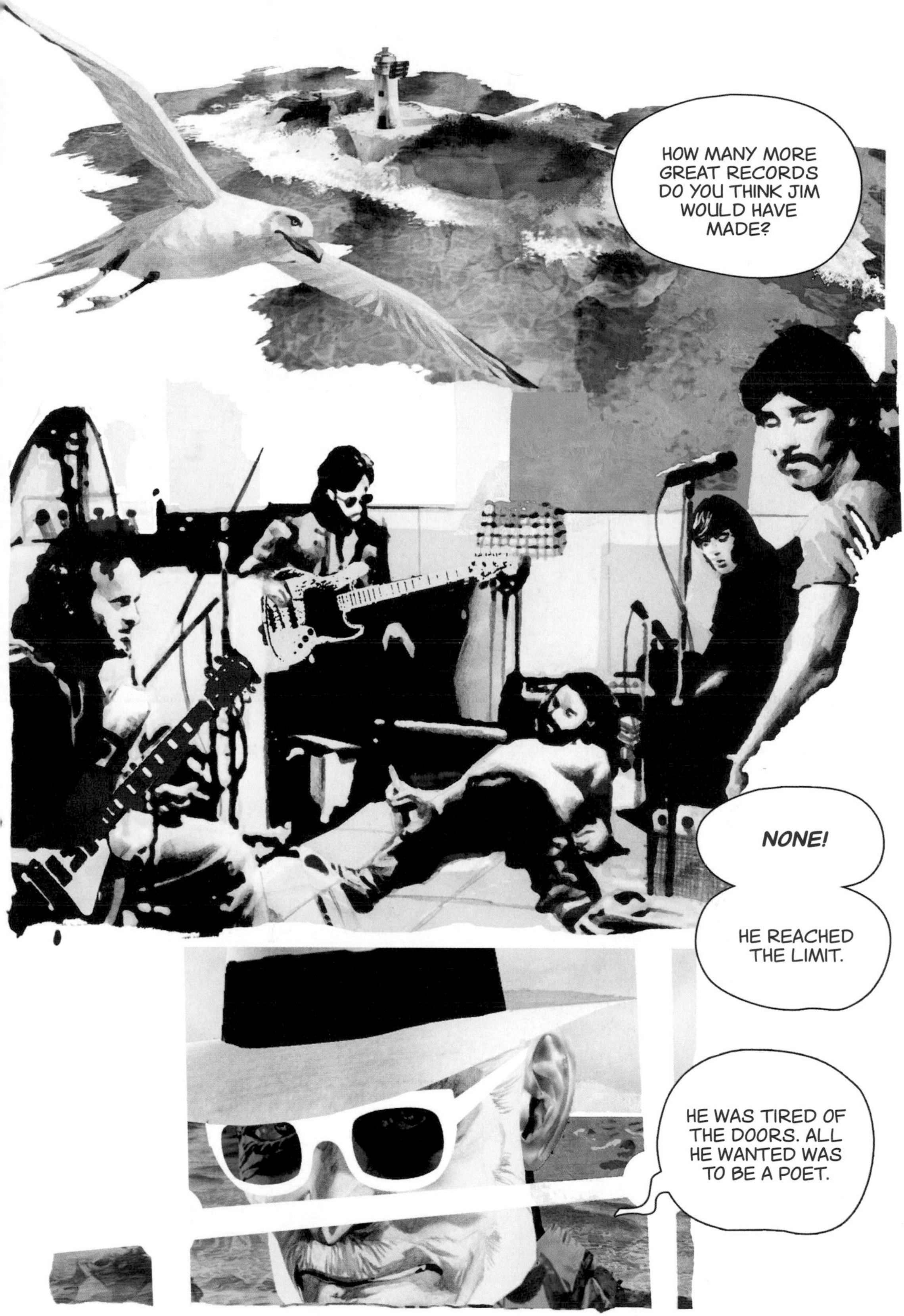
HOW MANY MORE GREAT RECORDS DO YOU THINK JIM WOULD HAVE MADE?
NONE!
HE REACHED THE LIMIT.
HE WAS TIRED OF THE DOORS. ALL HE WANTED WAS TO BE A POET.

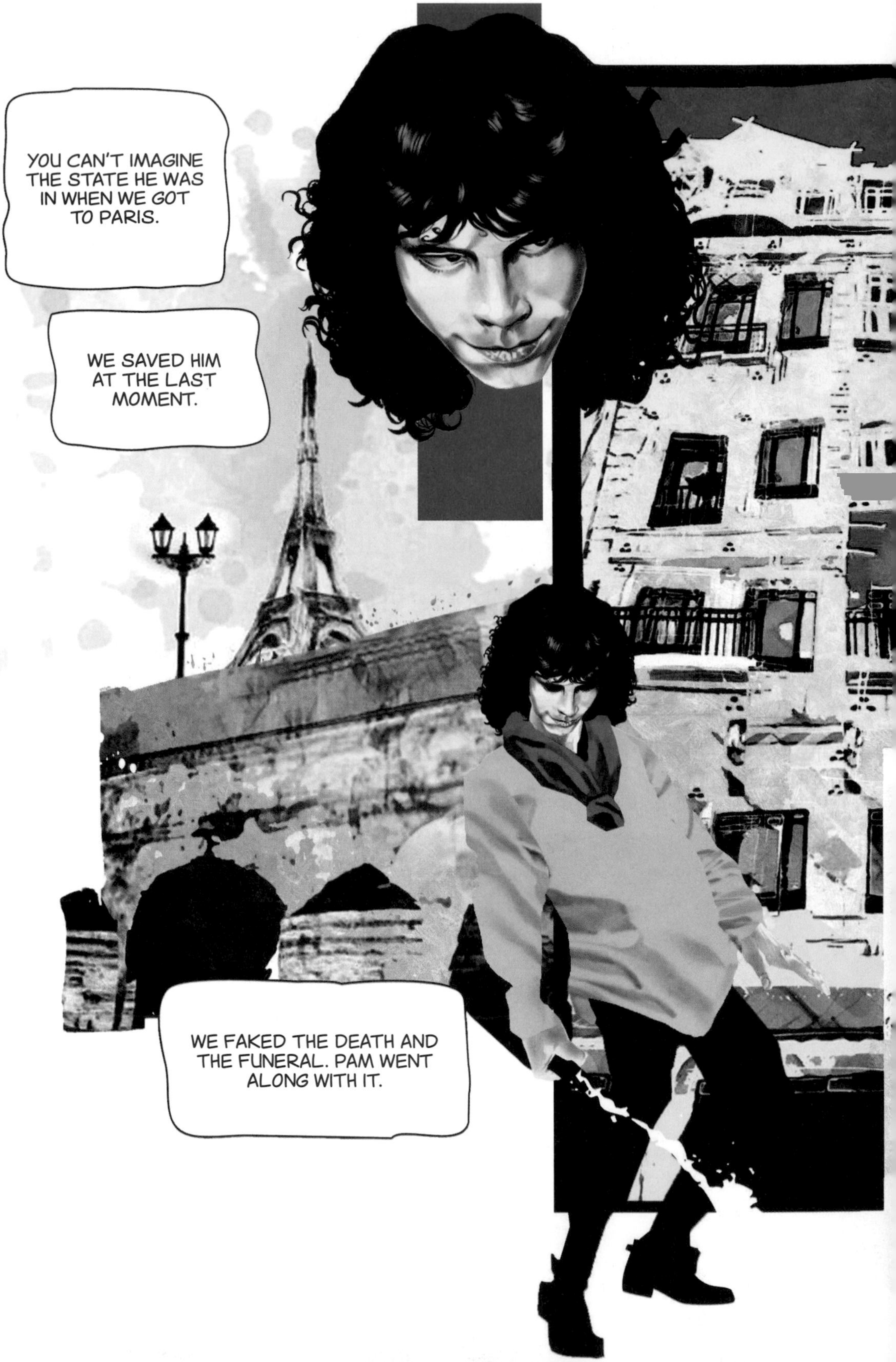
YOU CAN'T IMAGINE THE STATE HE WAS IN WHEN WE GOT TO PARIS.
WE SAVED HIM AT THE LAST MOMENT.
WE FAKED THE DEATH AND THE FUNERAL. PAM WENT ALONG WITH IT.

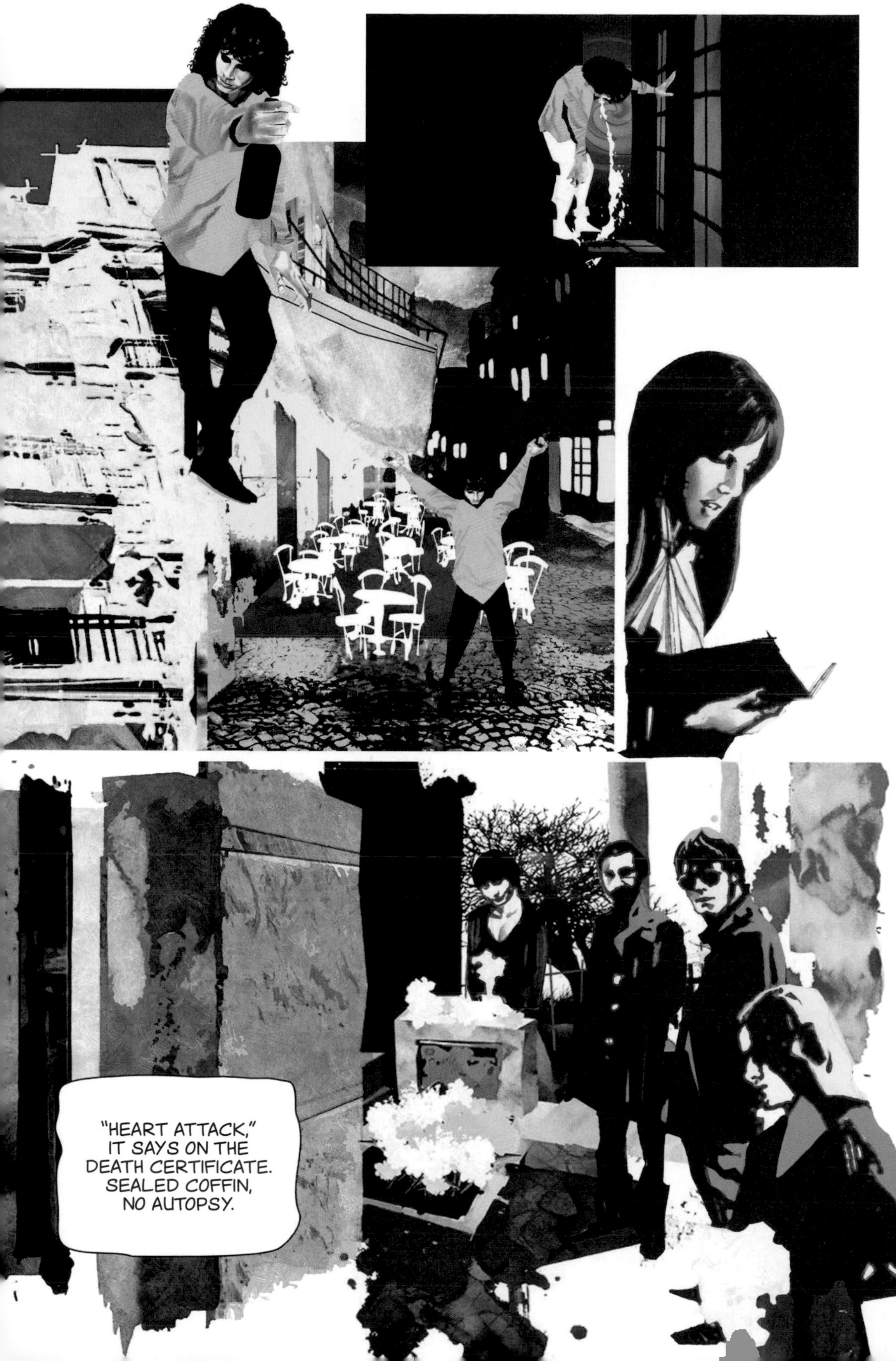
"HEART ATTACK," IT SAYS ON THE DEATH CERTIFICATE. SEALED COFFIN, NO AUTOPSY.

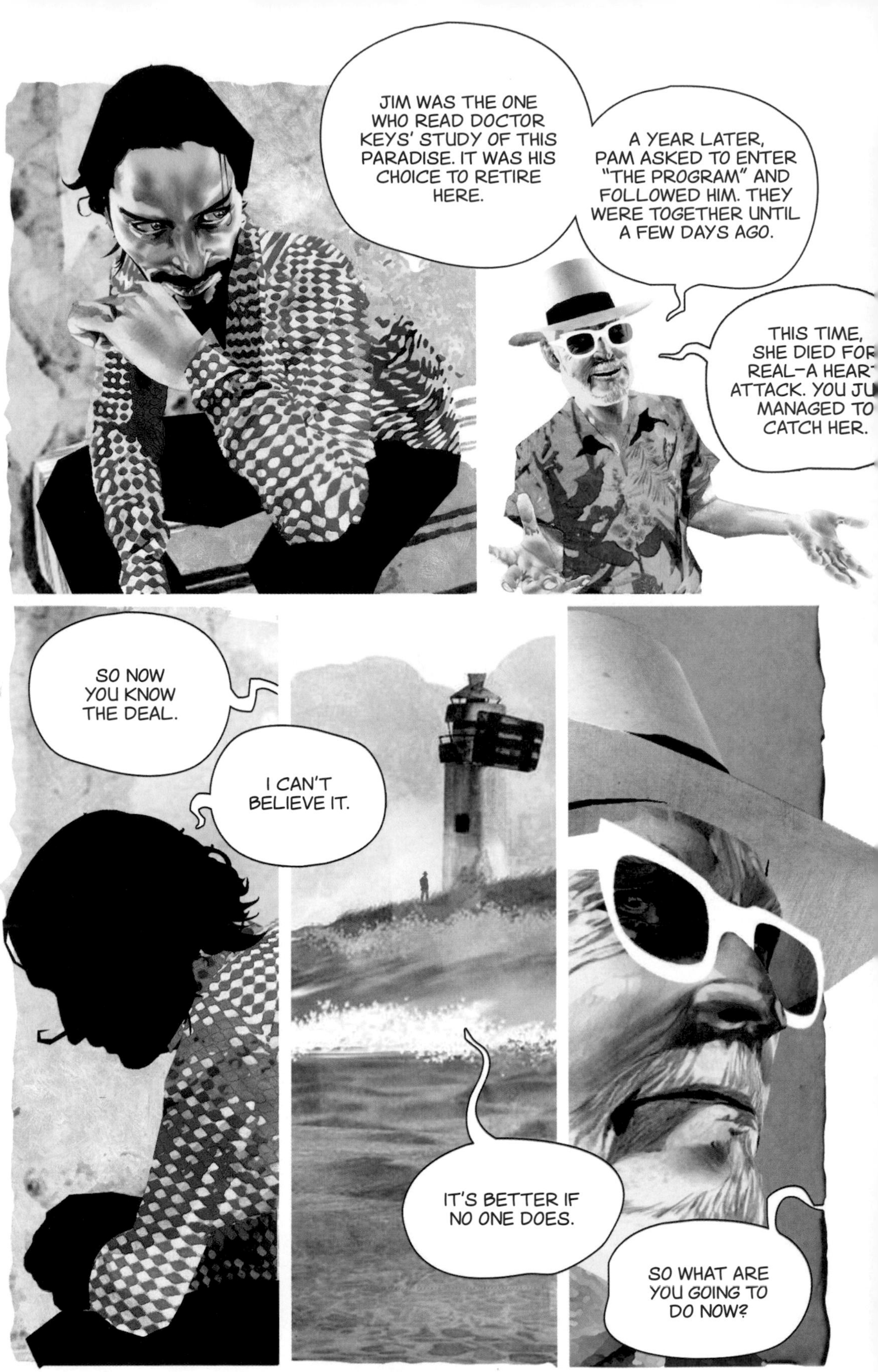
JIM WAS THE ONE WHO READ DOCTOR KEYS' STUDY OF THIS PARADISE. IT WAS HIS CHOICE TO RETIRE HERE.
A YEAR LATER, PAM ASKED TO ENTER "THE PROGRAM" AND FOLLOWED HIM. THEY WERE TOGETHER UNTIL A FEW DAYS AGO.
THIS TIME, SHE DIED FOR REAL—A HEART ATTACK. YOU JU MANAGED TO CATCH HER.
SO NOW YOU KNOW THE DEAL.
I CAN'T BELIEVE IT.
IT'S BETTER IF NO ONE DOES.
SO WHAT ARE YOU GOING TO DO NOW?

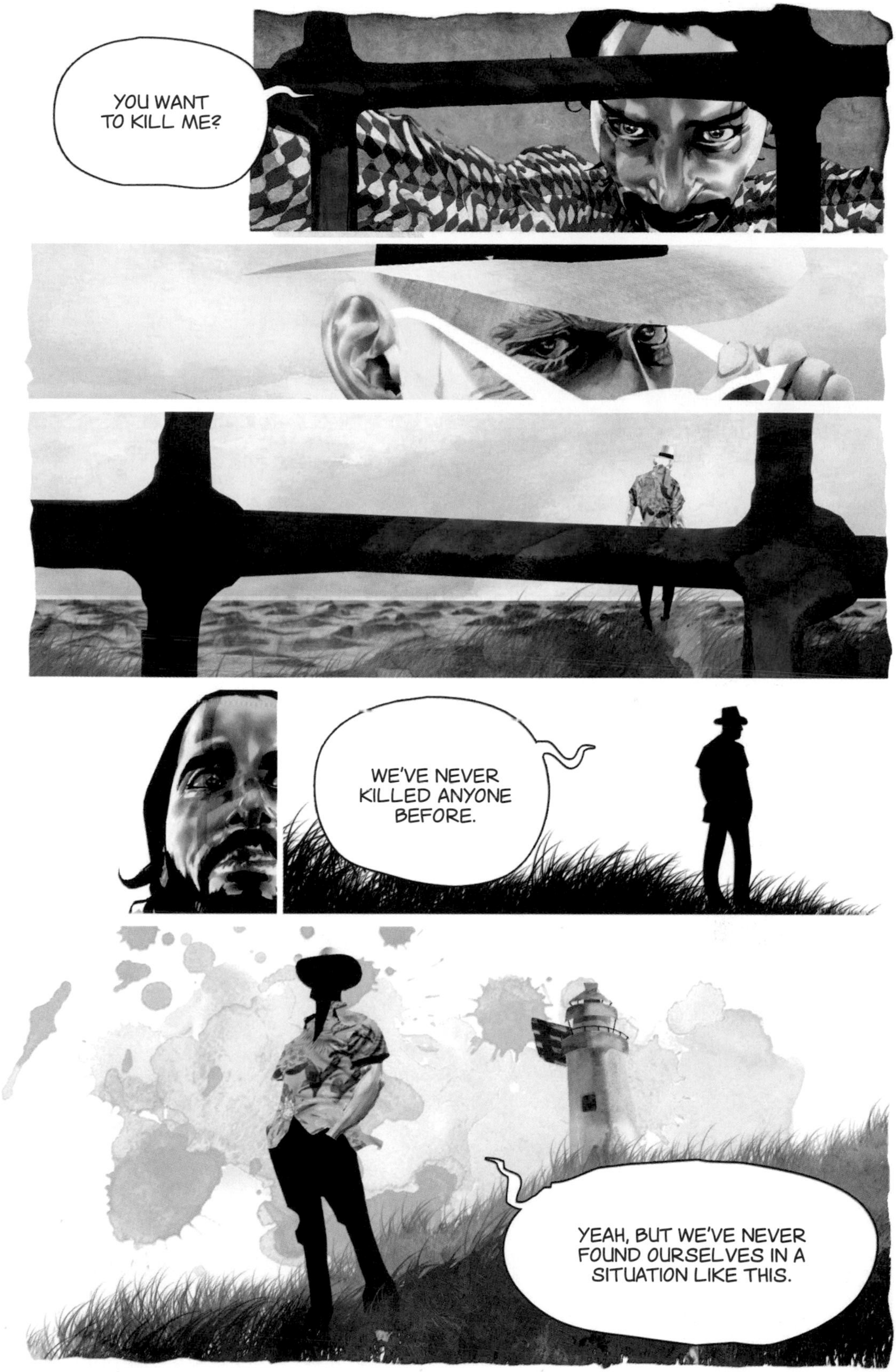
YOU WANT TO KILL ME?
WE'VE NEVER KILLED ANYONE BEFORE.
YEAH, BUT WE'VE NEVER FOUND OURSELVES IN A SITUATION LIKE THIS.

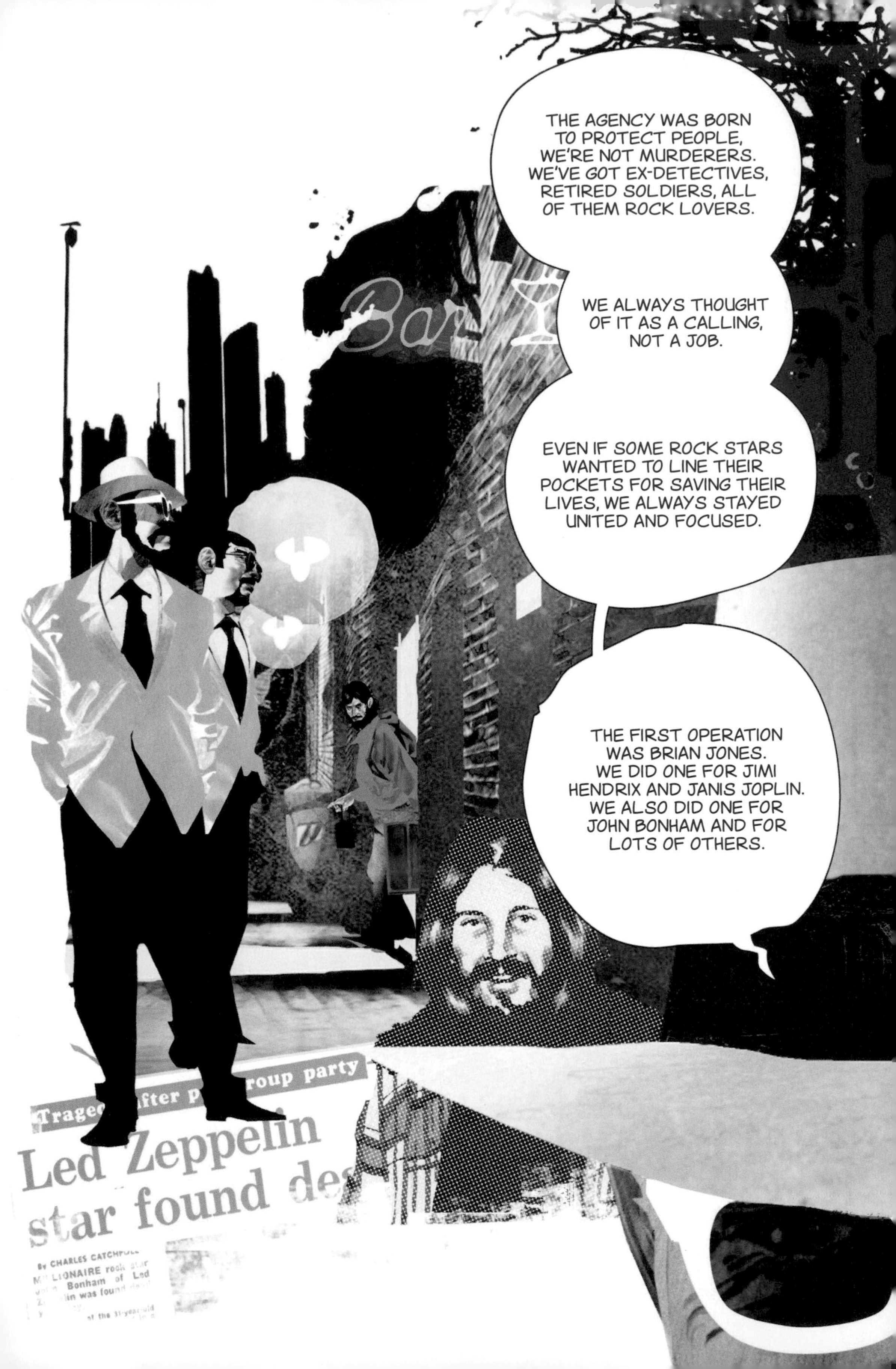
THE AGENCY WAS BORN TO PROTECT PEOPLE, WE'RE NOT MURDERERS. WE'VE GOT EX-DETECTIVES, RETIRED SOLDIERS, ALL OF THEM ROCK LOVERS.
WE ALWAYS THOUGHT OF IT AS A CALLING, NOT A JOB.
EVEN IF SOME ROCK STARS WANTED TO LINE THEIR POCKETS FOR SAVING THEIR LIVES, WE ALWAYS STAYED UNITED AND FOCUSED.
THE FIRST OPERATION WAS BRIAN JONES. WE DID ONE FOR JIMI HENDRIX AND JANIS JOPLIN. WE ALSO DID ONE FOR JOHN BONHAM AND FOR LOTS OF OTHERS.
Bar
Led Zeppelin
star found
By CHARLES CATCHPOLE

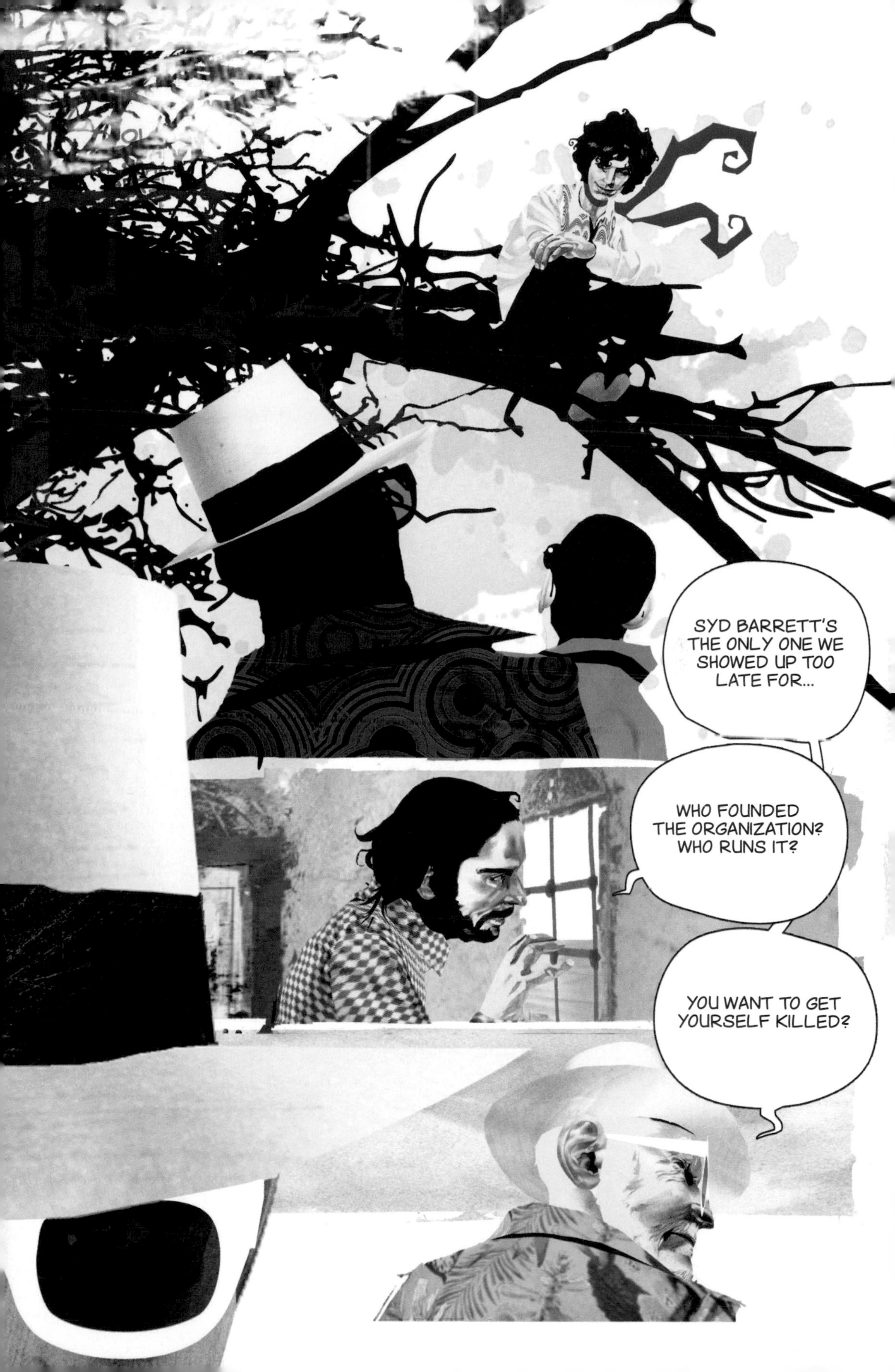
SYD BARRETT'S THE ONLY ONE WE SHOWED UP TOO LATE FOR...
WHO FOUNDED THE ORGANIZATION? WHO RUNS IT?
YOU WANT TO GET YOURSELF KILLED?

PAPA , HE WAS THROWIN' STONES

What did you ask me?
If I got a boat?

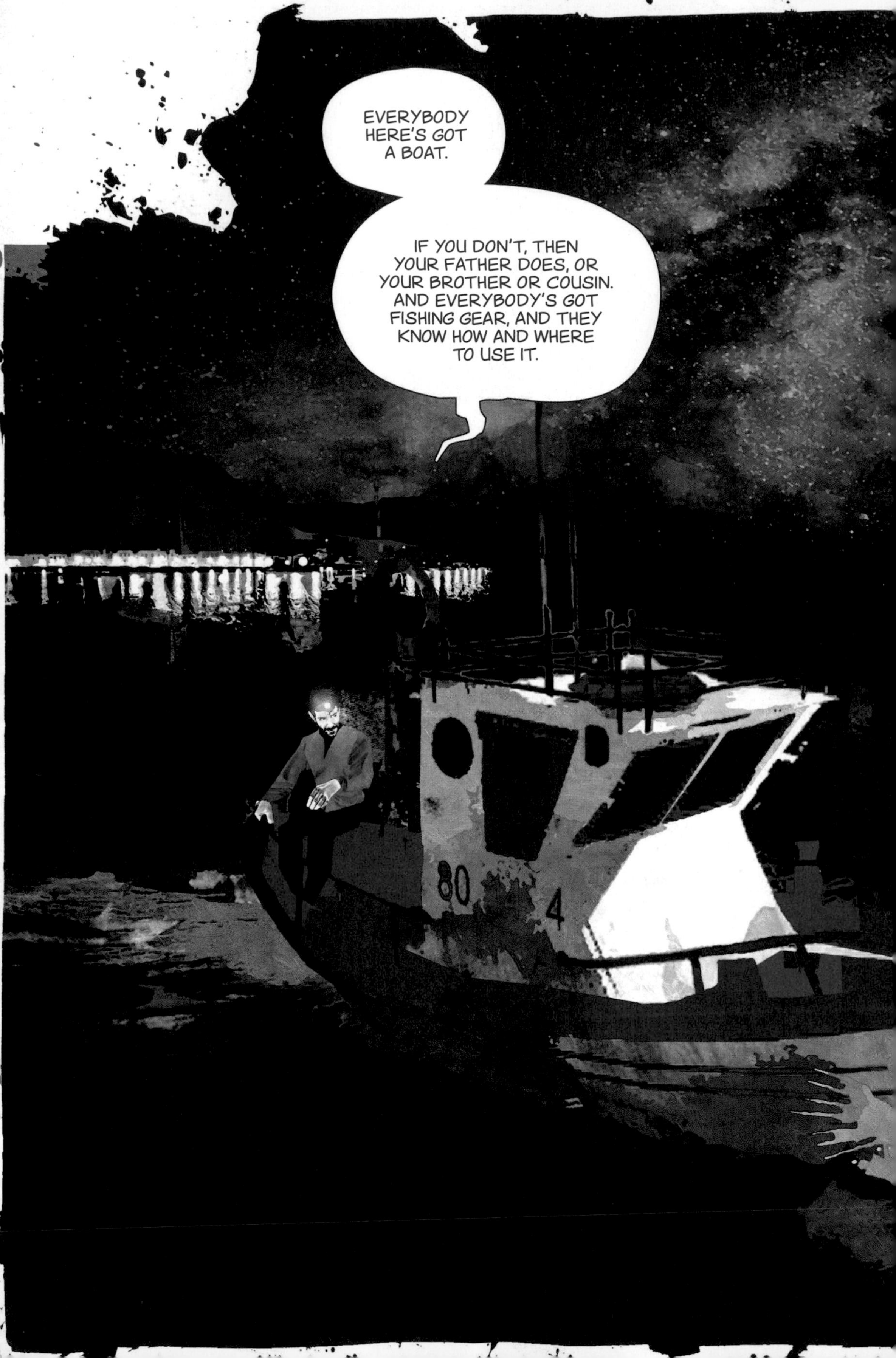
EVERYBODY HERE'S GOT A BOAT.
IF YOU DON'T, THEN YOUR FATHER DOES, OR YOUR BROTHER OR COUSIN. AND EVERYBODY'S GOT FISHING GEAR, AND THEY KNOW HOW AND WHERE TO USE IT.
80 4

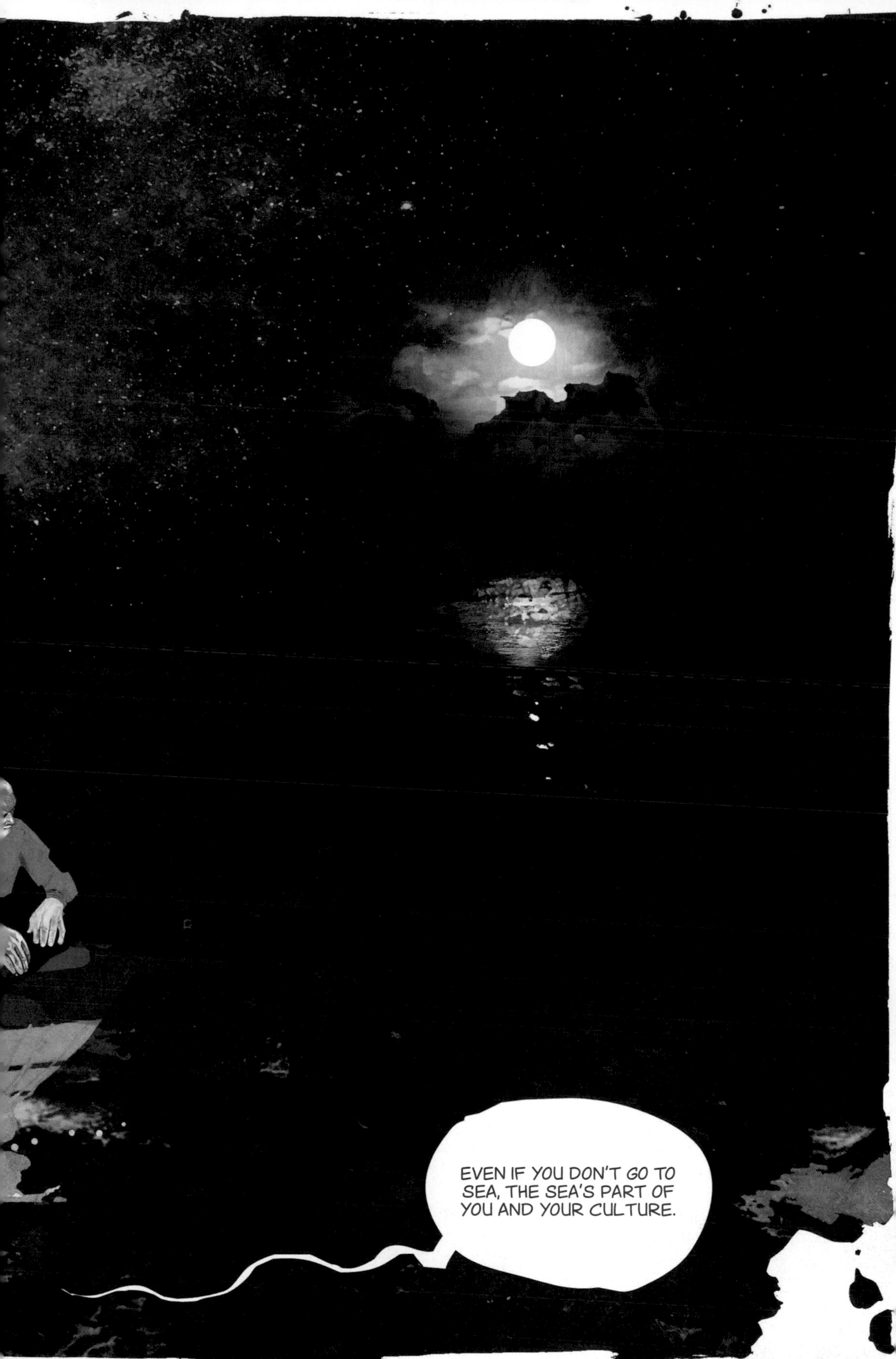
EVEN IF YOU DON'T GO TO SEA, THE SEA'S PART OF YOU AND YOUR CULTURE.

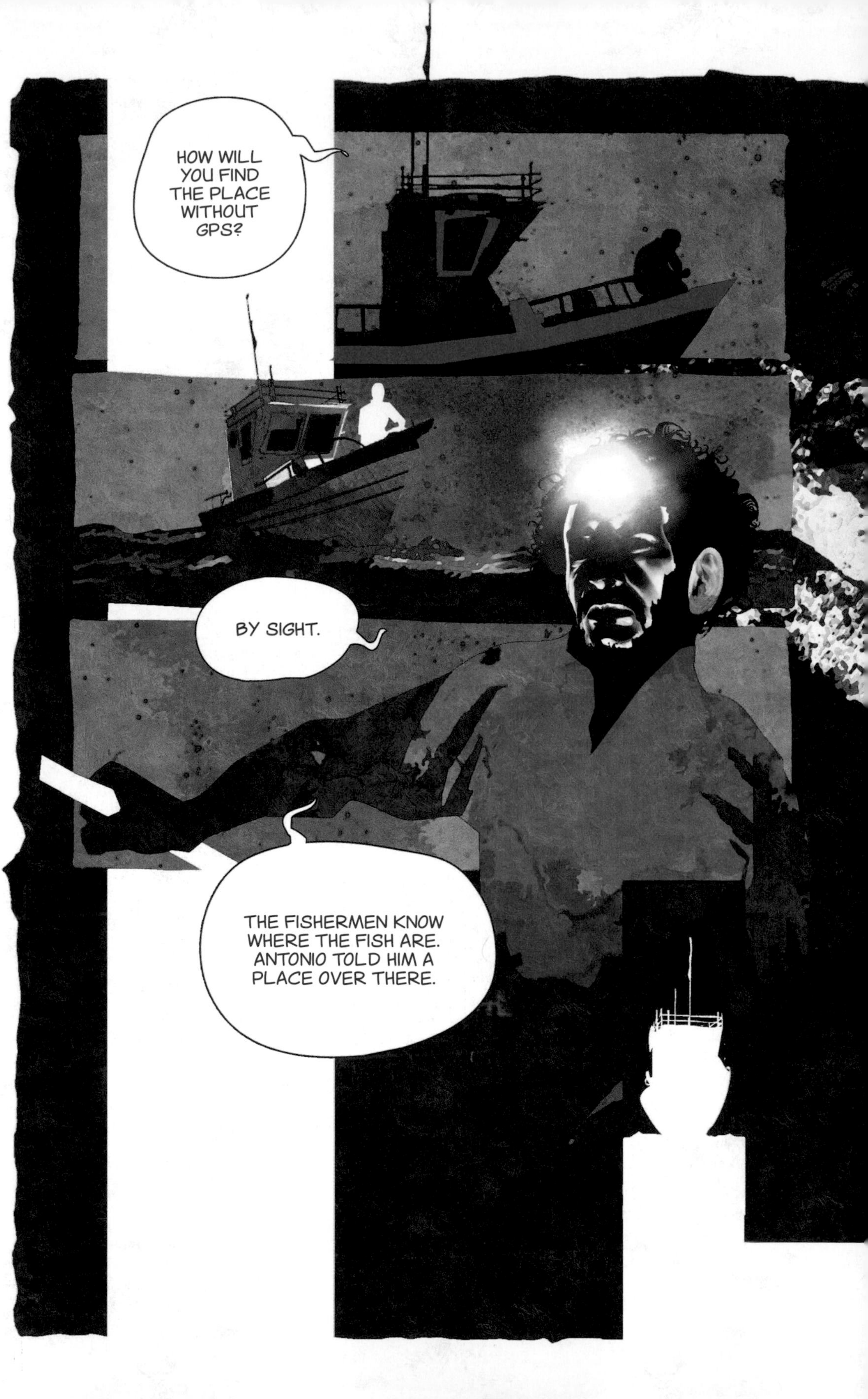
HOW WILL YOU FIND THE PLACE WITHOUT GPS?
BY SIGHT.
THE FISHERMEN KNOW WHERE THE FISH ARE. ANTONIO TOLD HIM A PLACE OVER THERE.

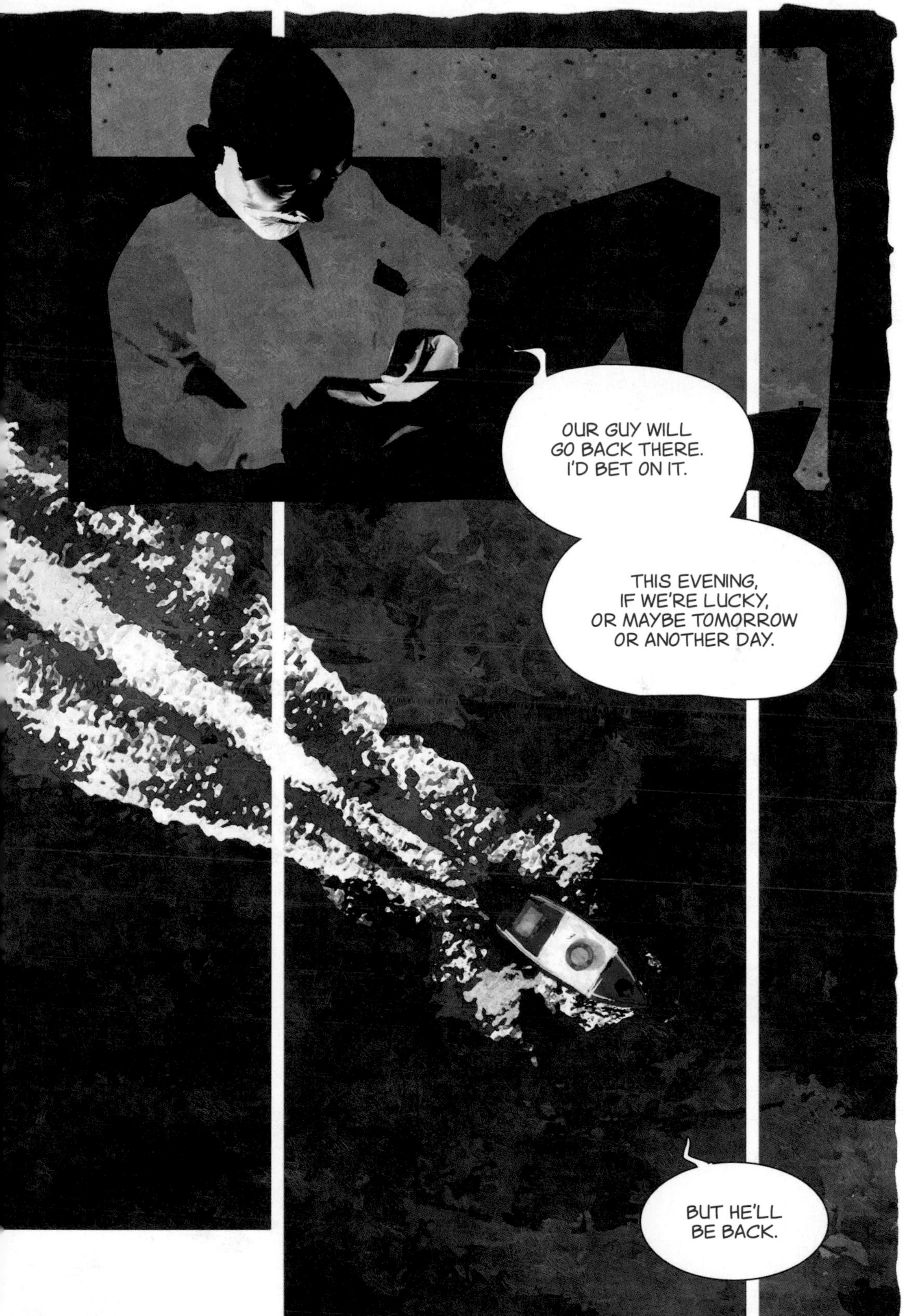
OUR GUY WILL GO BACK THERE. I'D BET ON IT.
THIS EVENING, IF WE'RE LUCKY, OR MAYBE TOMORROW OR ANOTHER DAY.
BUT HE'LL BE BACK.

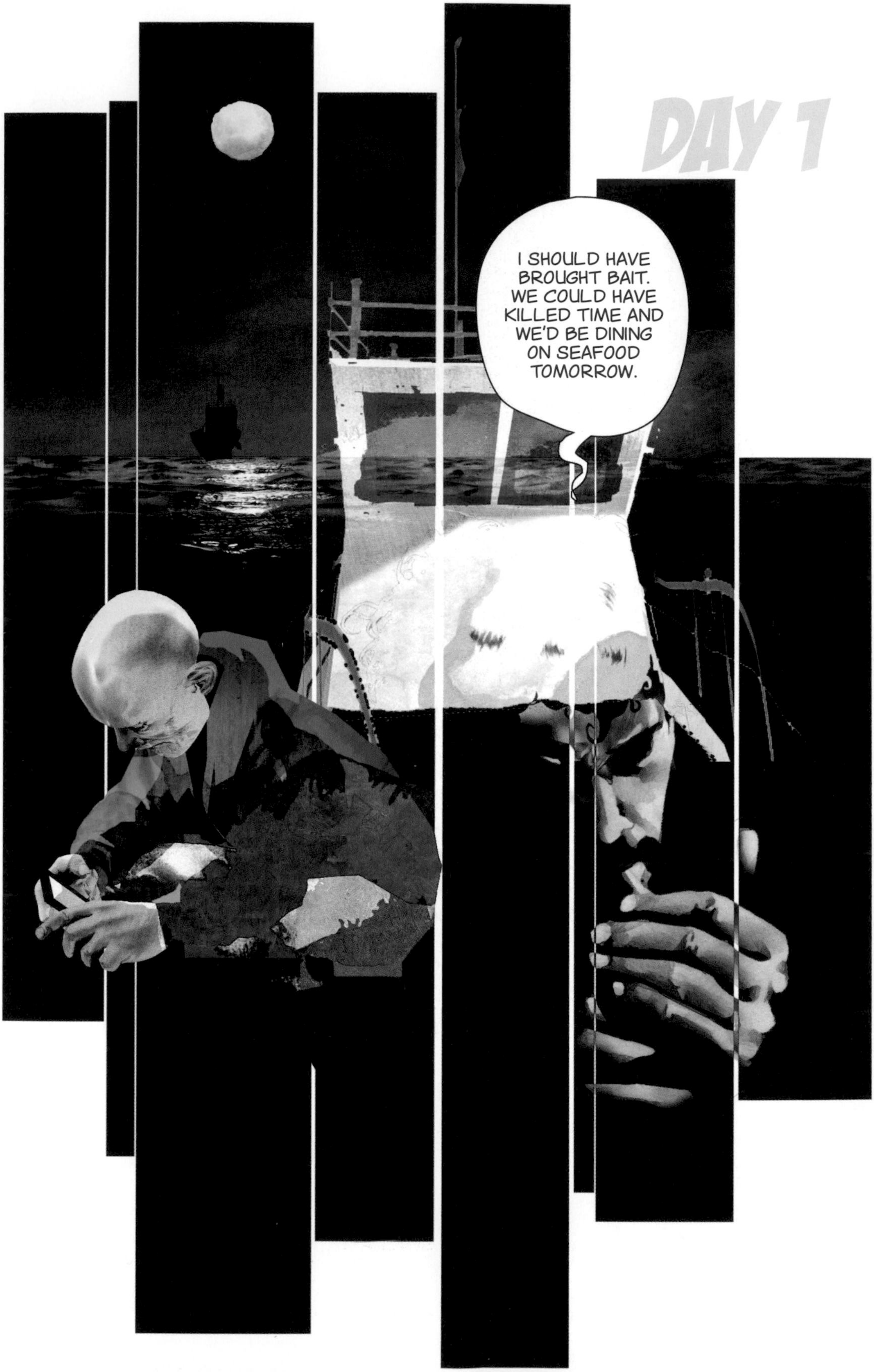
DAY 1
I SHOULD HAVE BROUGHT BAIT. WE COULD HAVE KILLED TIME AND WE'D BE DINING ON SEAFOOD TOMORROW.

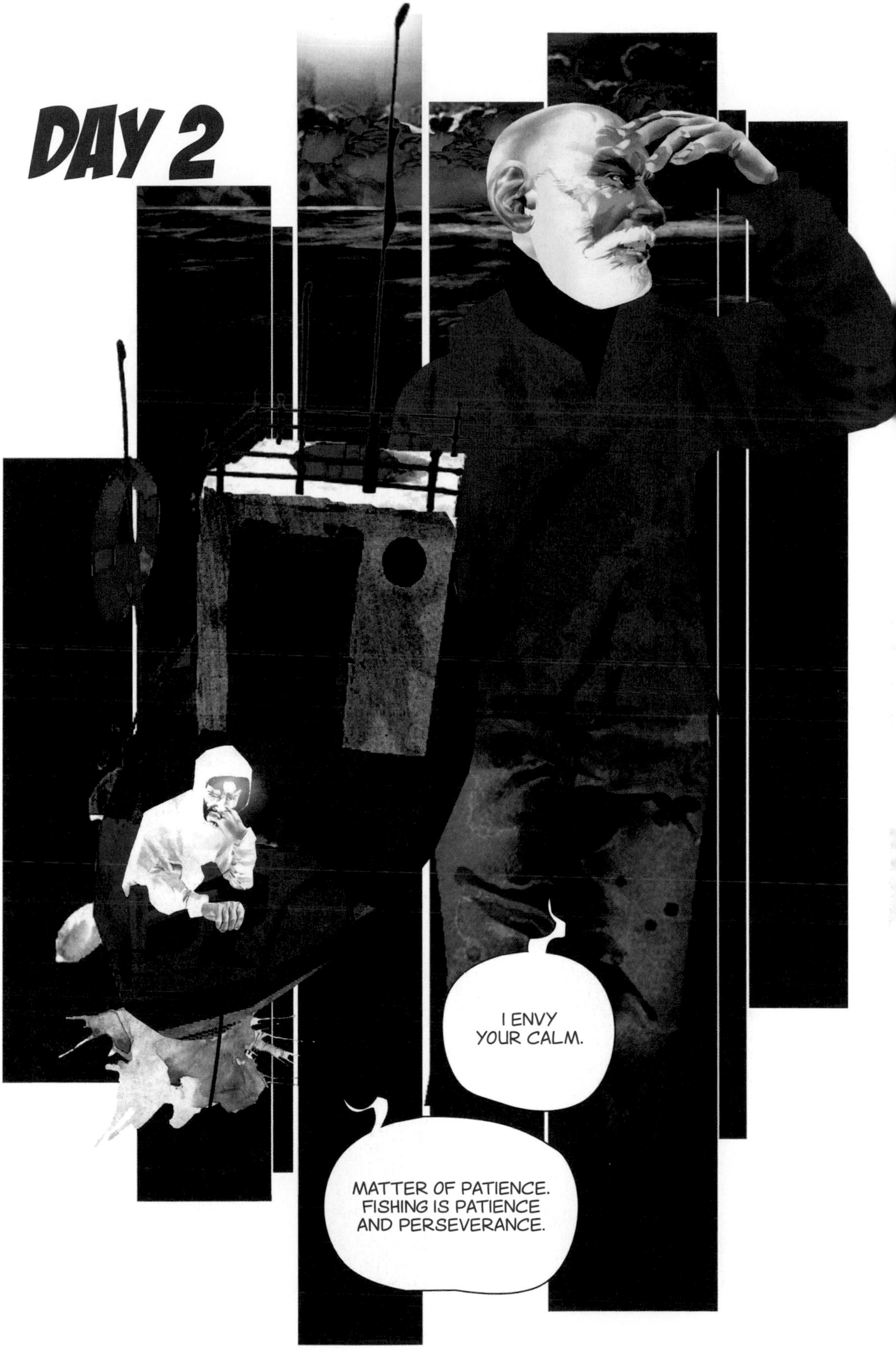
DAY 2
I ENVY YOUR CALM.
MATTER OF PATIENCE. FISHING IS PATIENCE AND PERSEVERANCE.

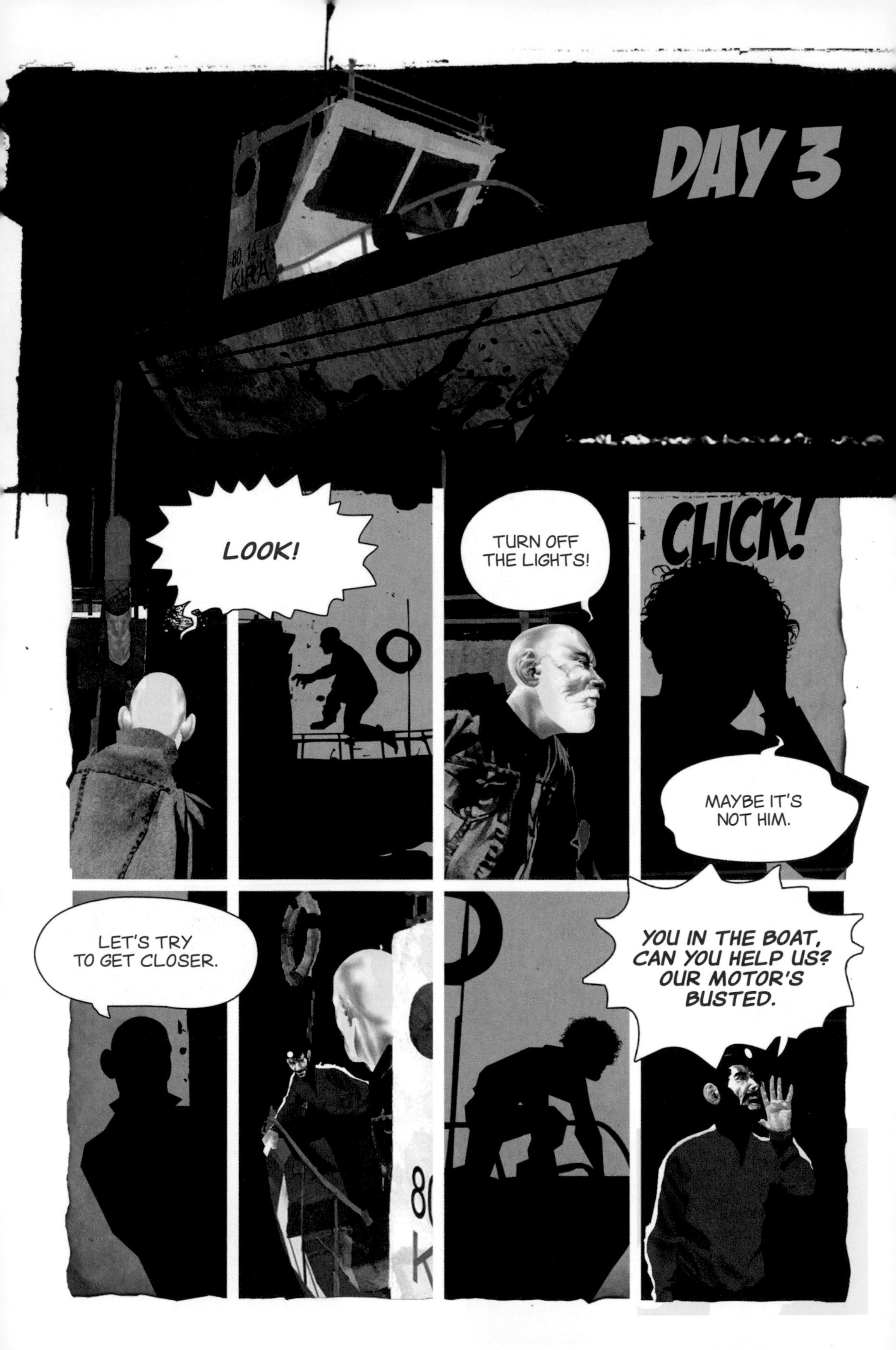
DAY 3
LOOK!
TURN OFF THE LIGHTS!
CLICK!
MAYBE IT'S NOT HIM.
LET'S TRY TO GET CLOSER.
YOU IN THE BOAT, CAN YOU HELP US? OUR MOTOR'S BUSTED.

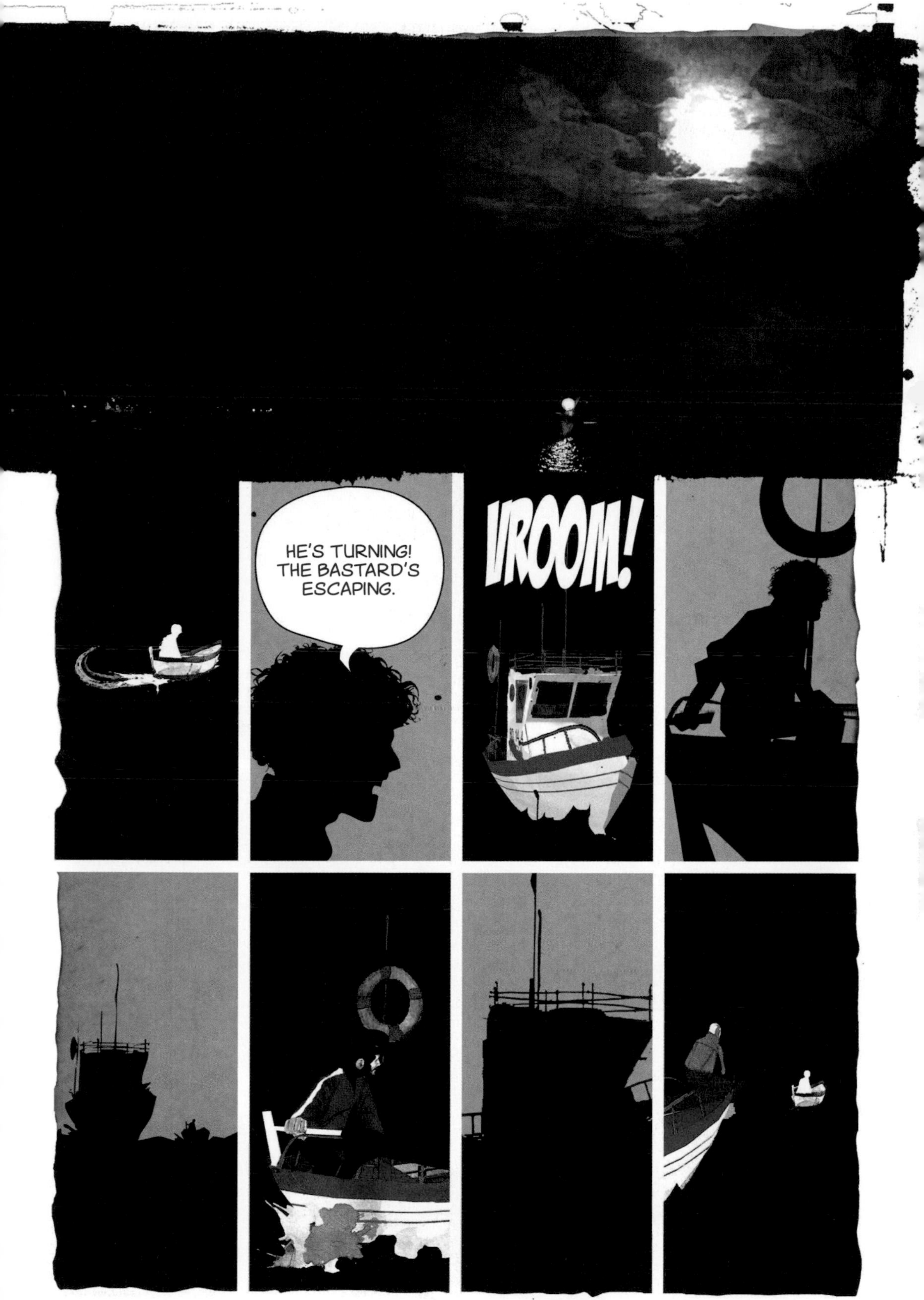
HE'S TURNING! THE BASTARD'S ESCAPING.
VROOM!

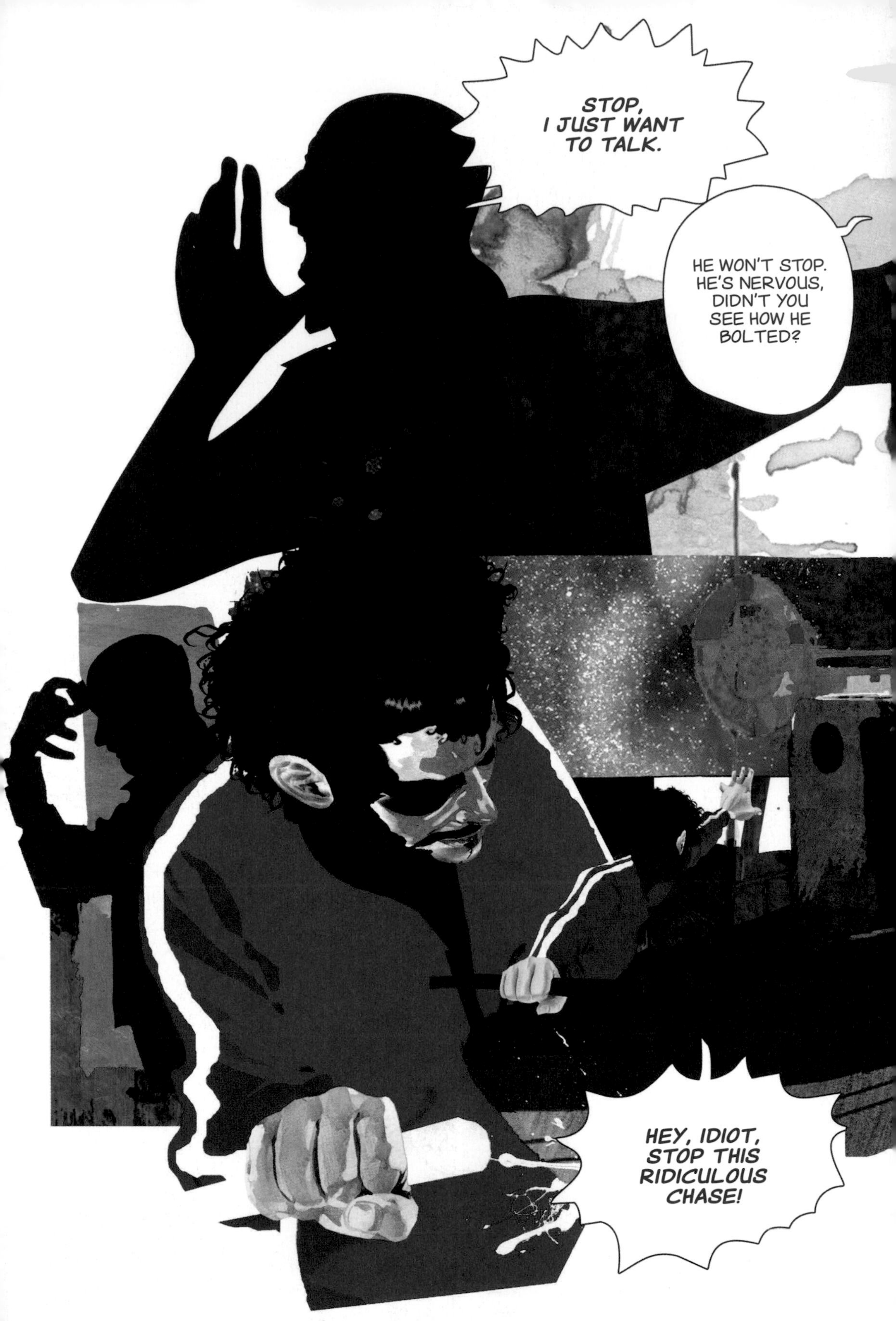
STOP, I JUST WANT TO TALK.
HE WON'T STOP. HE'S NERVOUS, DIDN'T YOU SEE HOW HE BOLTED?
HEY, IDIOT, STOP THIS RIDICULOUS CHASE!

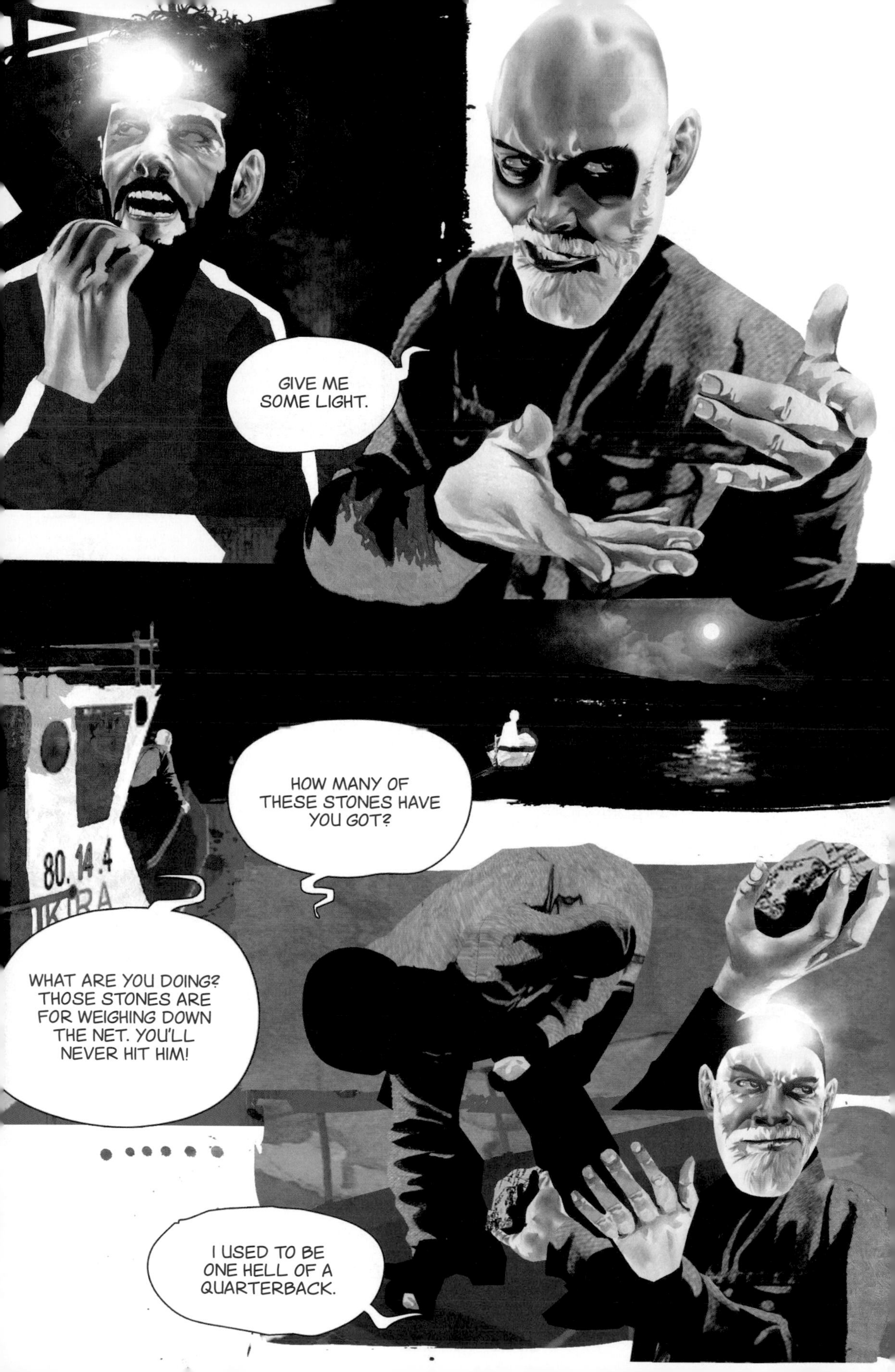
GIVE ME SOME LIGHT.
HOW MANY OF THESE STONES HAVE YOU GOT?
80. 14.4
WHAT ARE YOU DOING? THOSE STONES ARE FOR WEIGHING DOWN THE NET. YOU'LL NEVER HIT HIM!
I USED TO BE ONE HELL OF A QUARTERBACK.

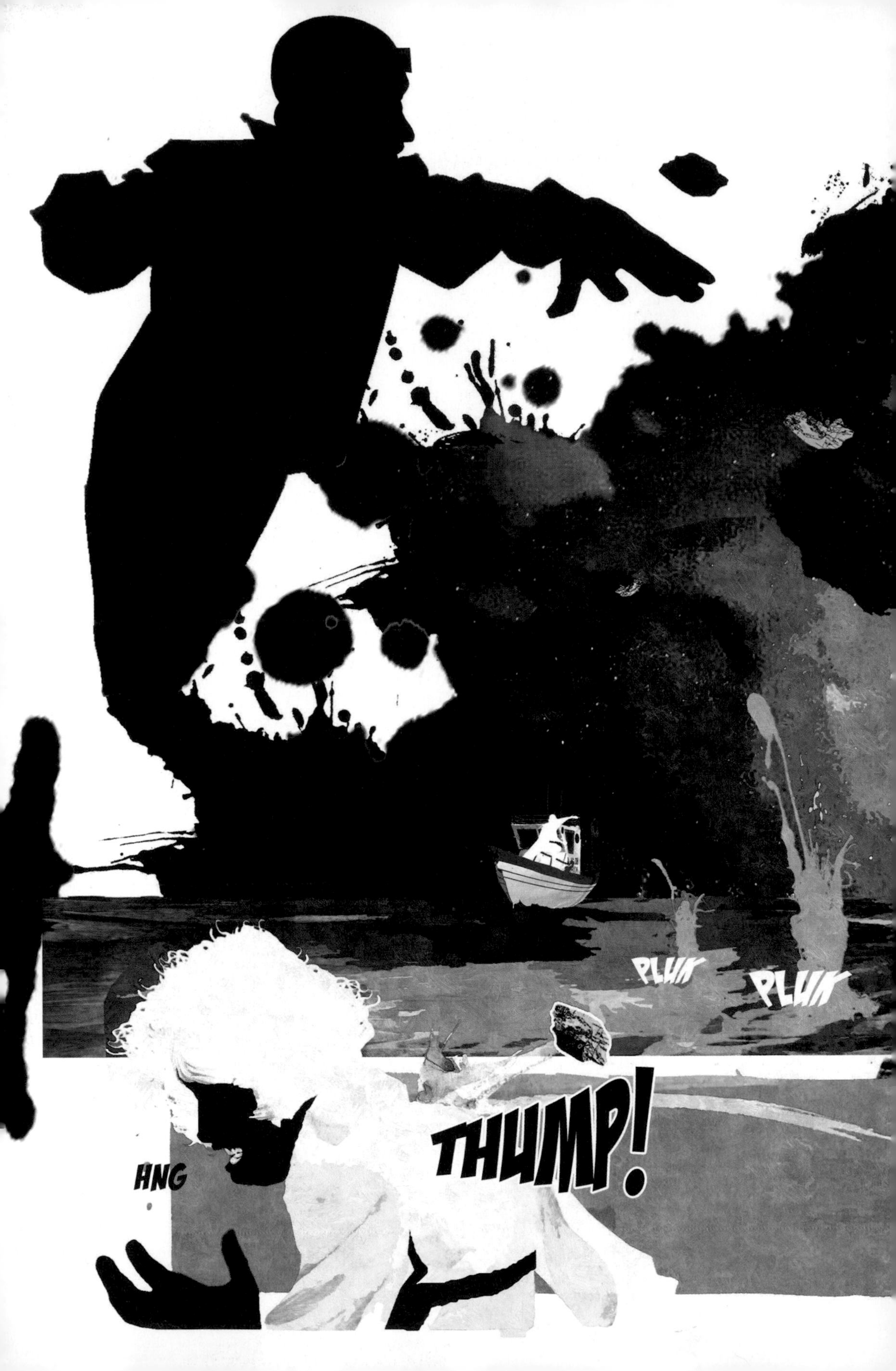
PLUK
PLUK
HNG
THUMP!

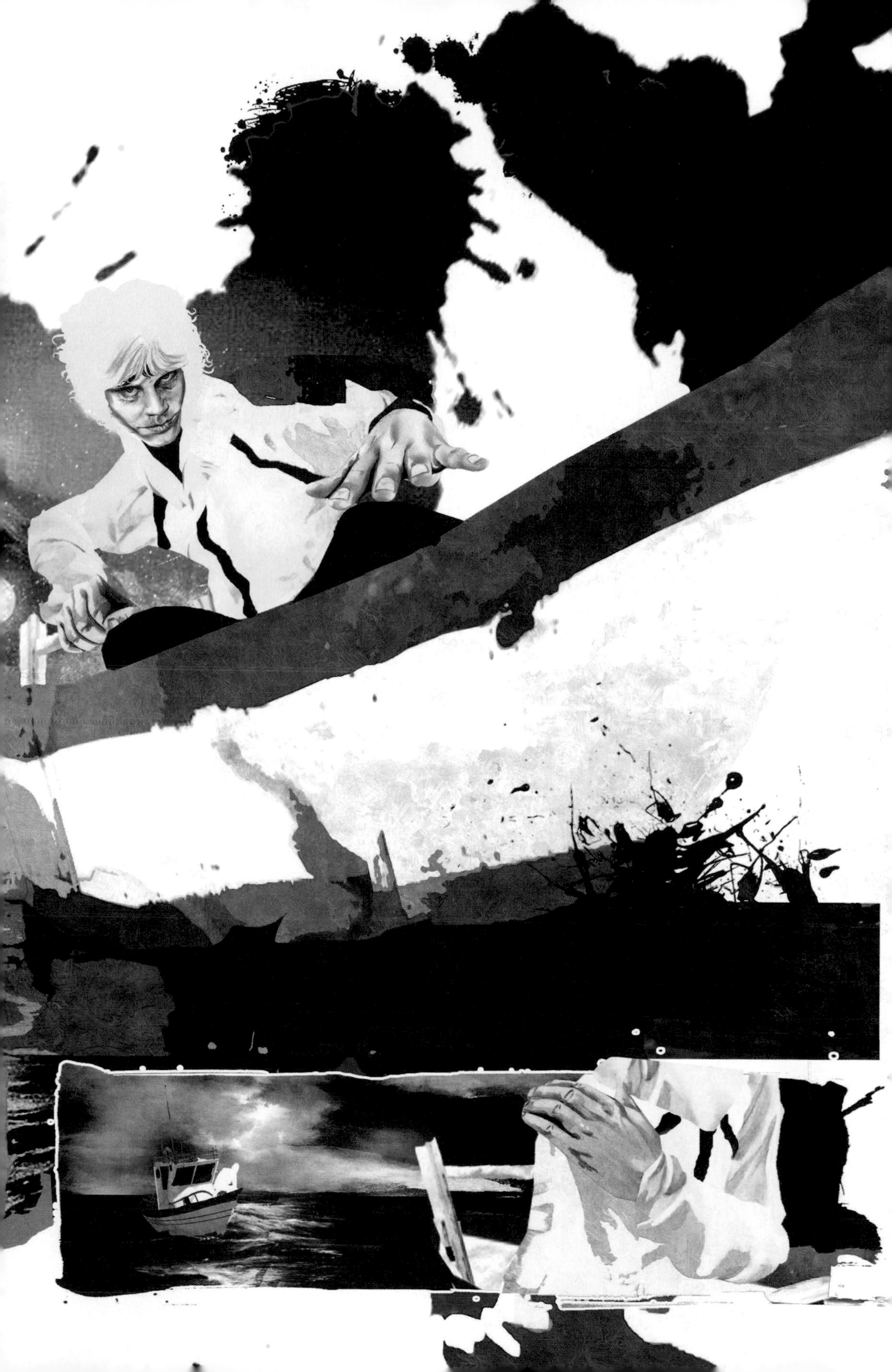

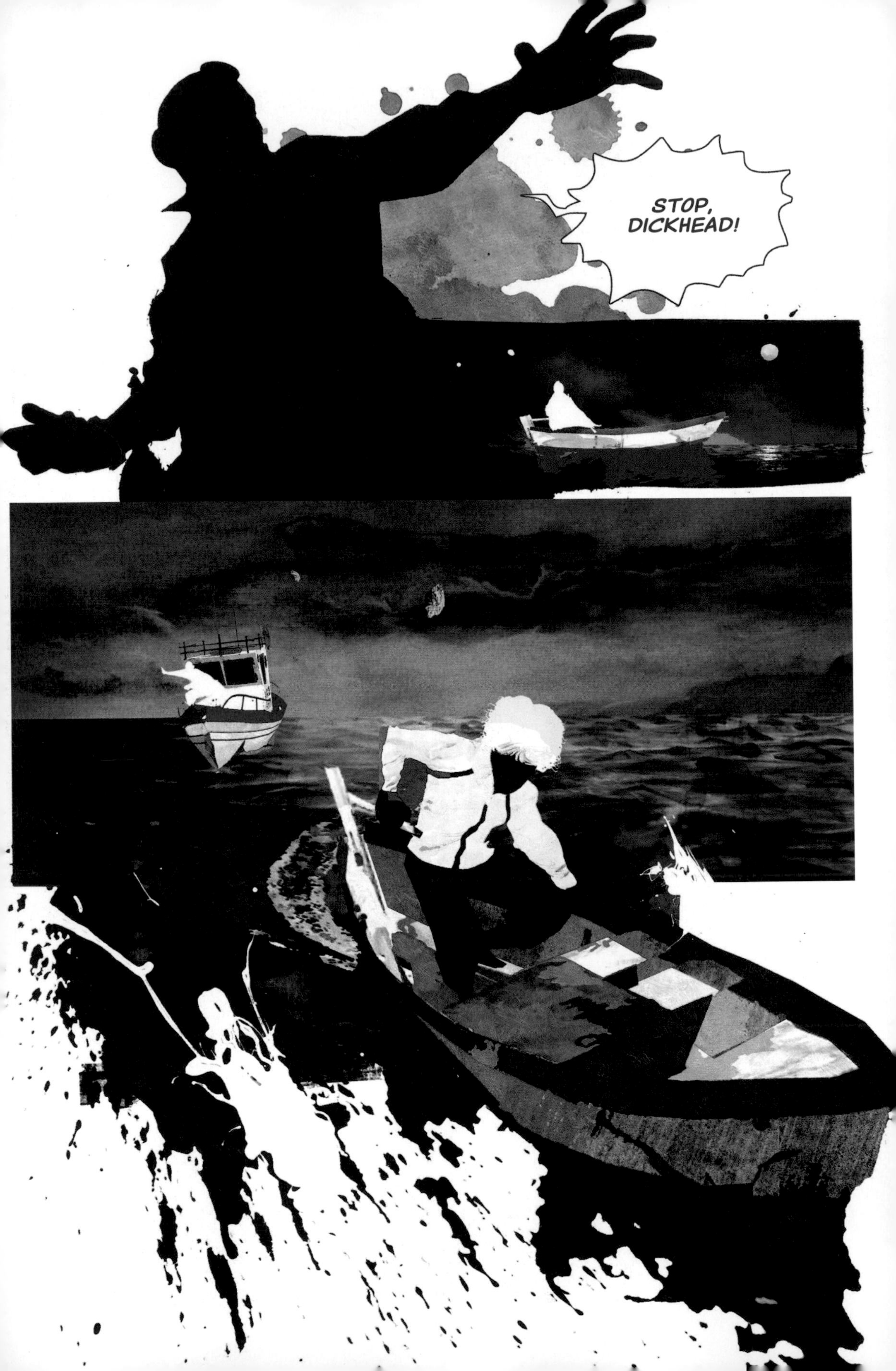
STOP, DICKHEAD!

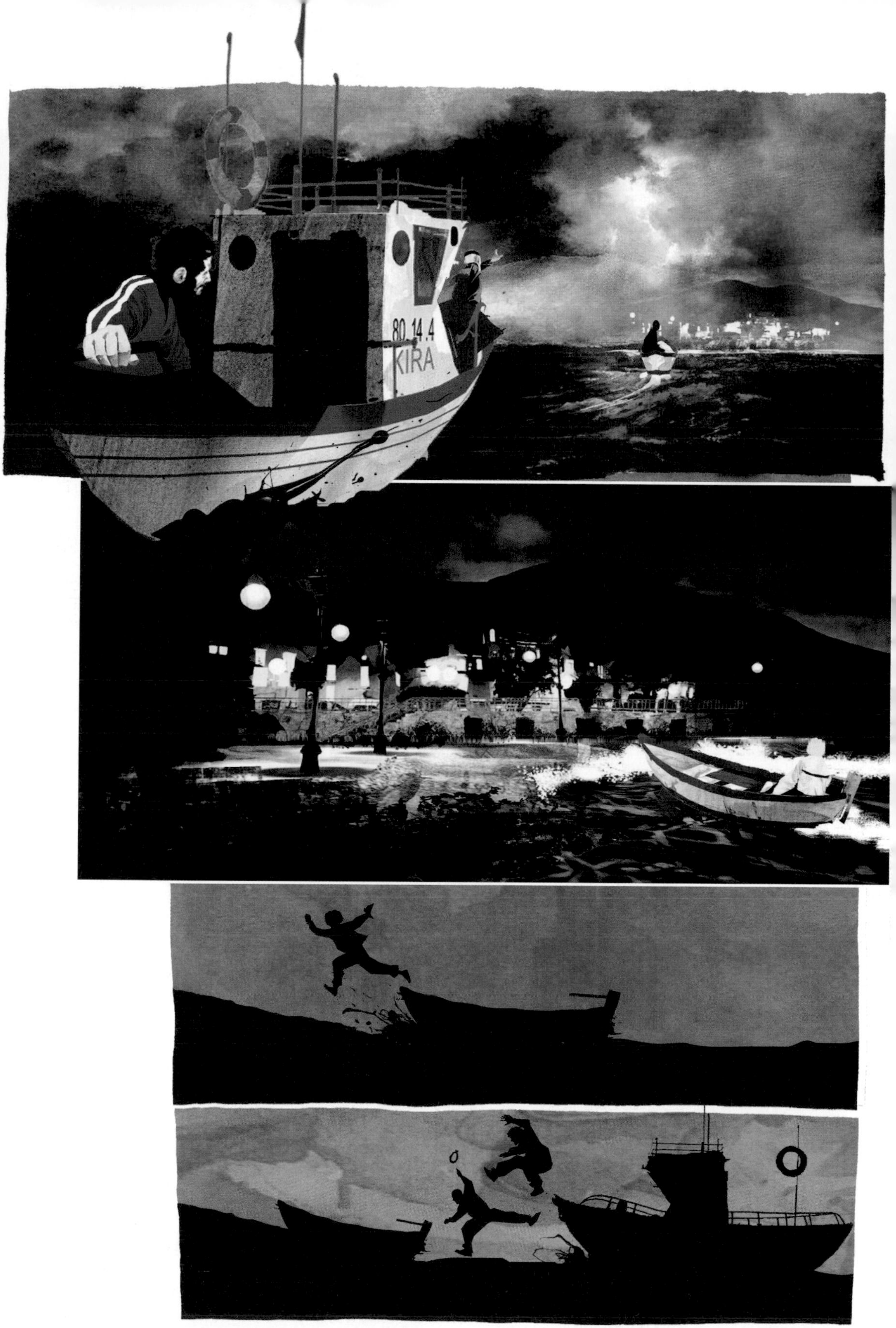
80.14.4
KIRA

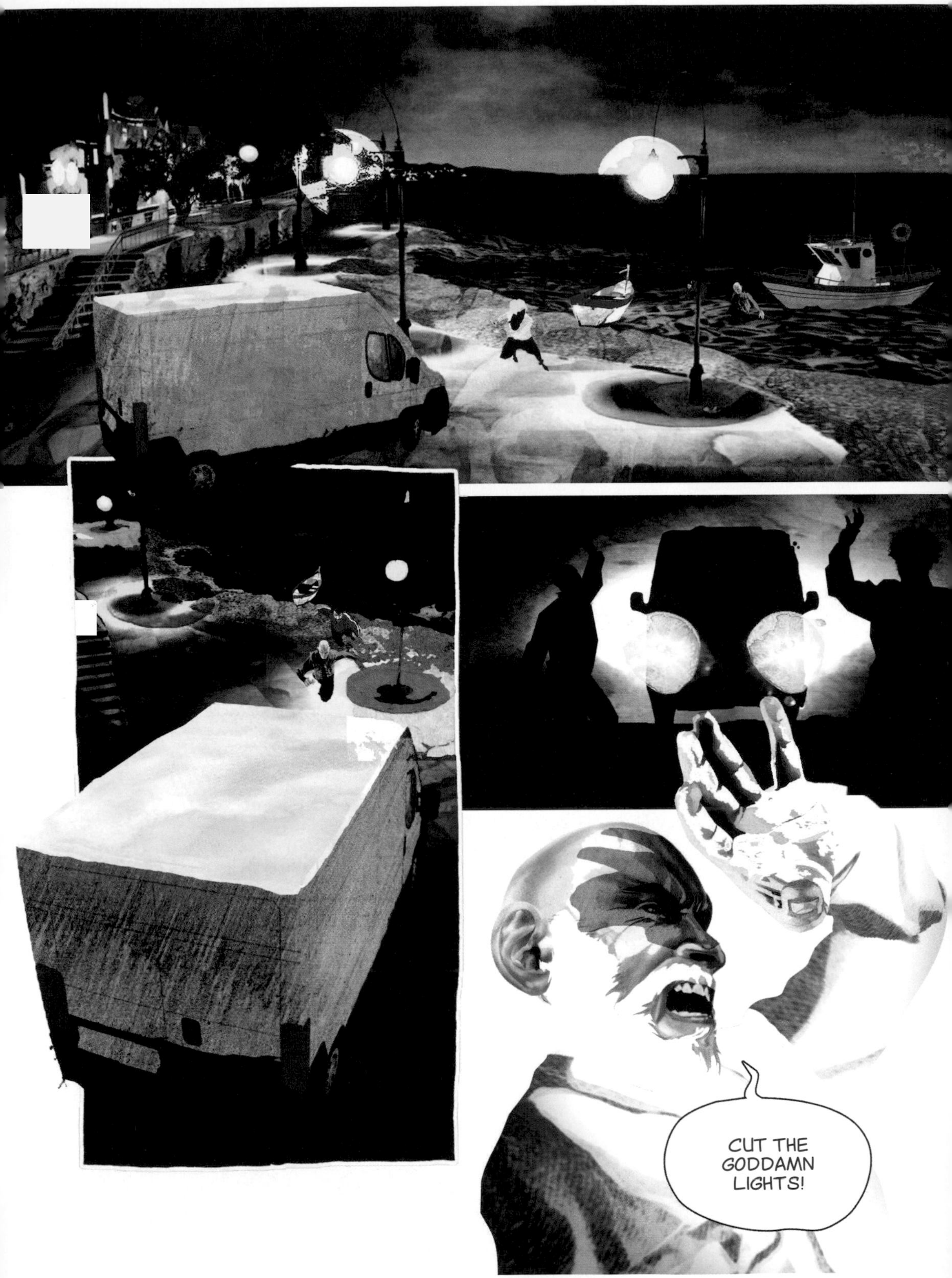
CUT THE
GODDAMN
LIGHTS!

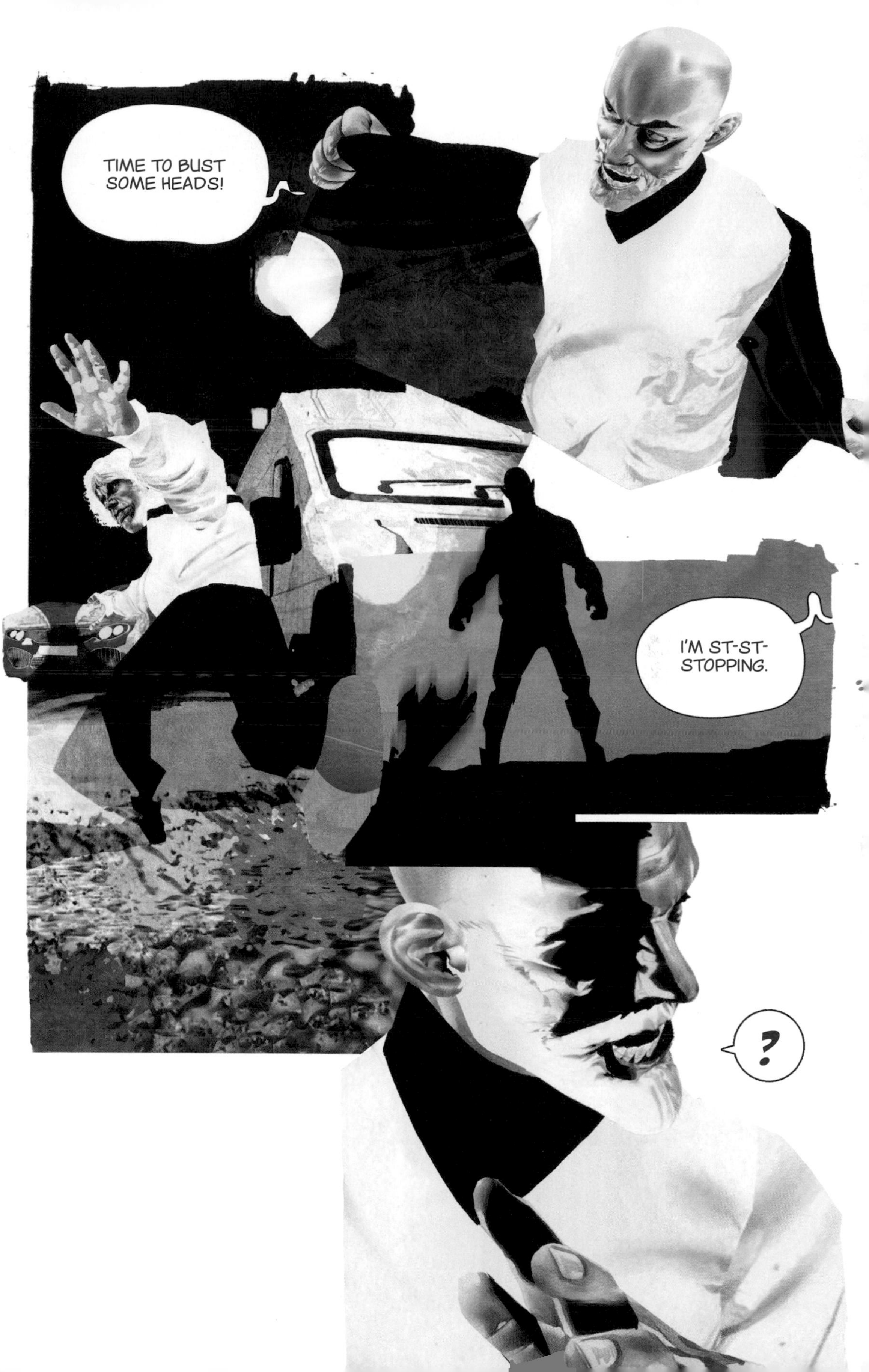
TIME TO BUST
SOME HEADS!
I'M ST-ST-
STOPPING.
?

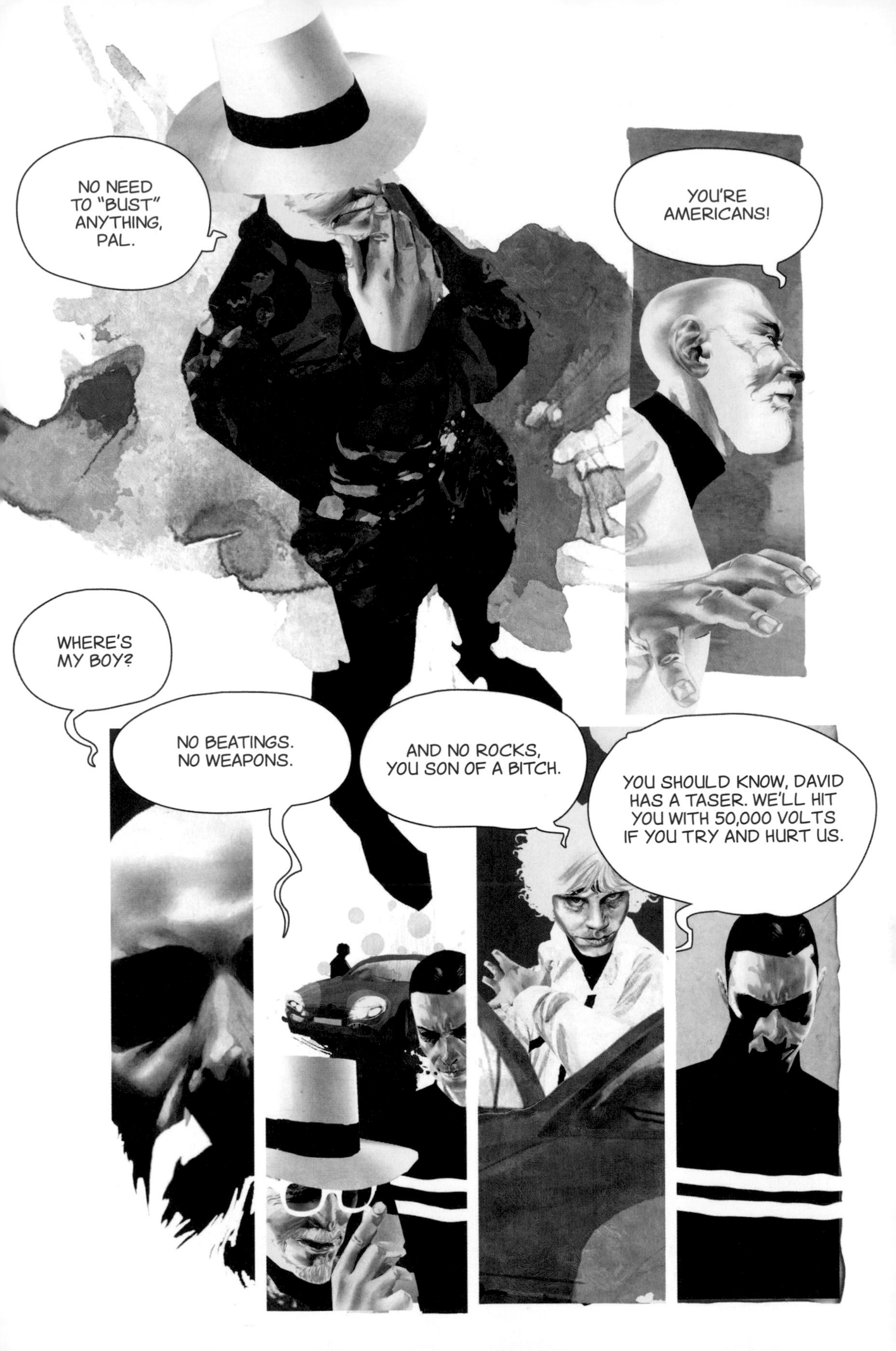
NO NEED TO "BUST" ANYTHING, PAL.
YOU'RE AMERICANS!
WHERE'S MY BOY?
NO BEATINGS. NO WEAPONS.
AND NO ROCKS, YOU SON OF A BITCH.
YOU SHOULD KNOW, DAVID HAS A TASER. WE'LL HIT YOU WITH 50,000 VOLTS IF YOU TRY AND HURT US.

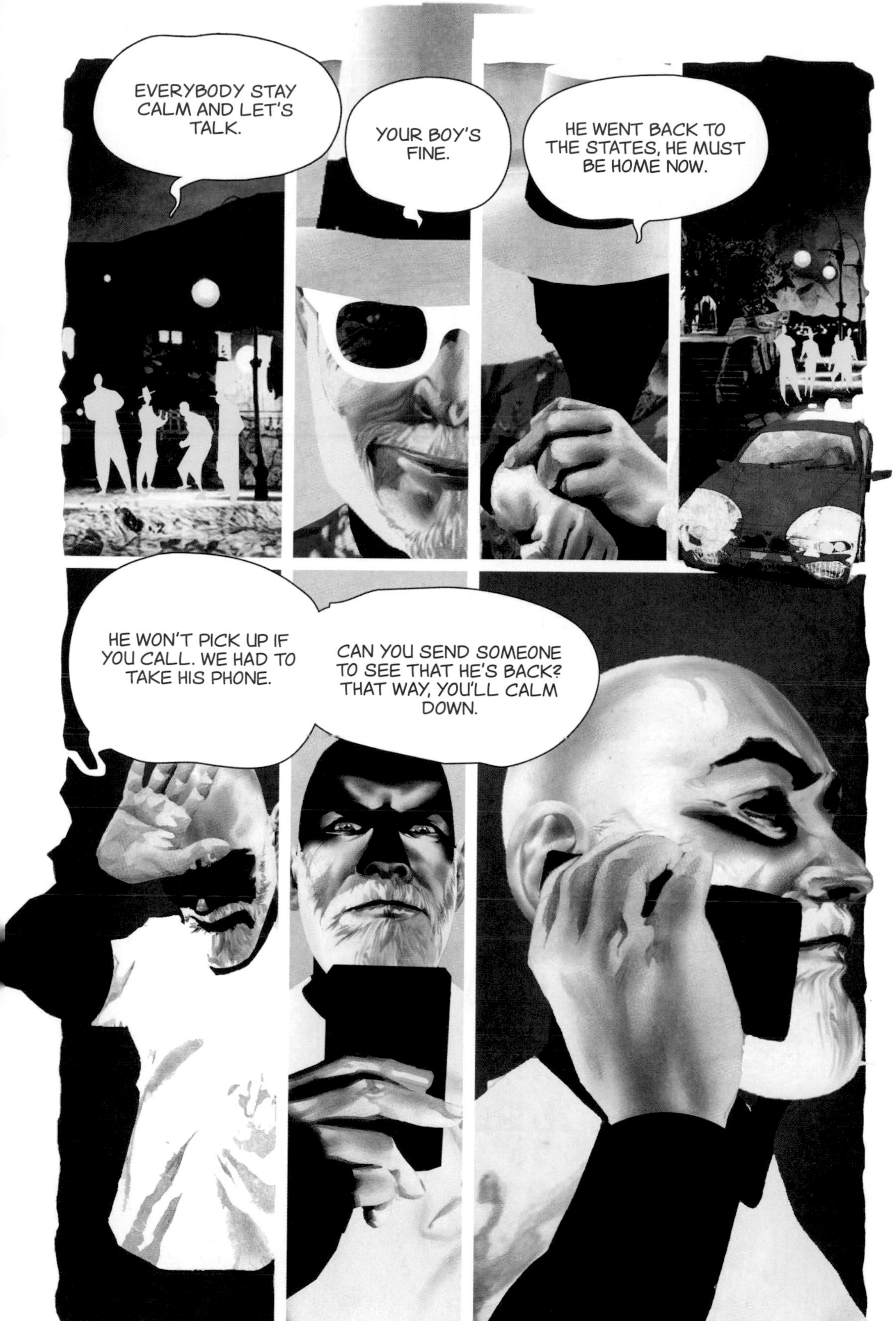
EVERYBODY STAY CALM AND LET'S TALK.
YOUR BOY'S FINE.
HE WENT BACK TO THE STATES, HE MUST BE HOME NOW.
HE WON'T PICK UP IF YOU CALL. WE HAD TO TAKE HIS PHONE.
CAN YOU SEND SOMEONE TO SEE THAT HE'S BACK? THAT WAY, YOU'LL CALM DOWN.

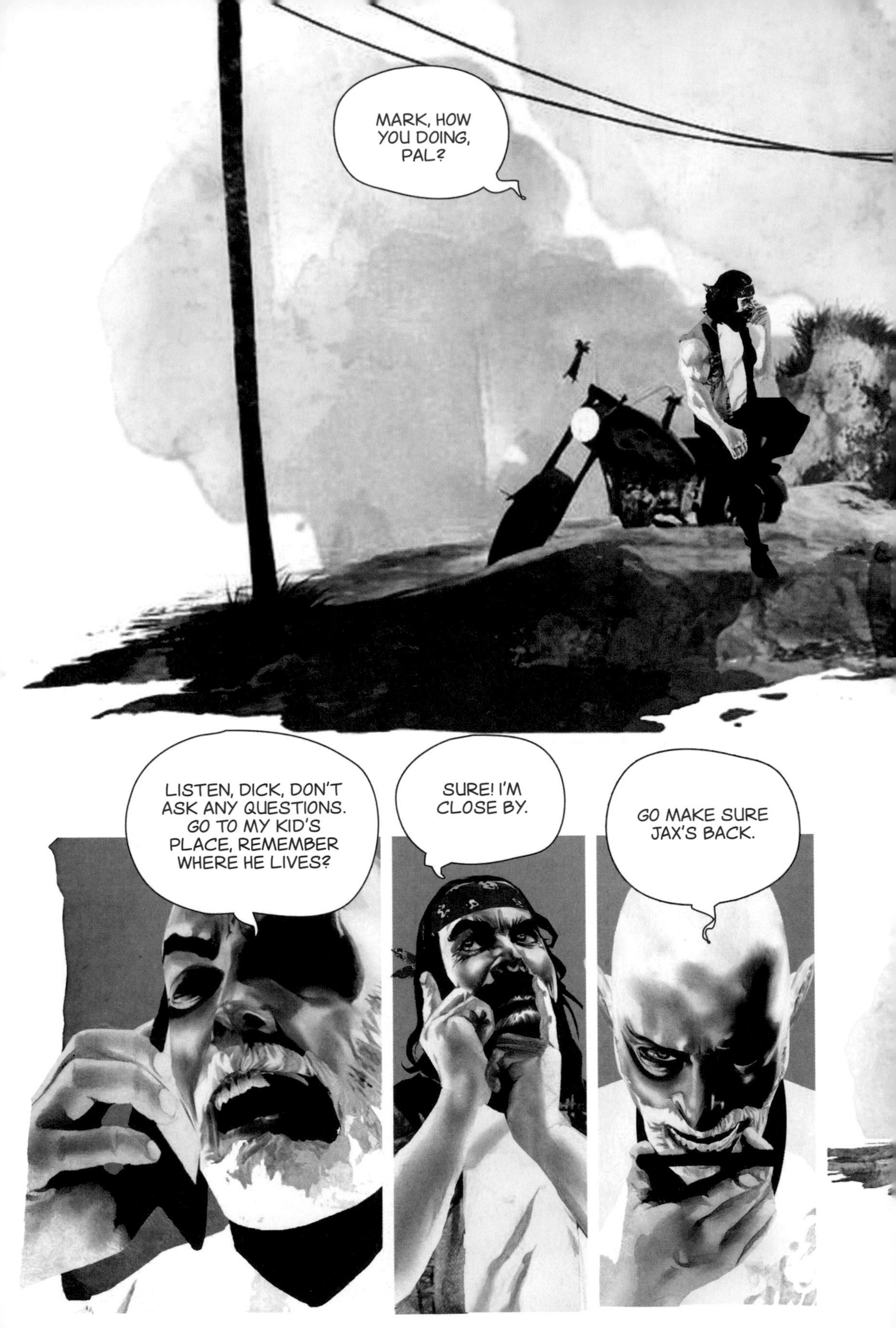
MARK, HOW YOU DOING, PAL?
LISTEN, DICK, DON'T ASK ANY QUESTIONS. GO TO MY KID'S PLACE, REMEMBER WHERE HE LIVES?
SURE! I'M CLOSE BY.
GO MAKE SURE JAX'S BACK.

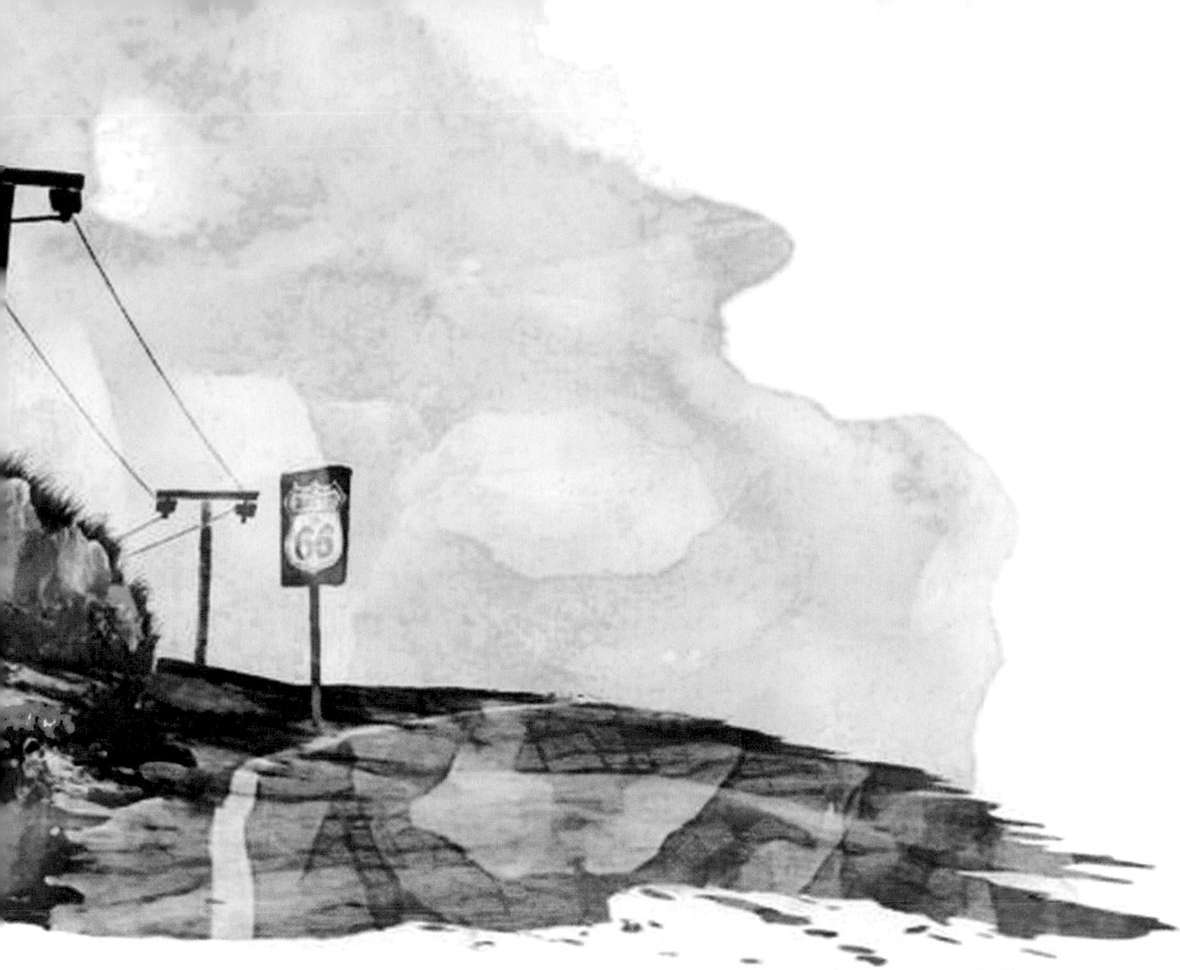

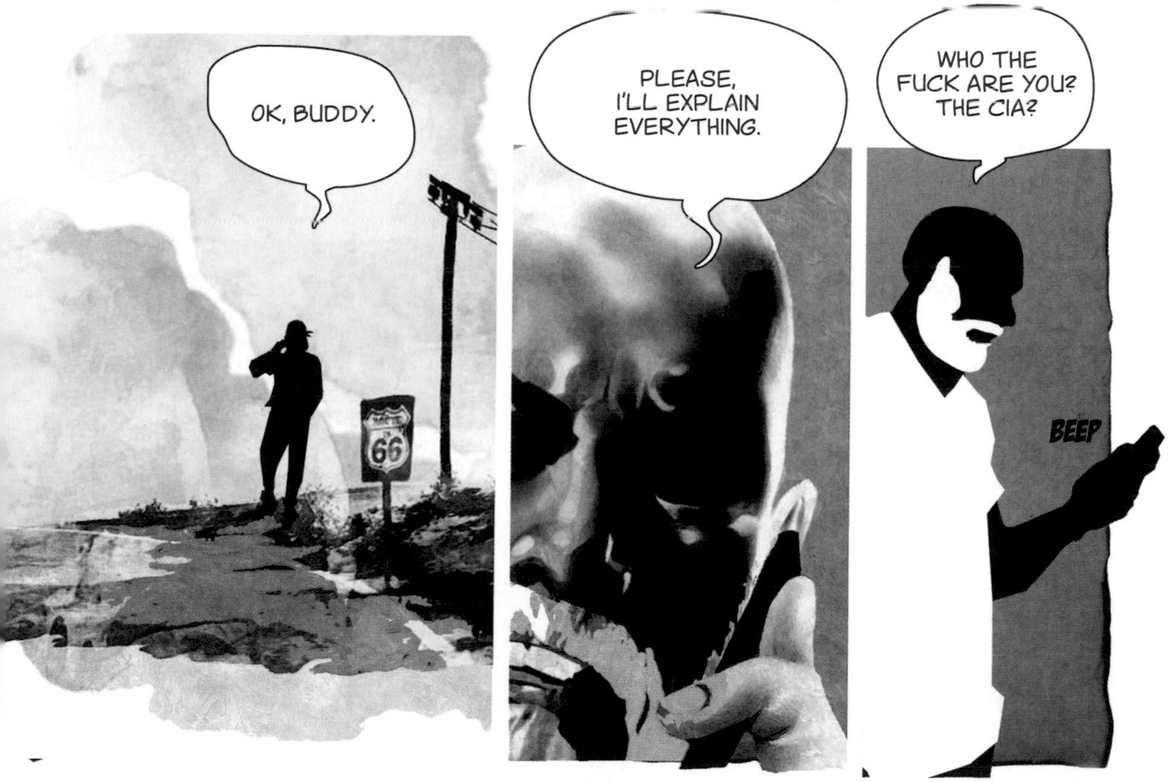
OK, BUDDY.
PLEASE, I'LL EXPLAIN EVERYTHING.
WHO THE FUCK ARE YOU? THE CIA?
BEEP

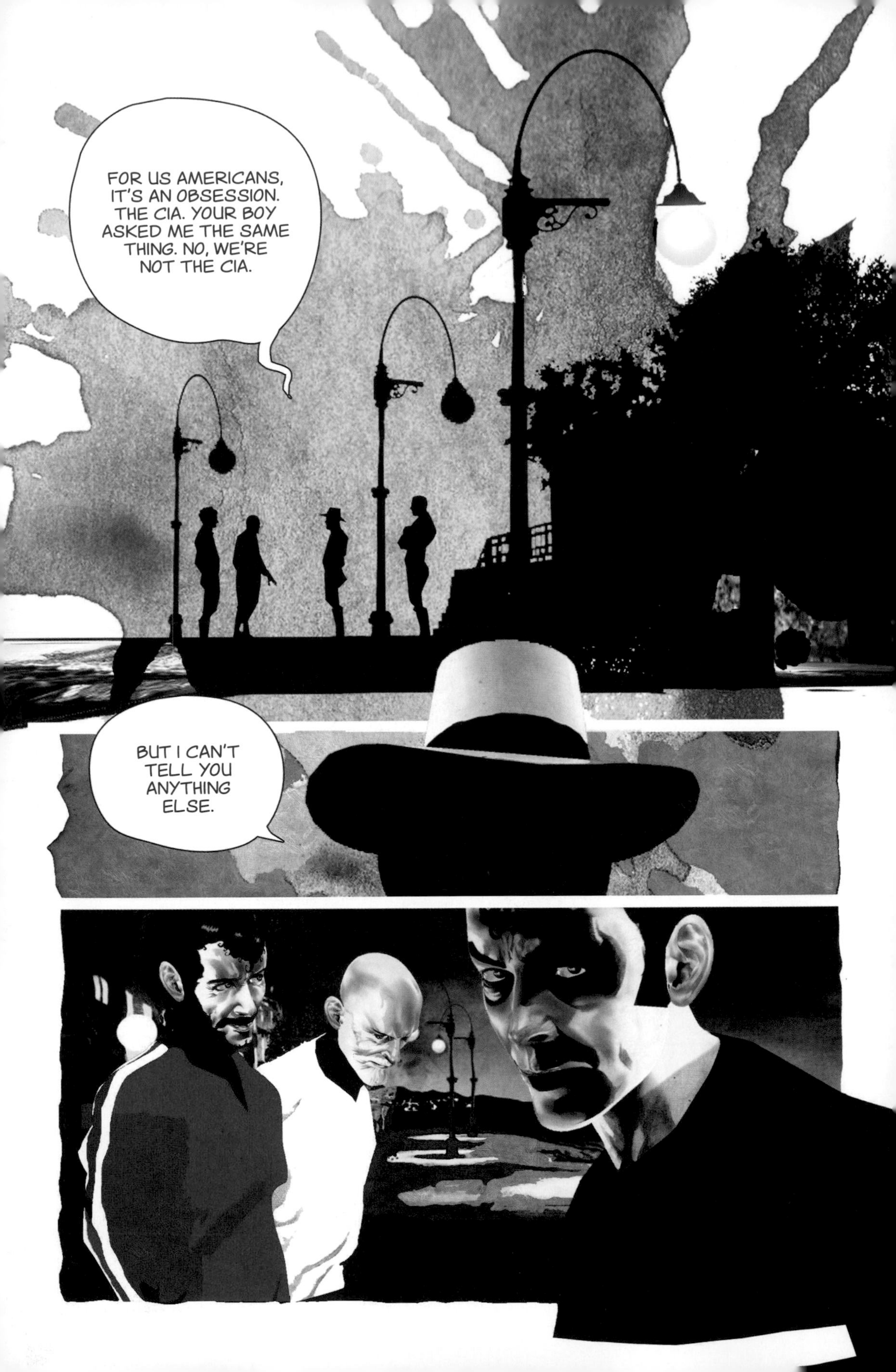
FOR US AMERICANS, IT'S AN OBSESSION. THE CIA. YOUR BOY ASKED ME THE SAME THING. NO, WE'RE NOT THE CIA.
BUT I CAN'T TELL YOU ANYTHING ELSE.

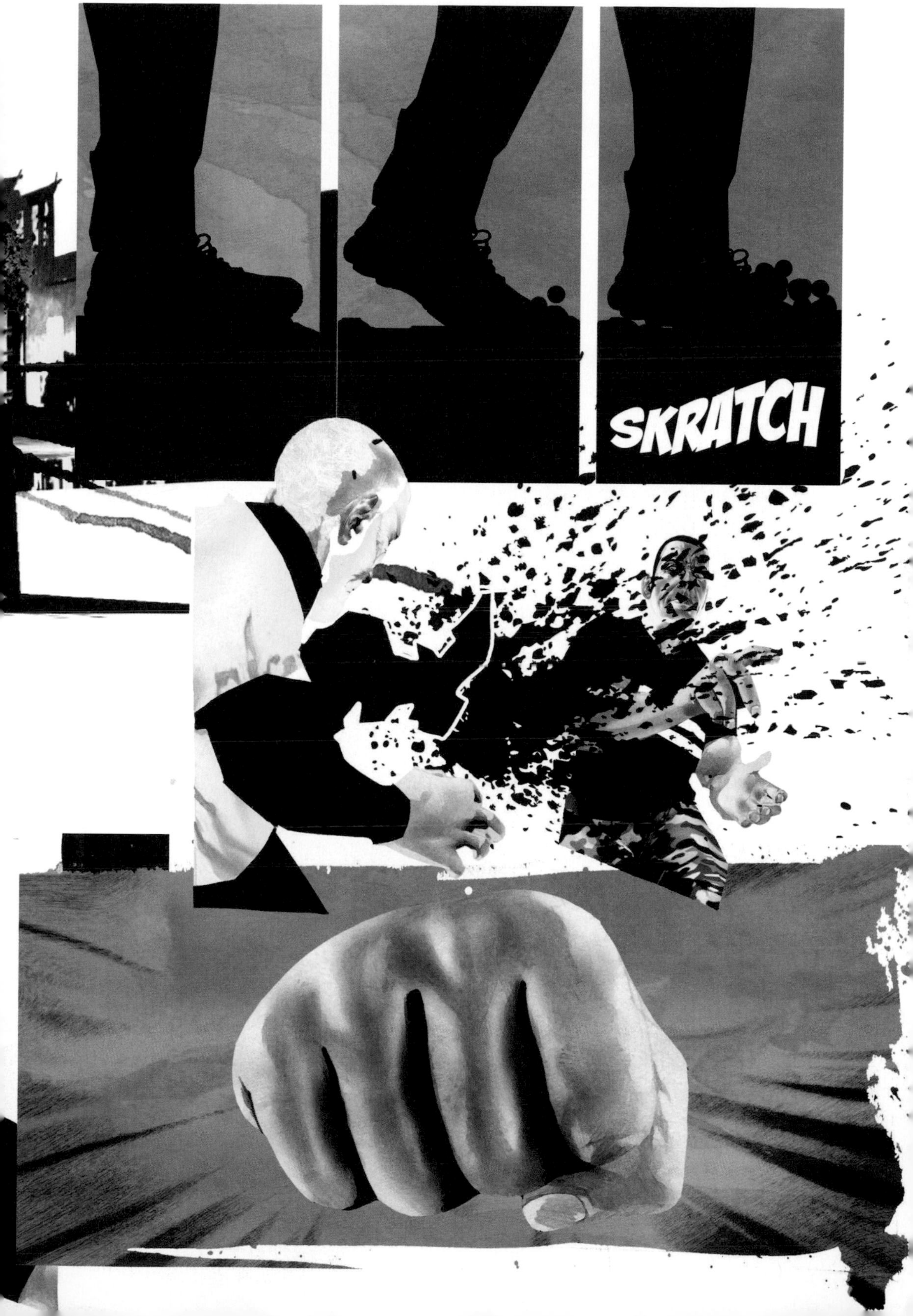
SKRATCH

JAX OVER THE PHONE
Springfield, Oregon - USA

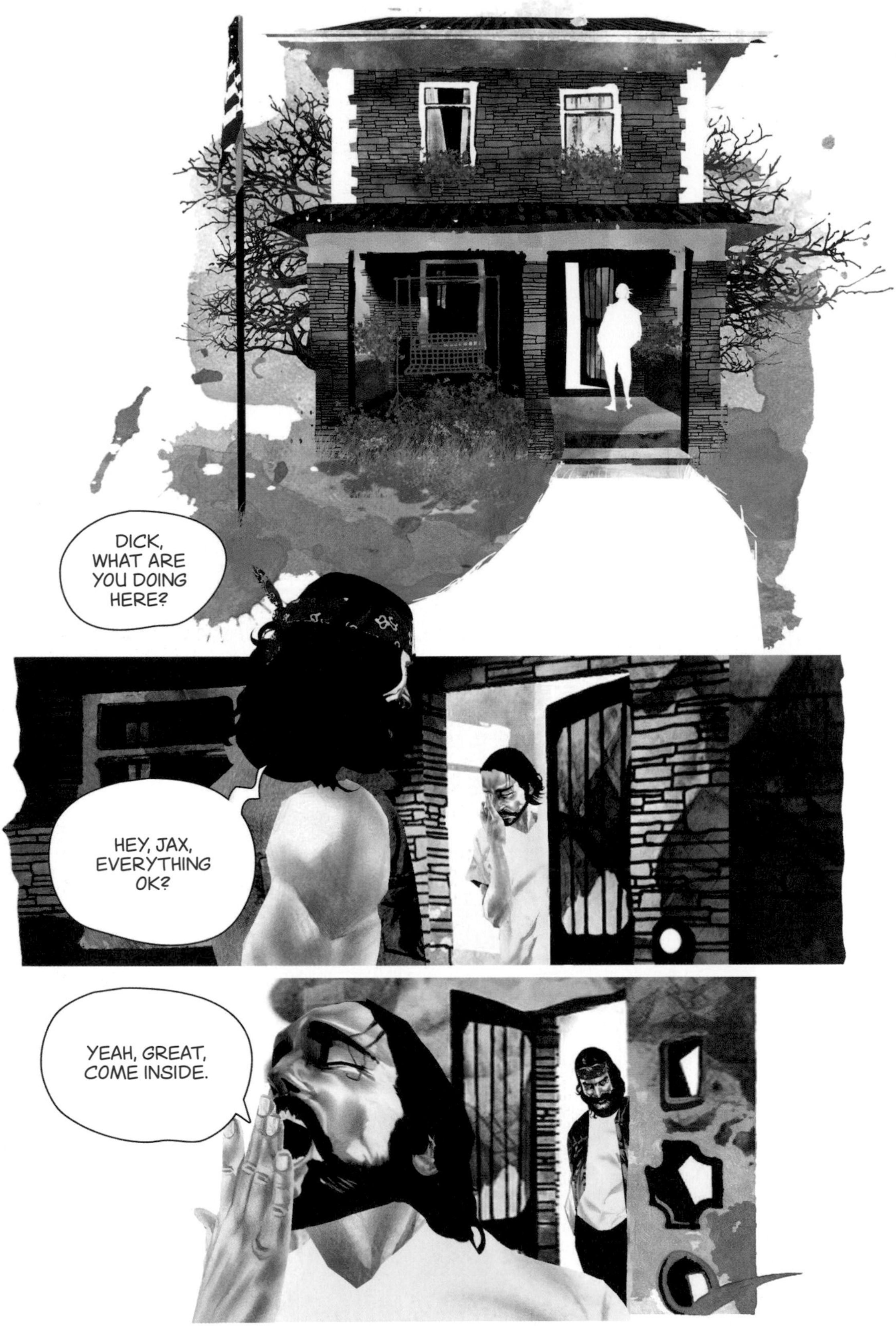
DICK, WHAT ARE YOU DOING HERE?
HEY, JAX, EVERYTHING OK?
YEAH, GREAT, COME INSIDE.

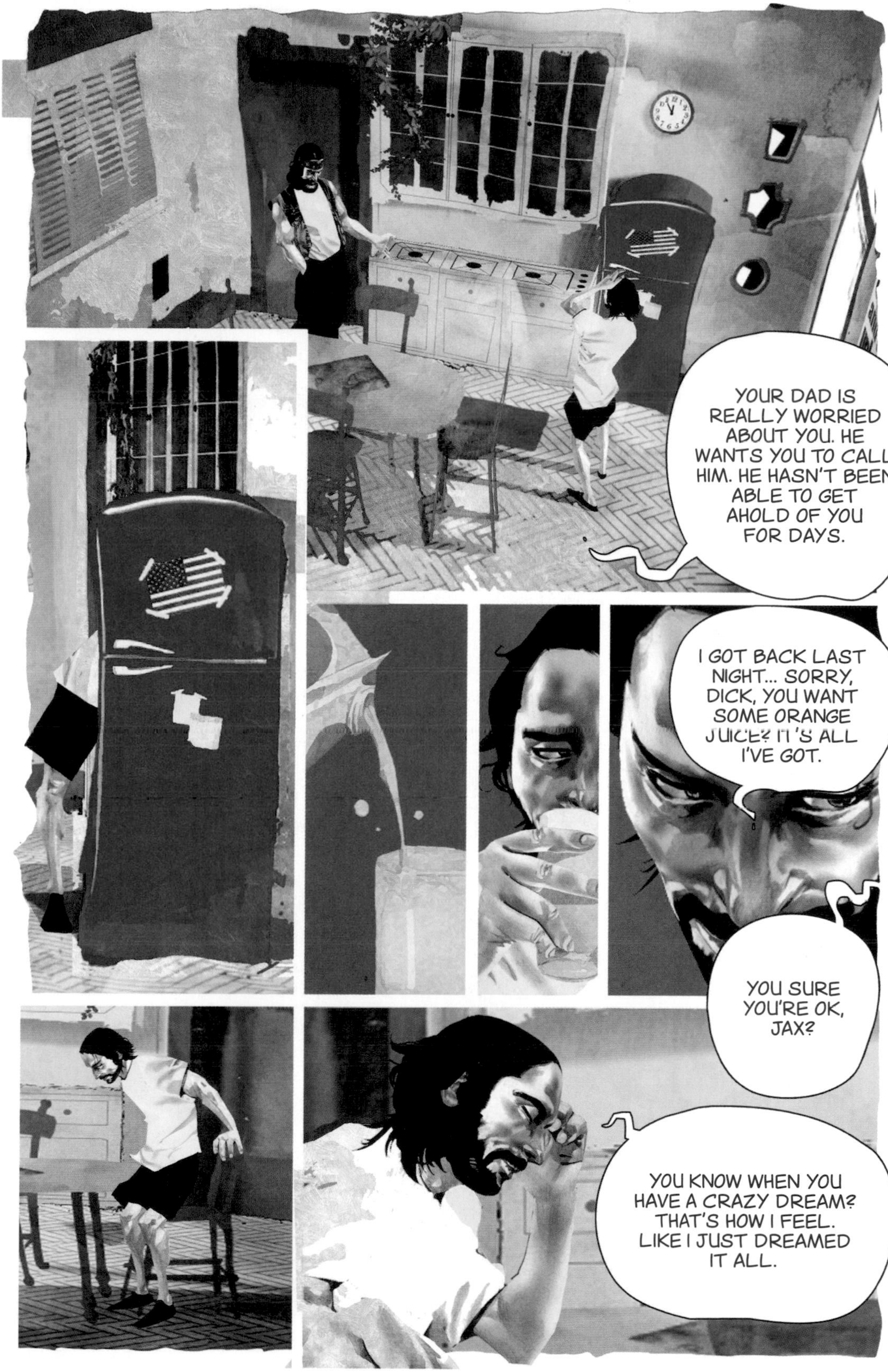
YOUR DAD IS REALLY WORRIED ABOUT YOU. HE WANTS YOU TO CALL HIM. HE HASN'T BEEN ABLE TO GET AHOLD OF YOU FOR DAYS.
I GOT BACK LAST NIGHT... SORRY, DICK, YOU WANT SOME ORANGE JUICE? IT'S ALL I'VE GOT.
YOU SURE YOU'RE OK, JAX?
YOU KNOW WHEN YOU HAVE A CRAZY DREAM? THAT'S HOW I FEEL. LIKE I JUST DREAMED IT ALL.

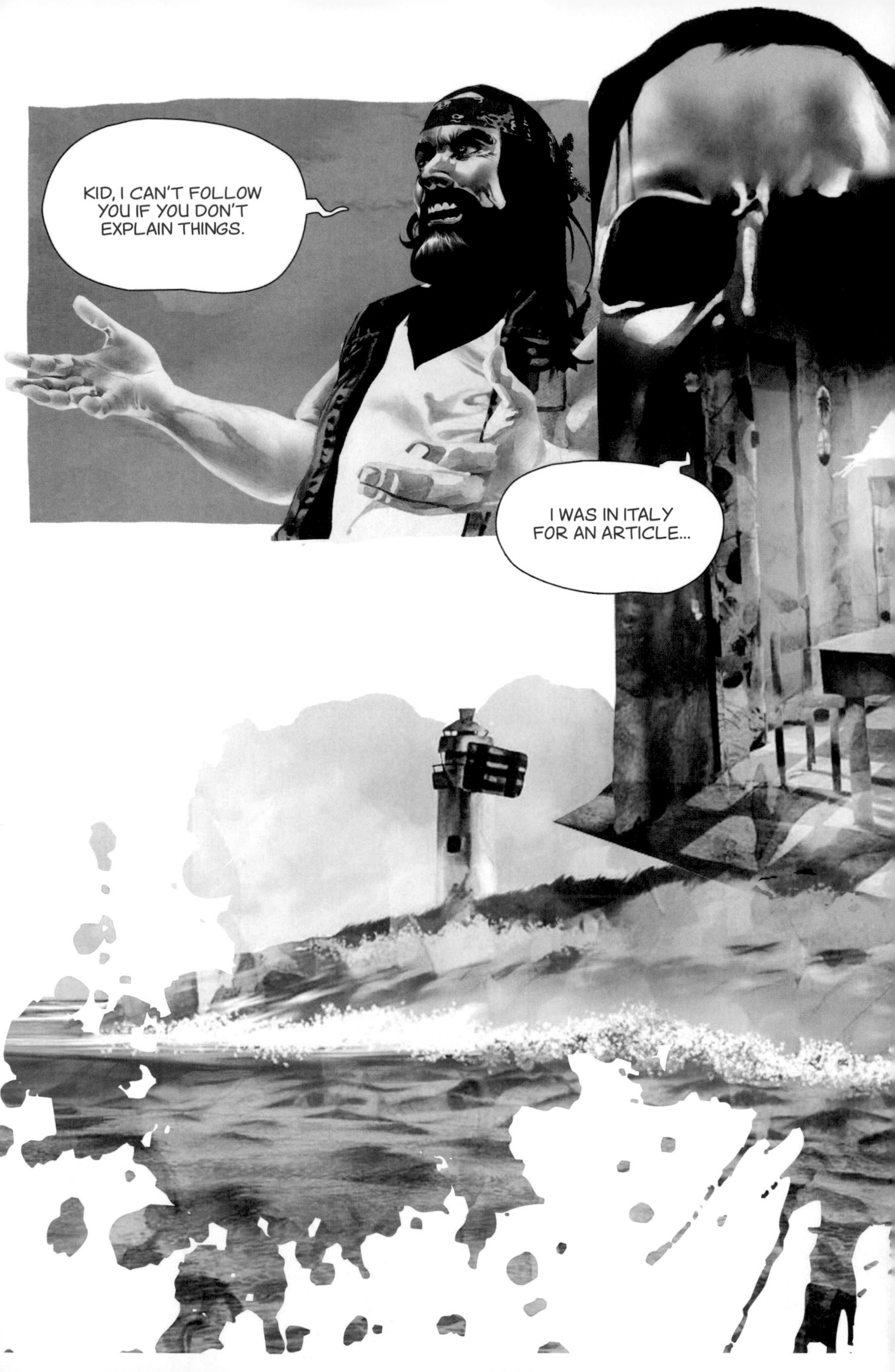
KID, I CAN'T FOLLOW YOU IF YOU DON'T EXPLAIN THINGS.
I WAS IN ITALY FOR AN ARTICLE...

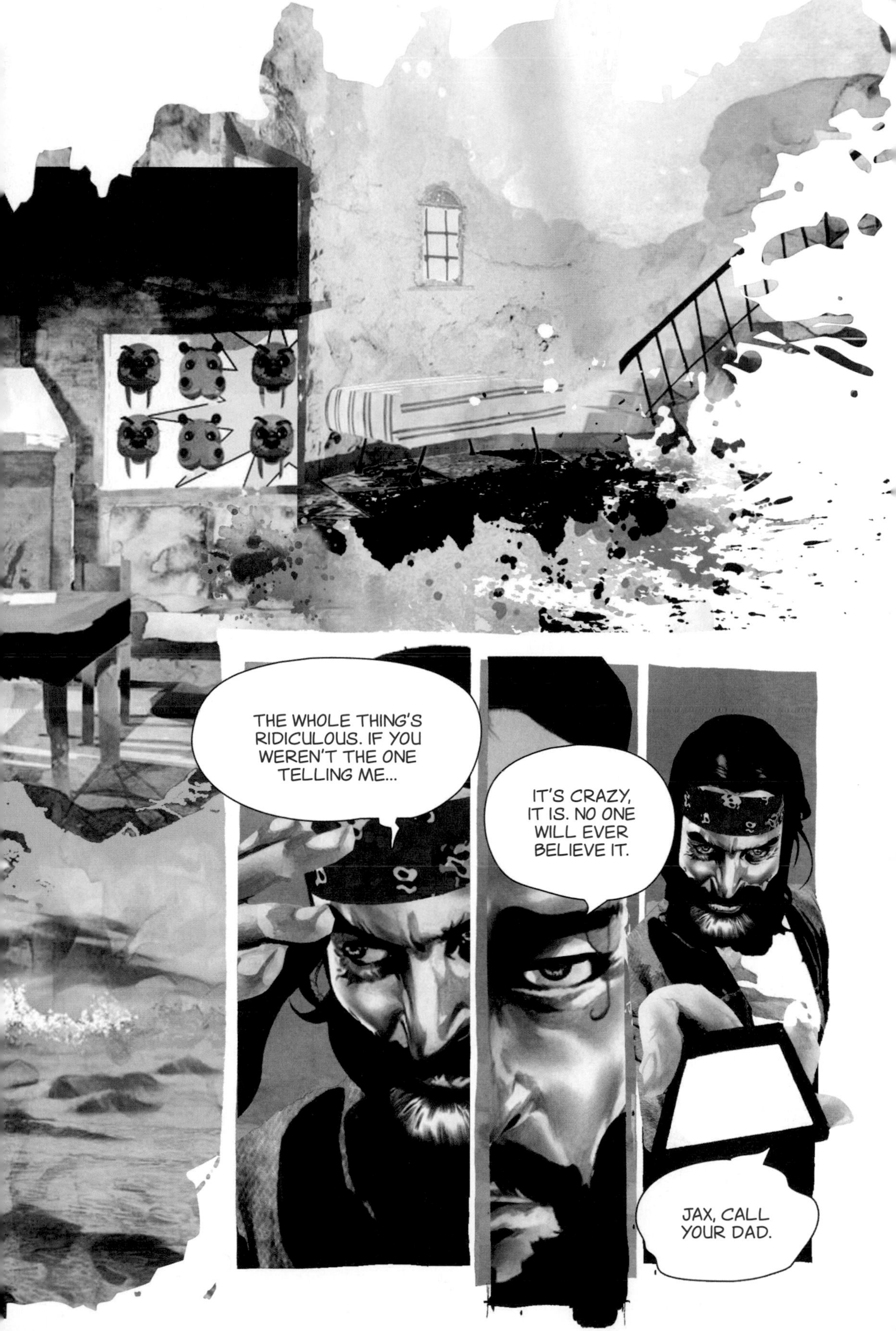
THE WHOLE THING'S RIDICULOUS. IF YOU WEREN'T THE ONE TELLING ME...
IT'S CRAZY, IT IS. NO ONE WILL EVER BELIEVE IT.
JAX, CALL YOUR DAD.

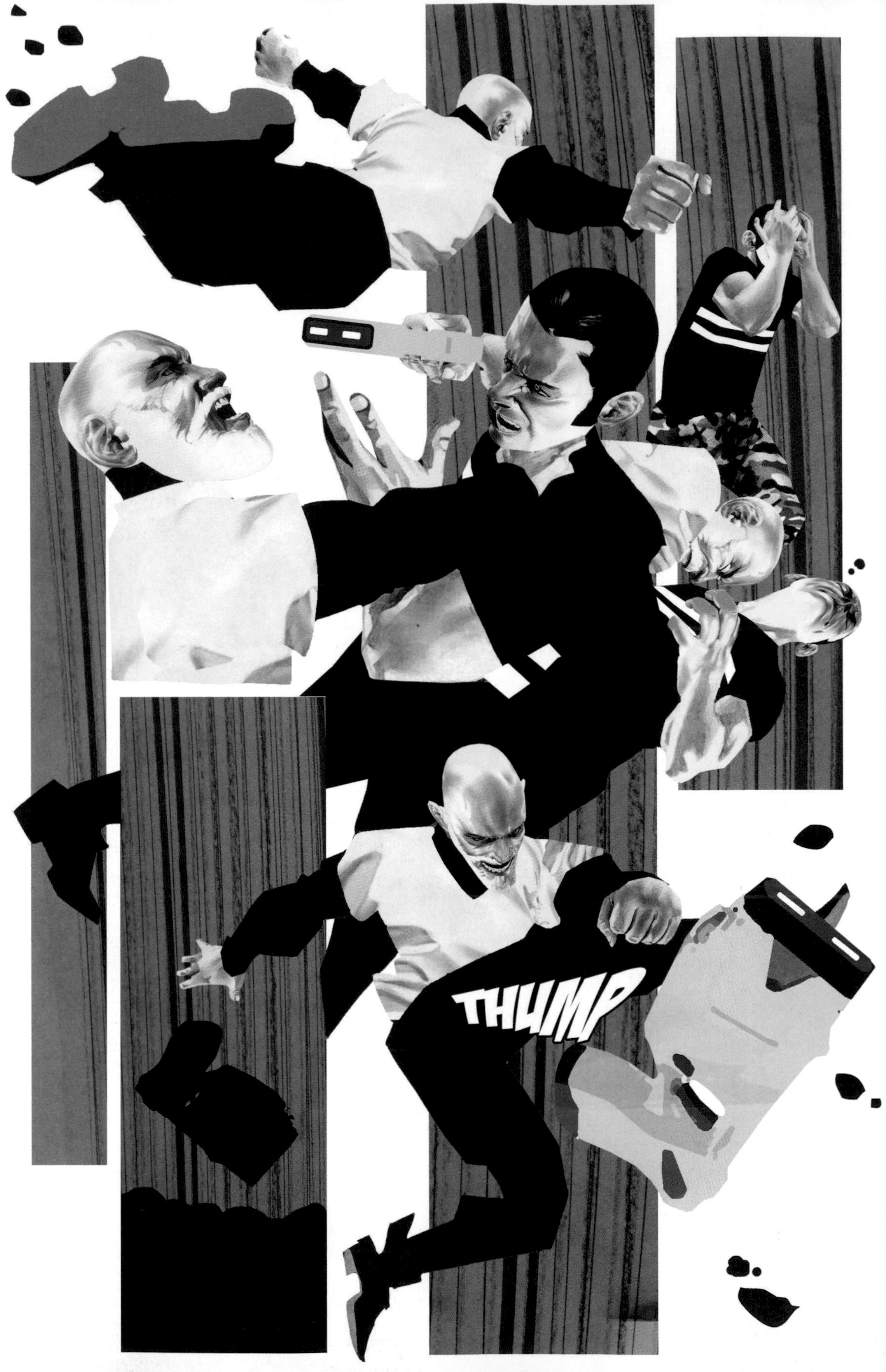
THUMP

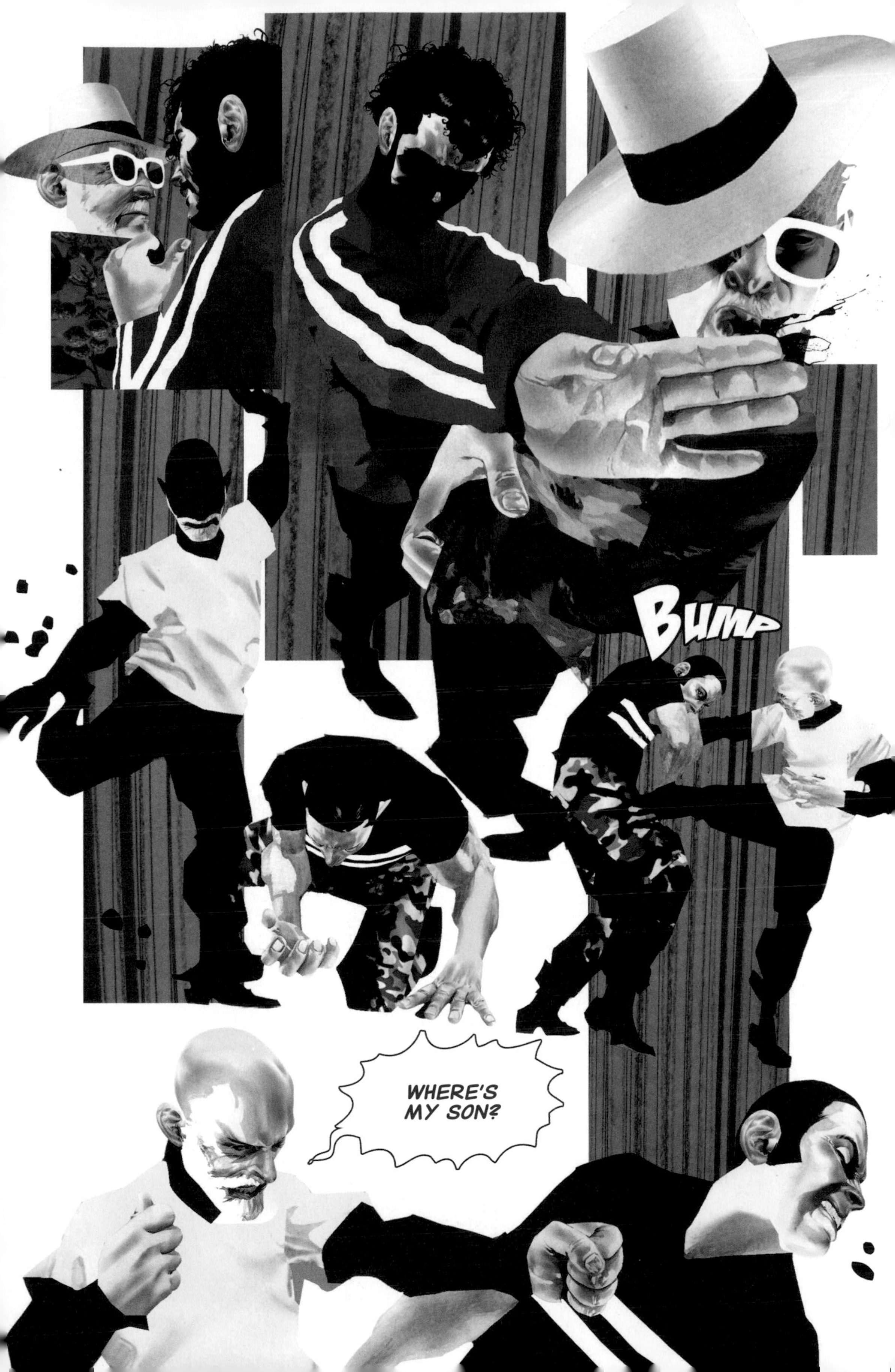
BUMP
WHERE'S MY SON?

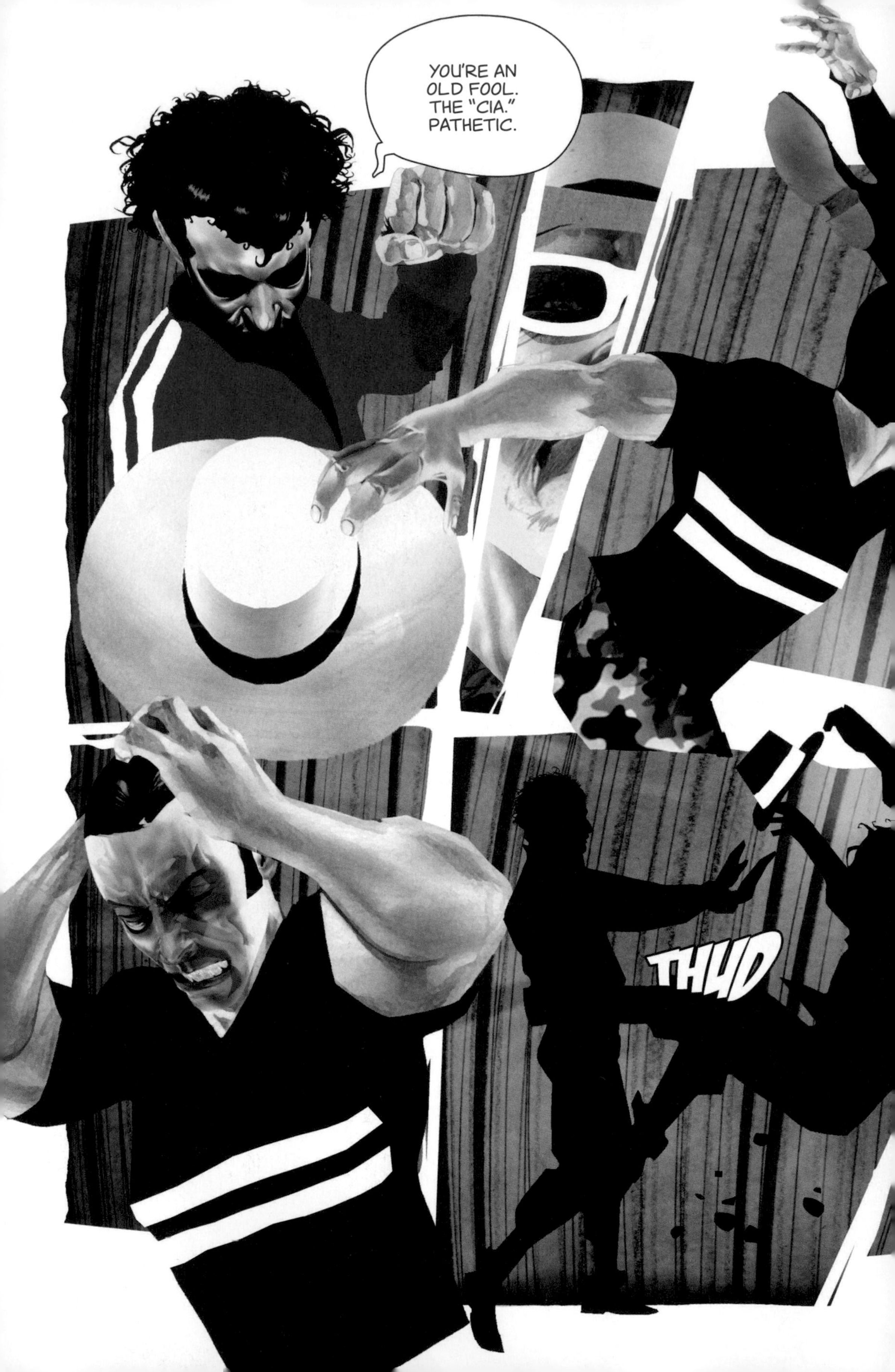
YOU'RE AN OLD FOOL. THE "CIA." PATHETIC.
THUD

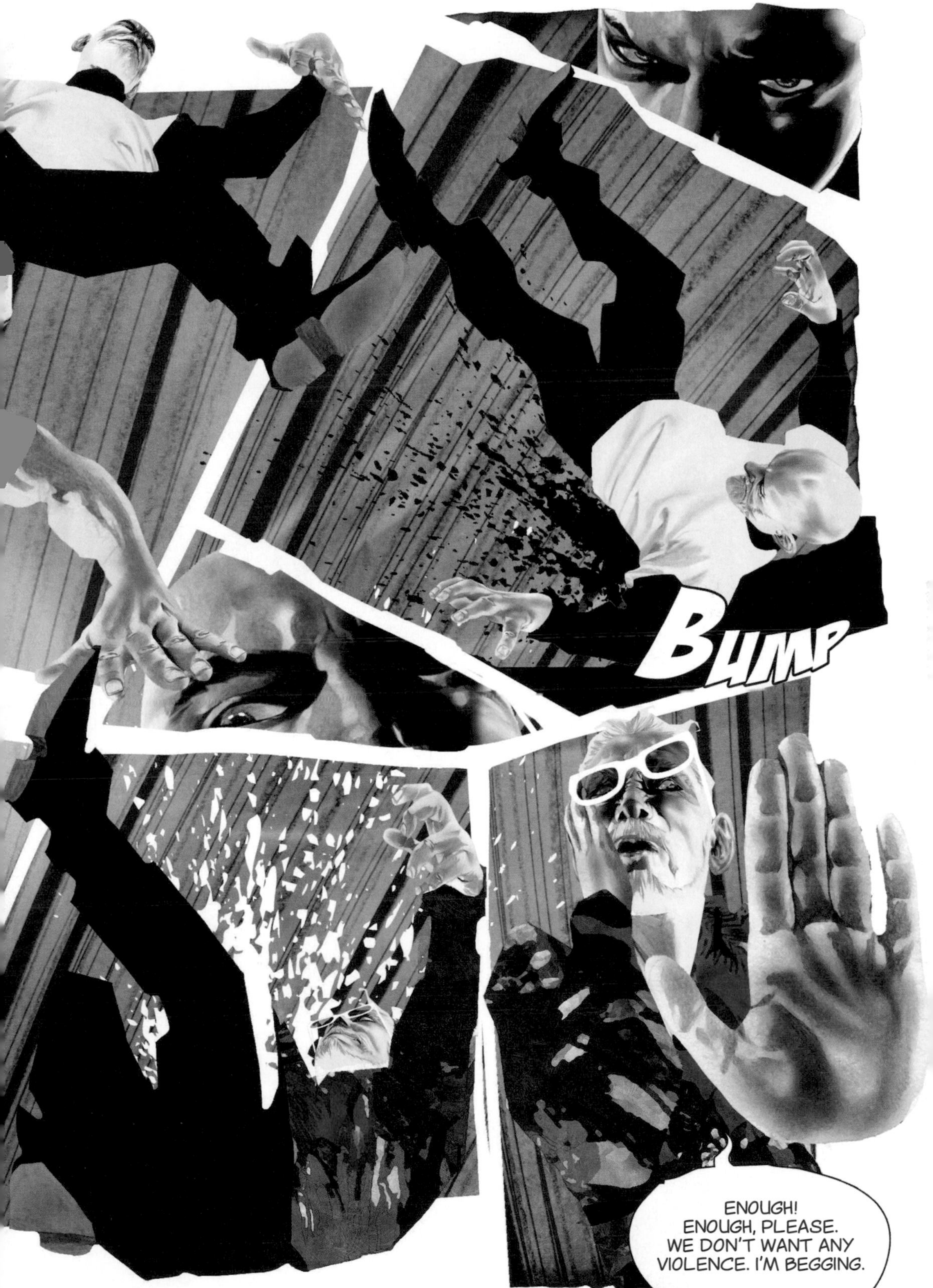
BUMP
ENOUGH! ENOUGH, PLEASE. WE DON'T WANT ANY VIOLENCE. I'M BEGGING.

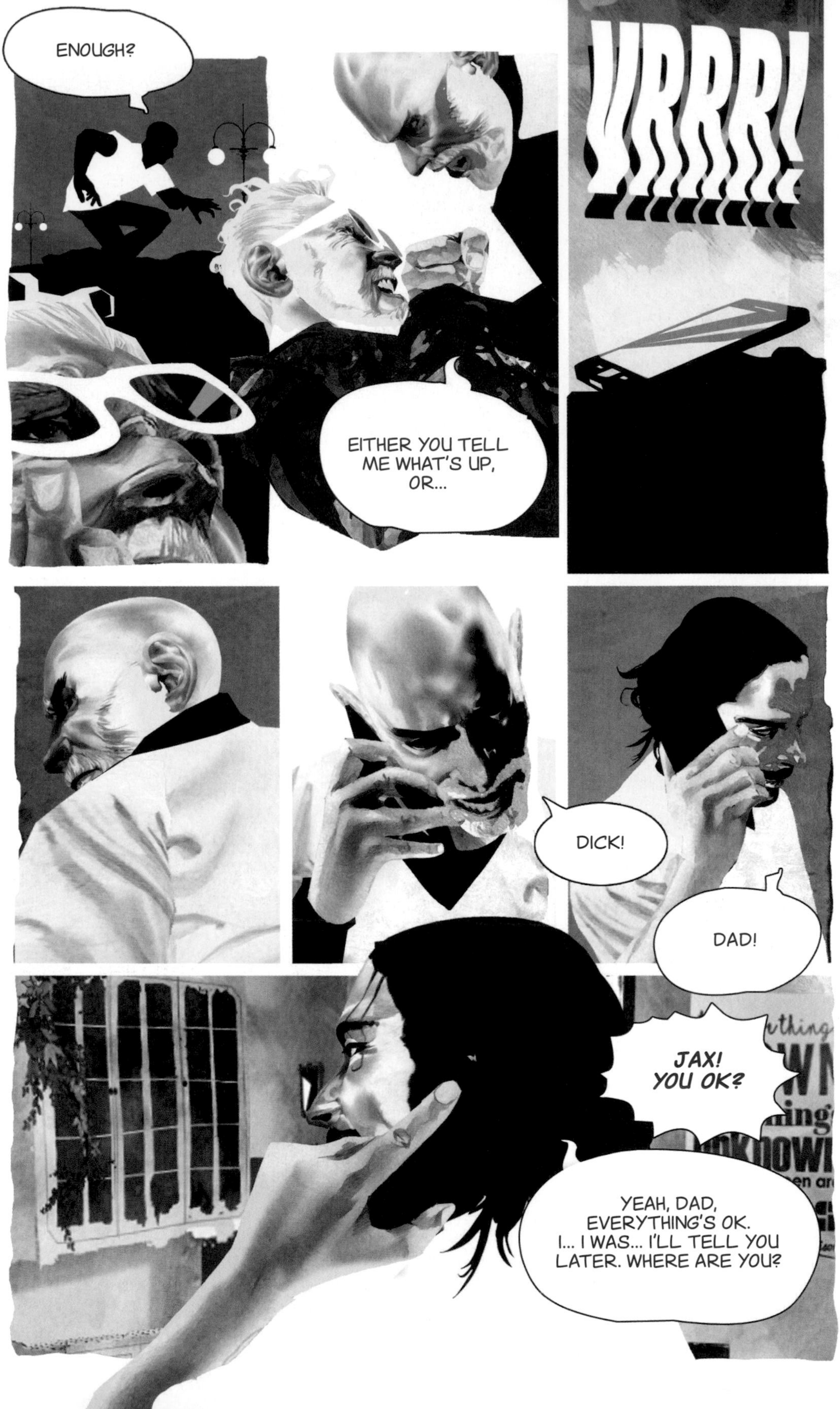
ENOUGH?
EITHER YOU TELL ME WHAT'S UP, OR...
VRRR!
DICK!
DAD!
JAX! YOU OK?
YEAH, DAD, EVERYTHING'S OK. I... I WAS... I'LL TELL YOU LATER. WHERE ARE YOU?

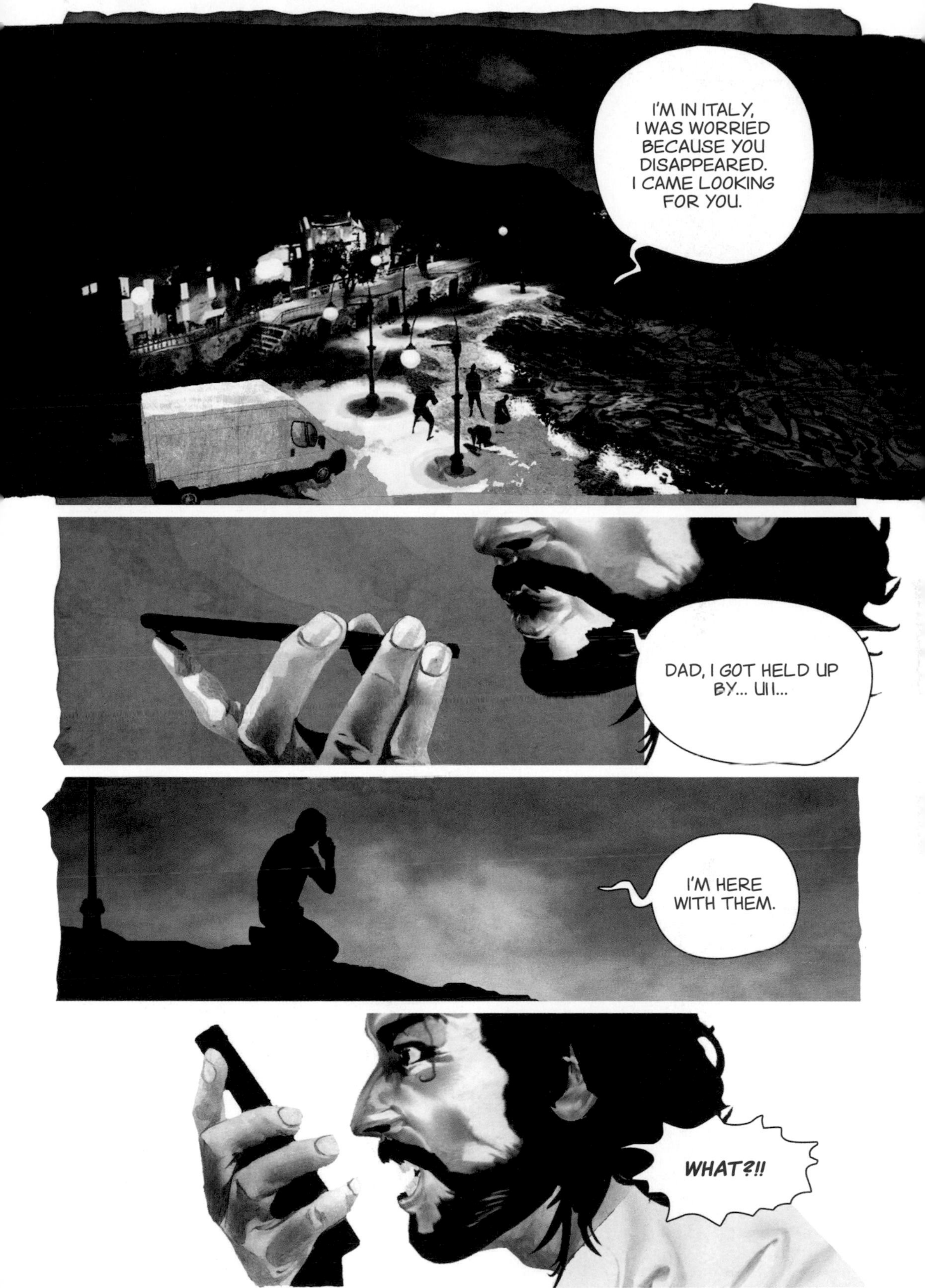
I'M IN ITALY, I WAS WORRIED BECAUSE YOU DISAPPEARED. I CAME LOOKING FOR YOU.
DAD, I GOT HELD UP BY... UH...
I'M HERE WITH THEM.
WHAT?!!

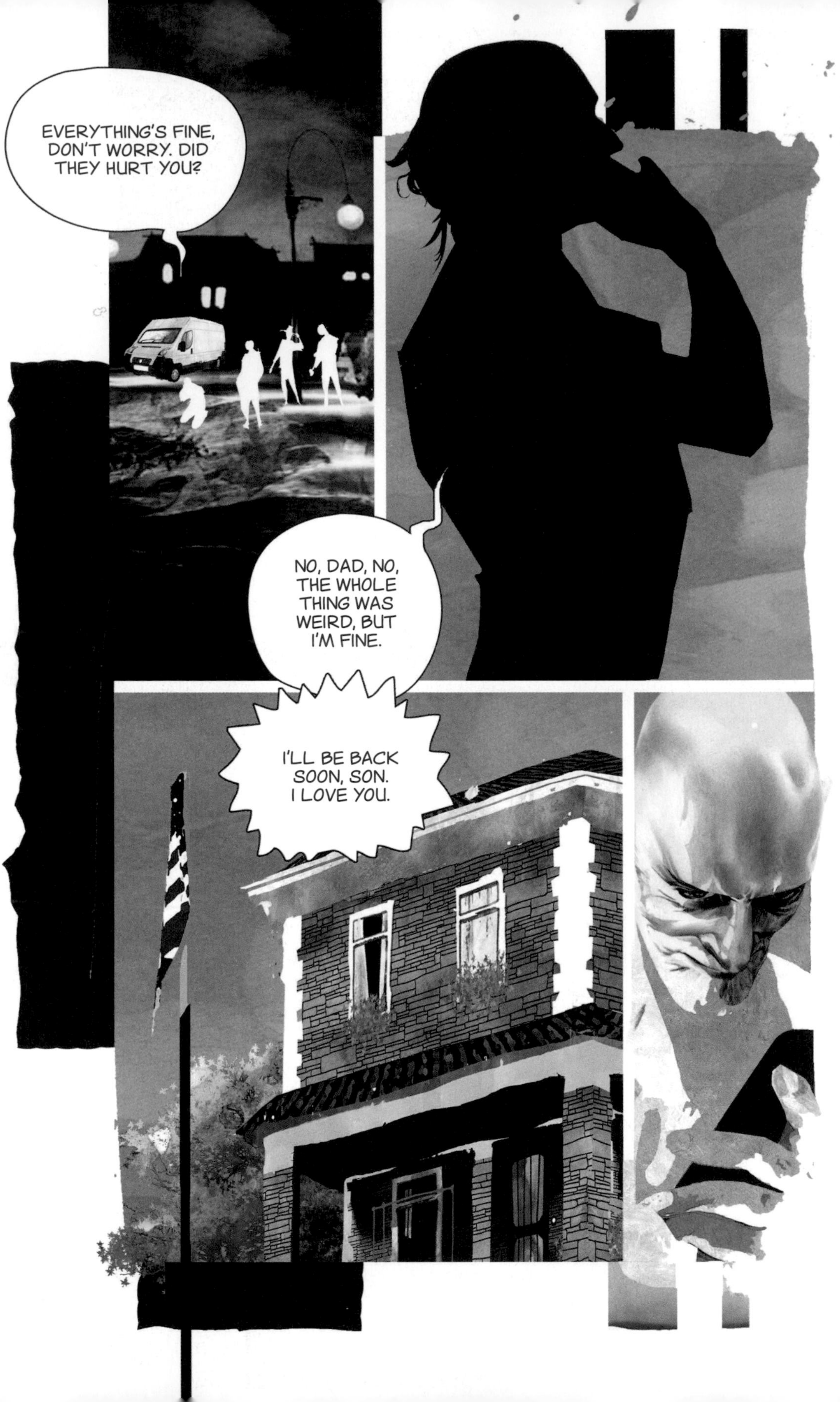
EVERYTHING'S FINE, DON'T WORRY. DID THEY HURT YOU?
NO, DAD, NO, THE WHOLE THING WAS WEIRD, BUT I'M FINE.
I'LL BE BACK SOON, SON. I LOVE YOU.

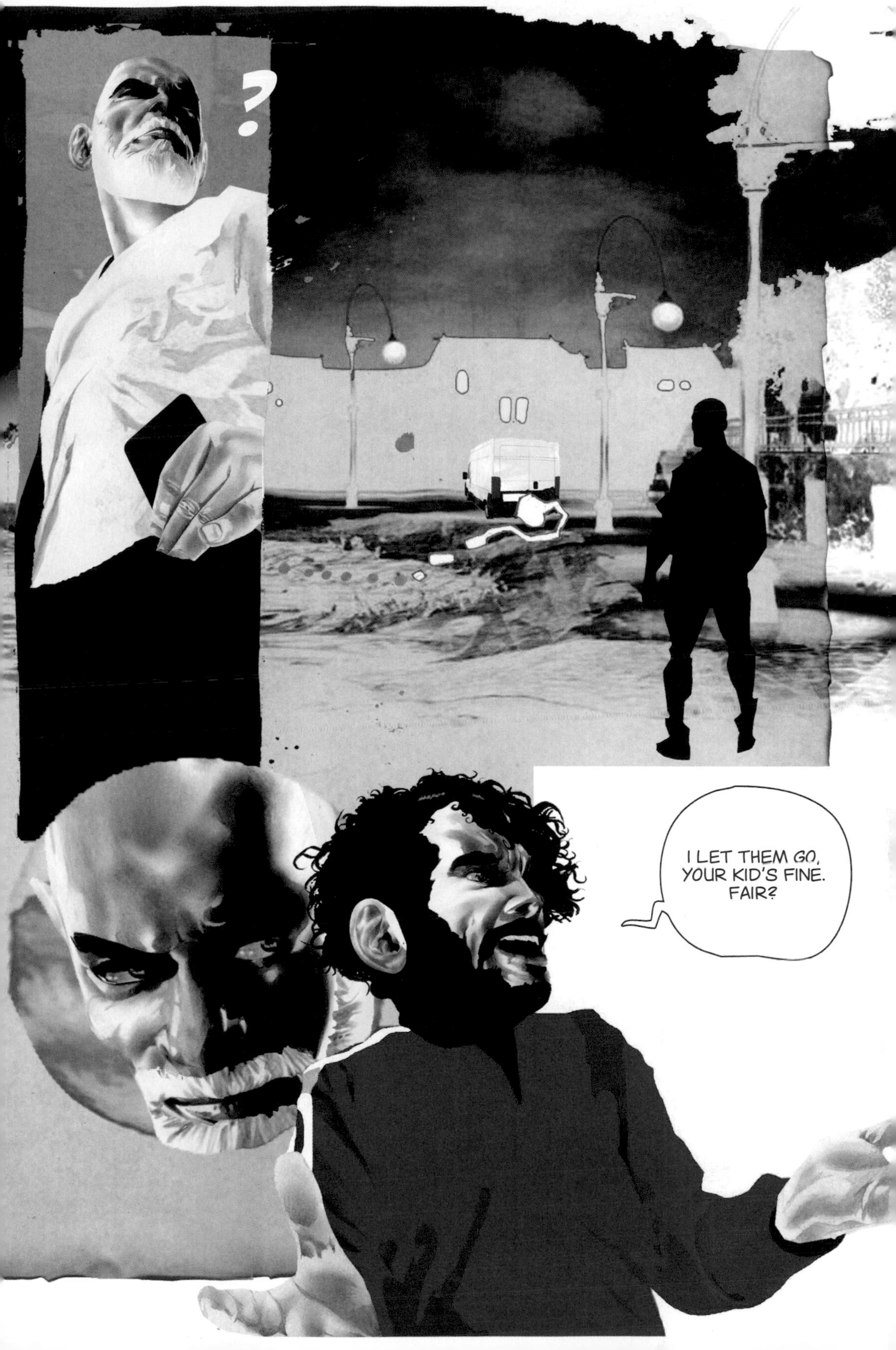
?
I LET THEM GO, YOUR KID'S FINE. FAIR?

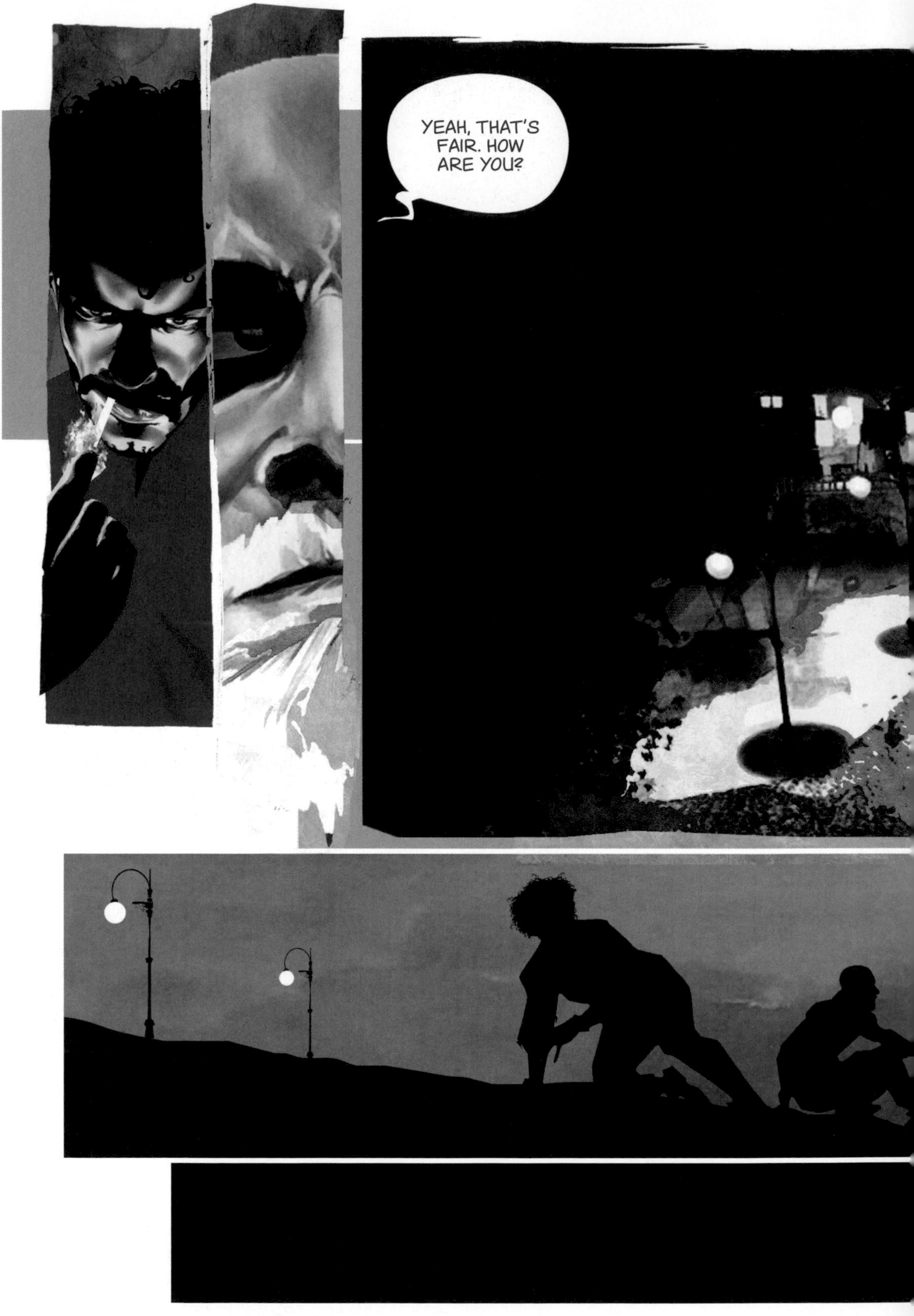
YEAH, THAT'S FAIR. HOW ARE YOU?

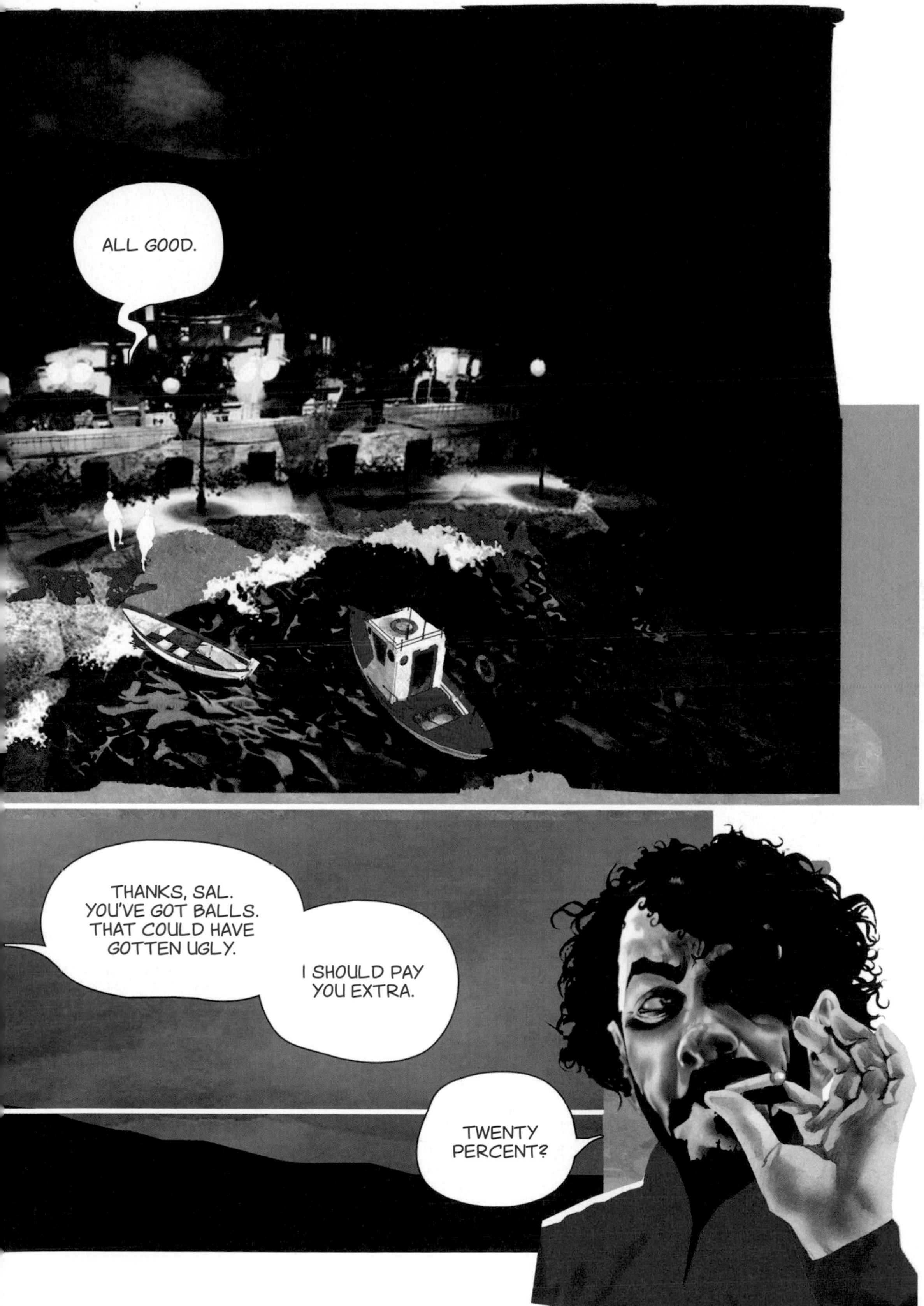
ALL GOOD.
THANKS, SAL. YOU'VE GOT BALLS. THAT COULD HAVE GOTTEN UGLY.
I SHOULD PAY YOU EXTRA.
TWENTY PERCENT?

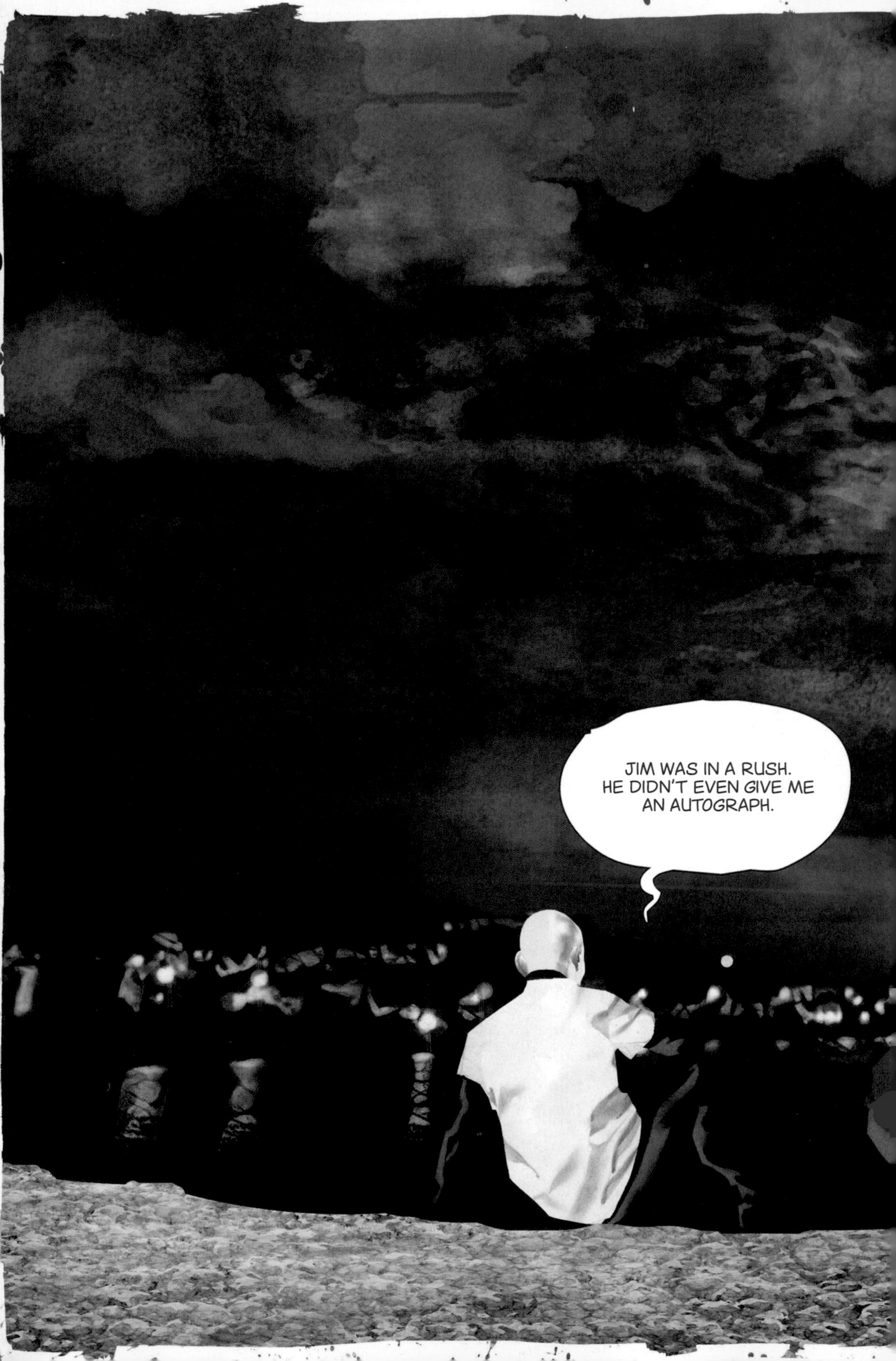
JIM WAS IN A RUSH. HE DIDN'T EVEN GIVE ME AN AUTOGRAPH.

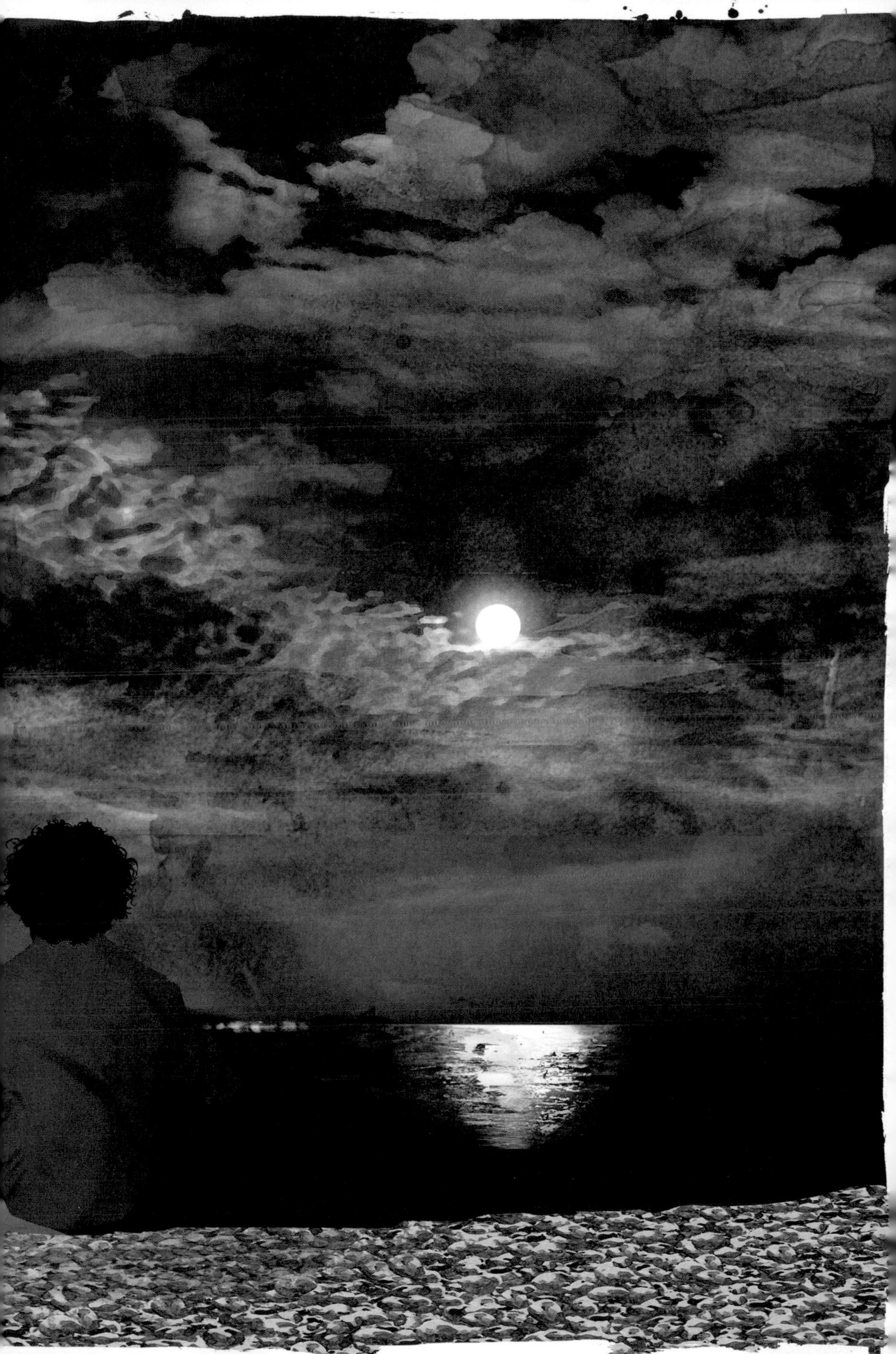

this is

the

end

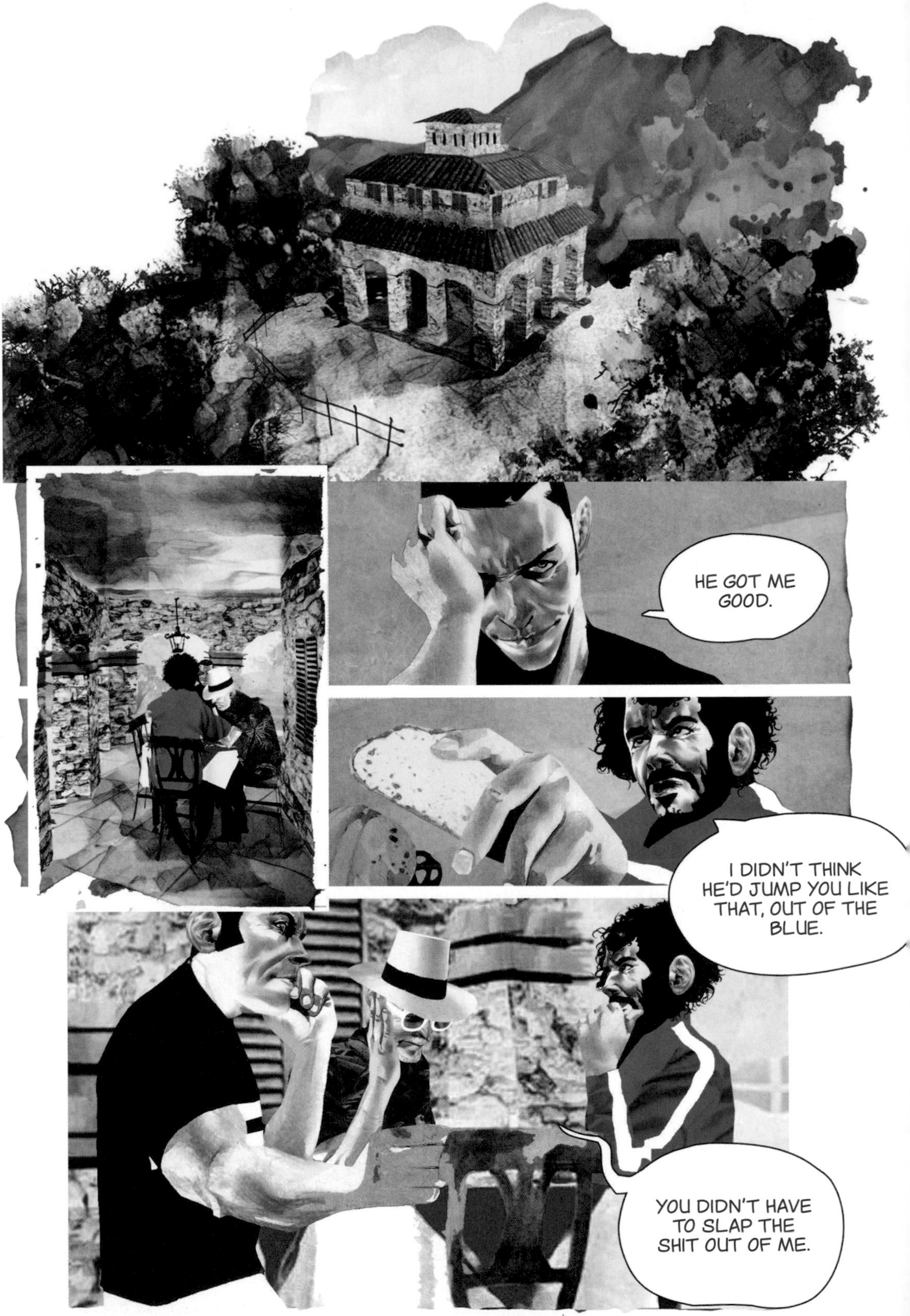
HE GOT ME GOOD.
I DIDN'T THINK HE'D JUMP YOU LIKE THAT, OUT OF THE BLUE.
YOU DIDN'T HAVE TO SLAP THE SHIT OUT OF ME.

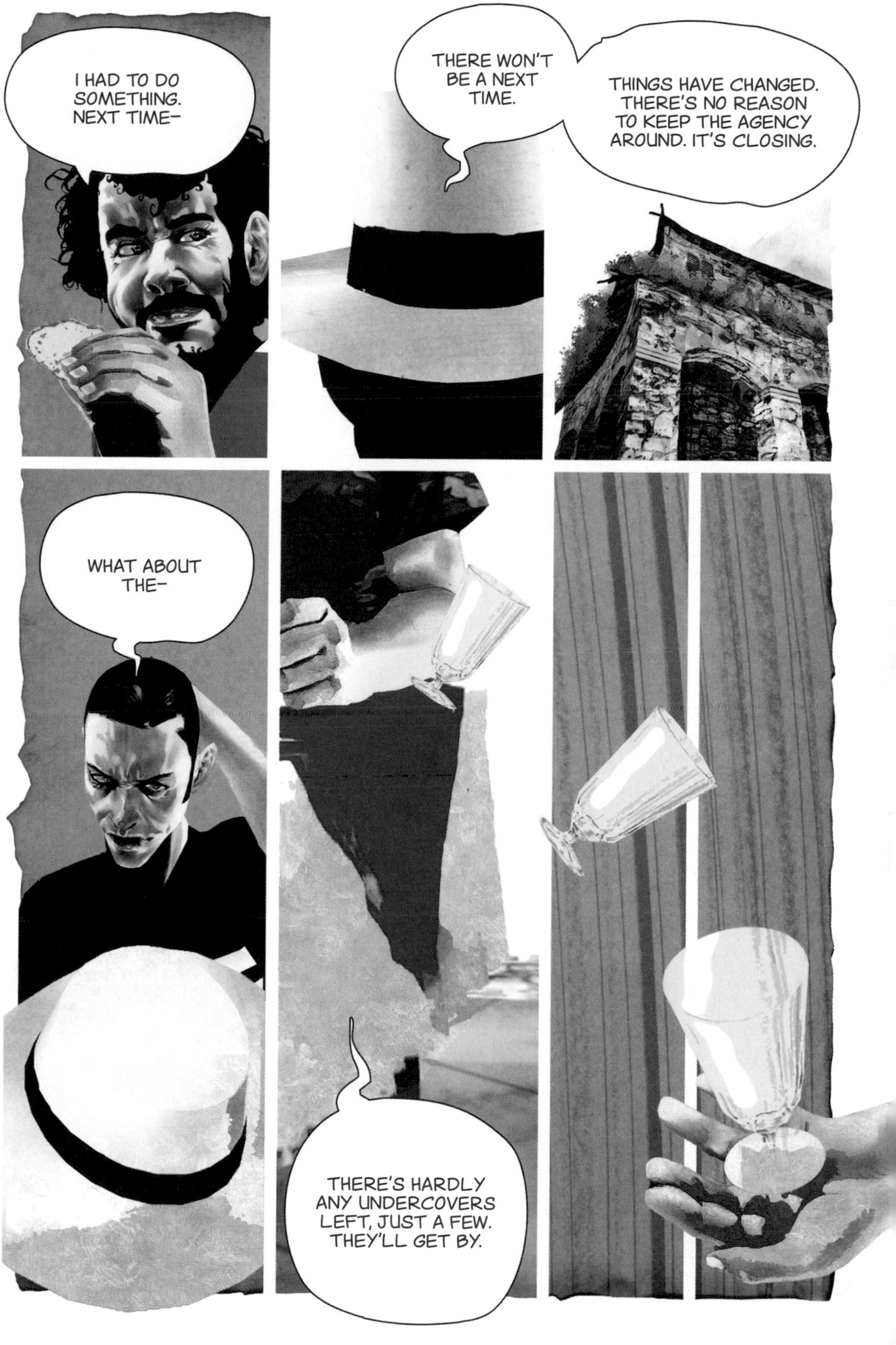
I HAD TO DO SOMETHING. NEXT TIME–
THERE WON'T BE A NEXT TIME.
THINGS HAVE CHANGED. THERE'S NO REASON TO KEEP THE AGENCY AROUND. IT'S CLOSING.
WHAT ABOUT THE–
THERE'S HARDLY ANY UNDERCOVERS LEFT, JUST A FEW. THEY'LL GET BY.

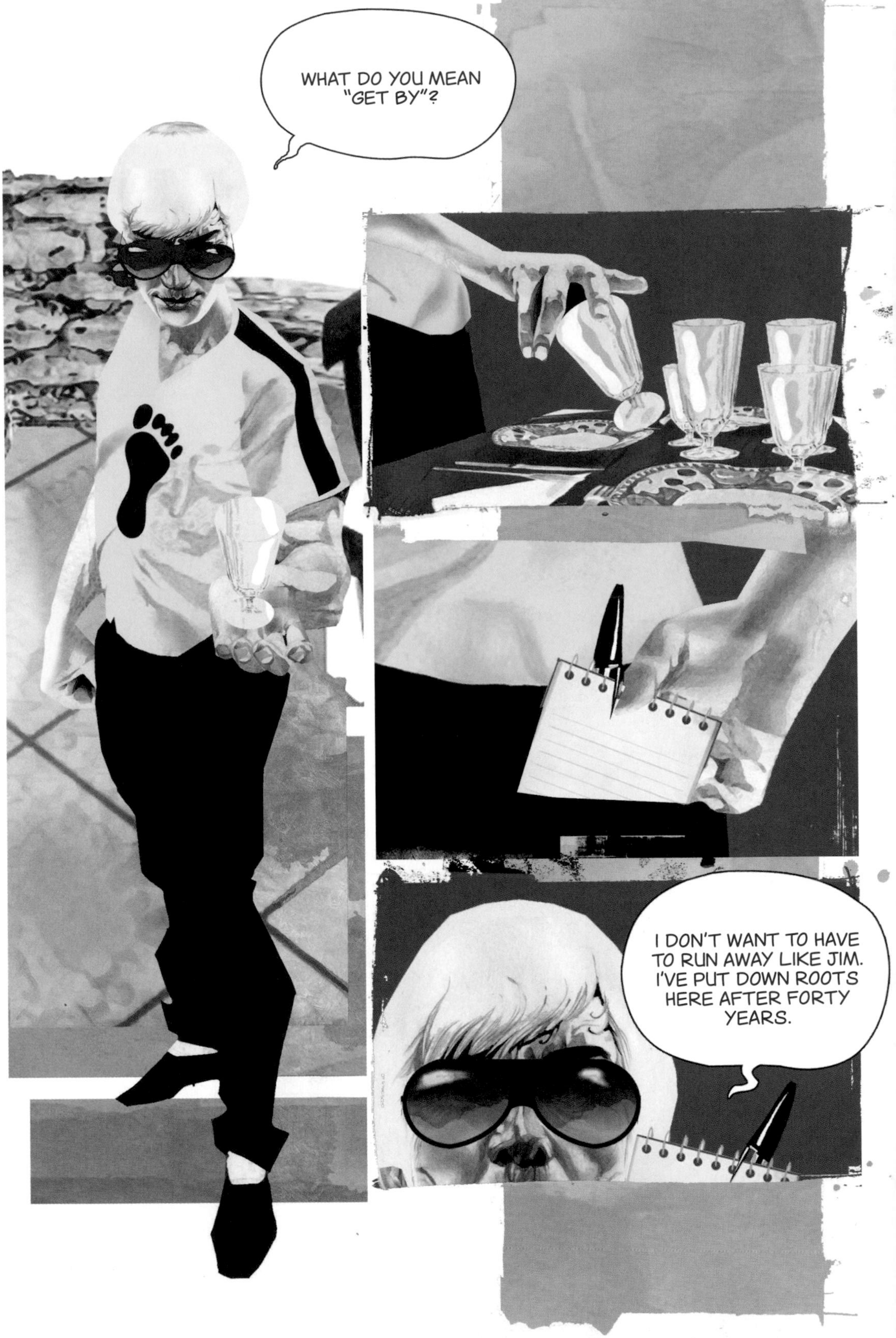
WHAT DO YOU MEAN "GET BY"?
I DON'T WANT TO HAVE TO RUN AWAY LIKE JIM. I'VE PUT DOWN ROOTS HERE AFTER FORTY YEARS.

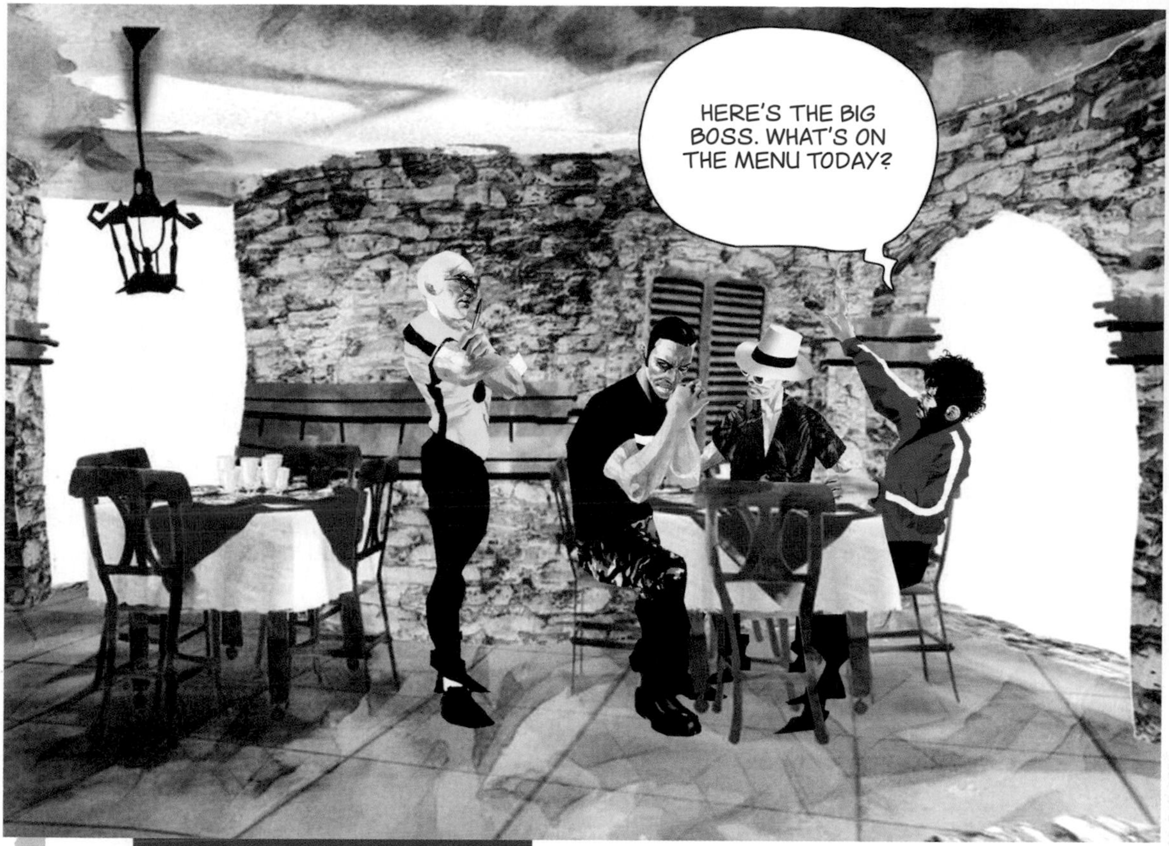
HERE'S THE BIG BOSS. WHAT'S ON THE MENU TODAY?

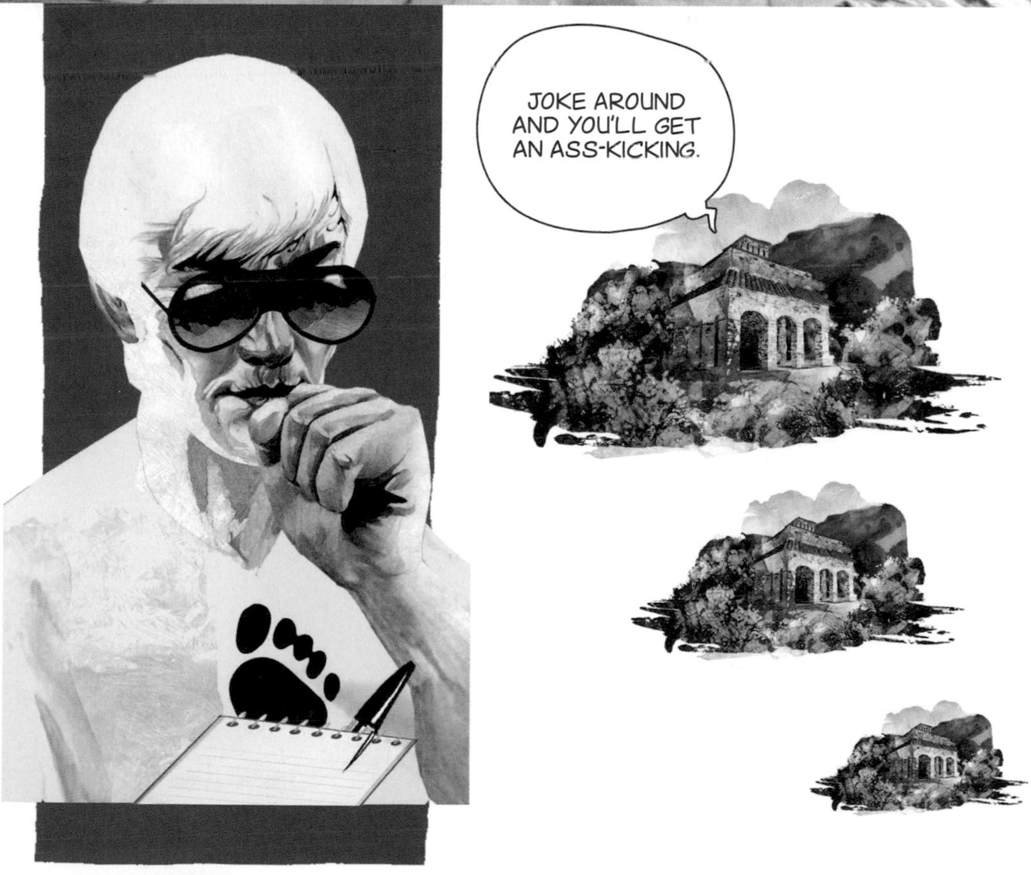
JOKE AROUND AND YOU'LL GET AN ASS-KICKING.

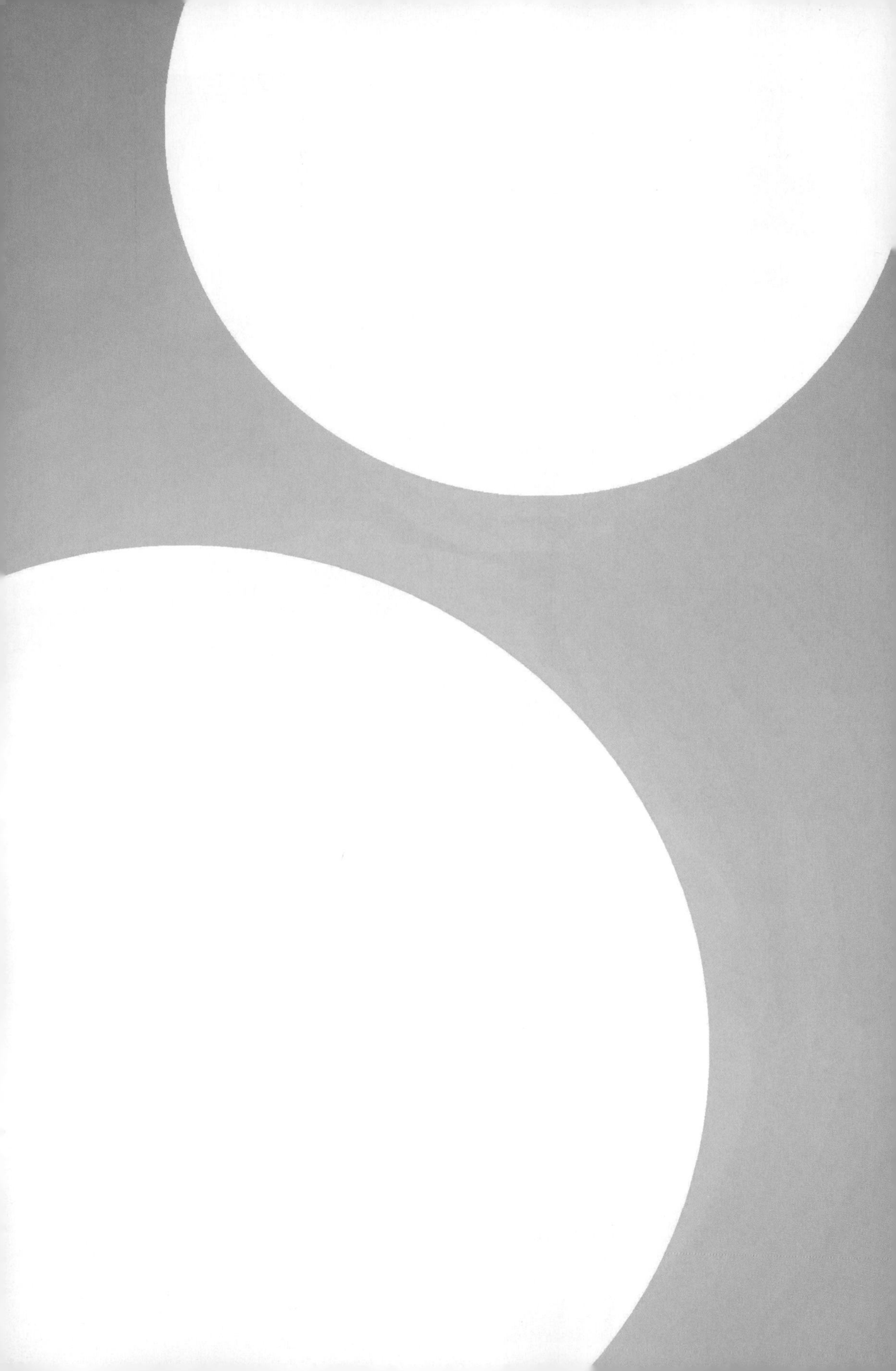

BLOOPERS

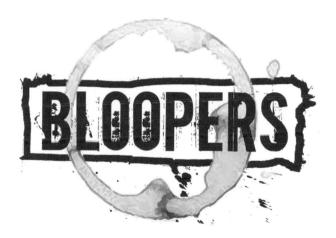

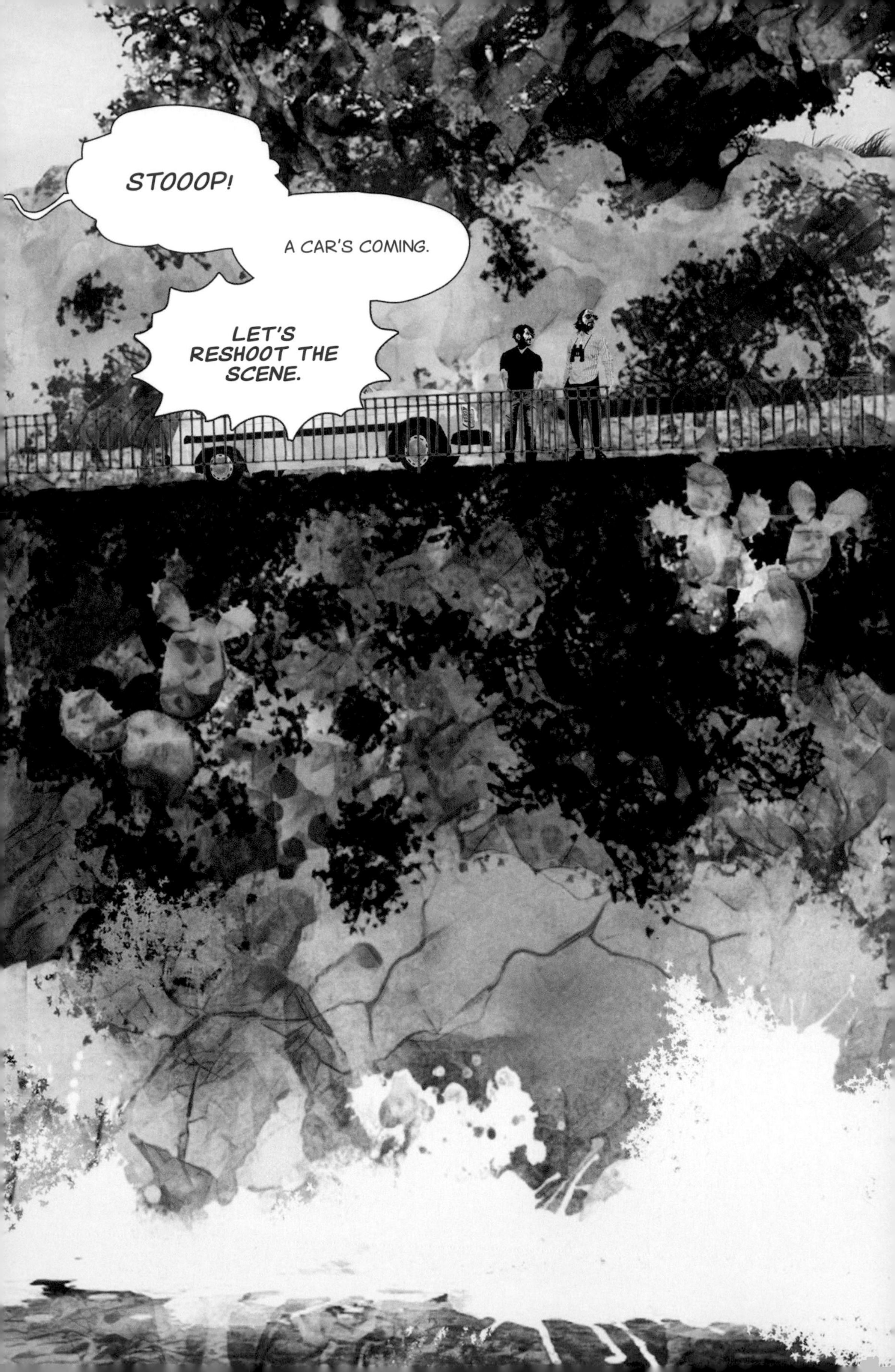
STOOOP!
A CAR'S COMING.
LET'S RESHOOT THE SCENE.

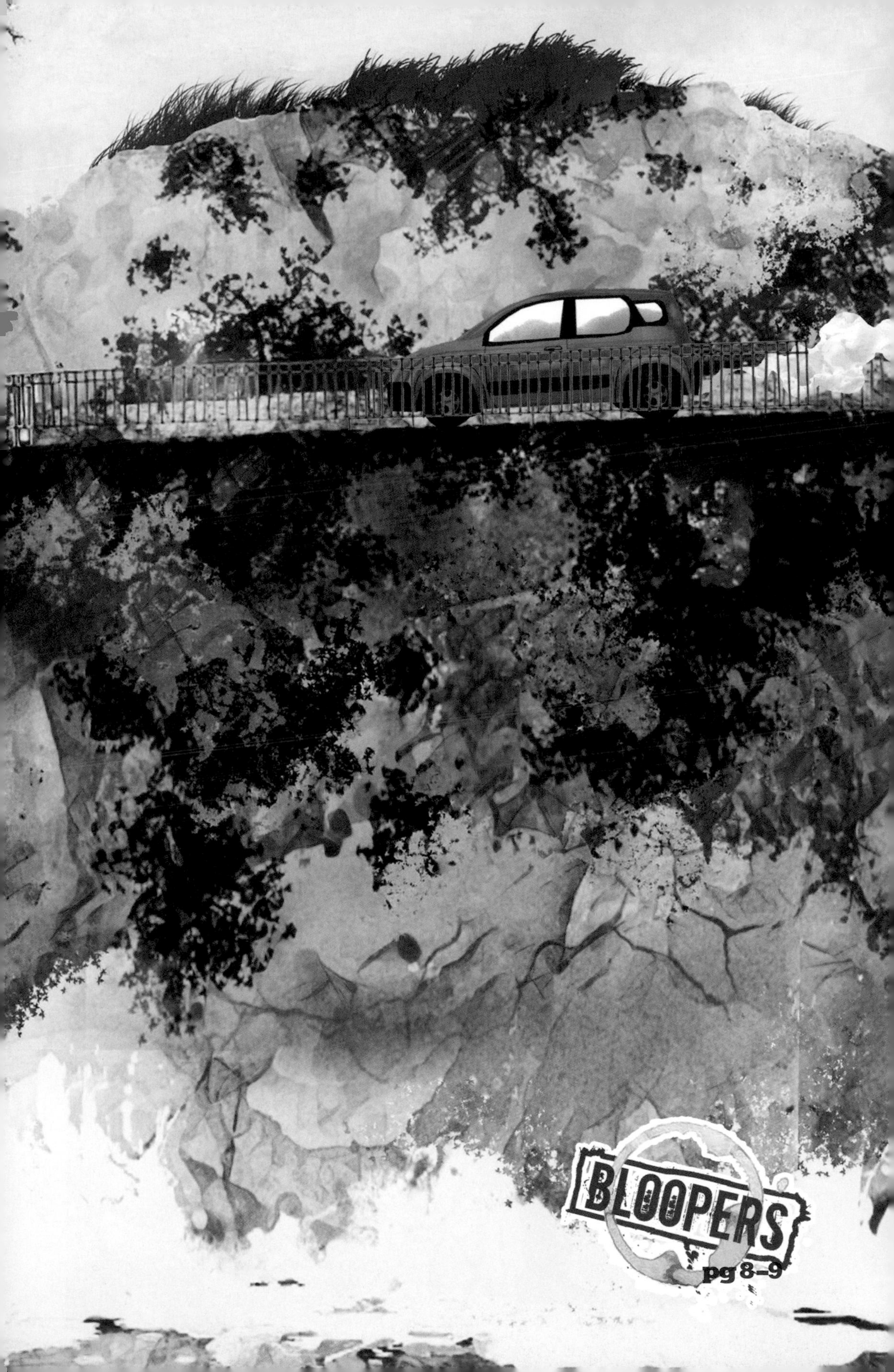
BLOOPERS
pg 8-9

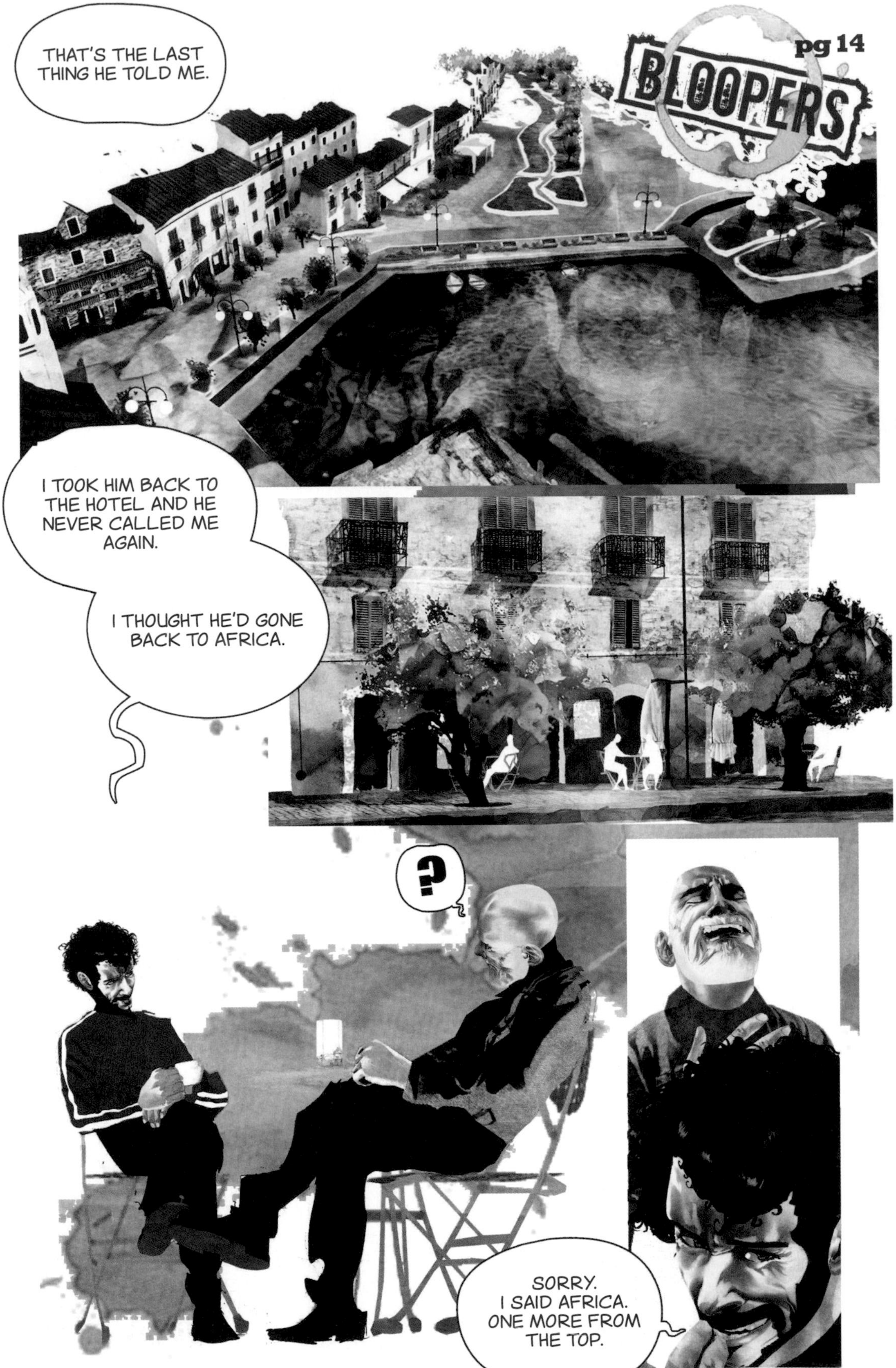
BLOOPERS
THAT'S THE LAST THING HE TOLD ME.
I TOOK HIM BACK TO THE HOTEL AND HE NEVER CALLED ME AGAIN.
I THOUGHT HE'D GONE BACK TO AFRICA.
?
SORRY. I SAID AFRICA. ONE MORE FROM THE TOP.

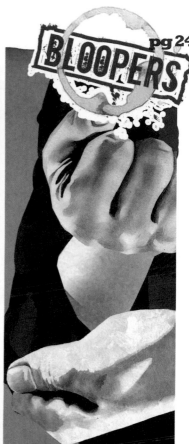

BLOOPERS

HE KNOWS YOU WELL.

HOW IS HE?

SPROOT

WHAT'D YOU PUT IN THIS GLASS?

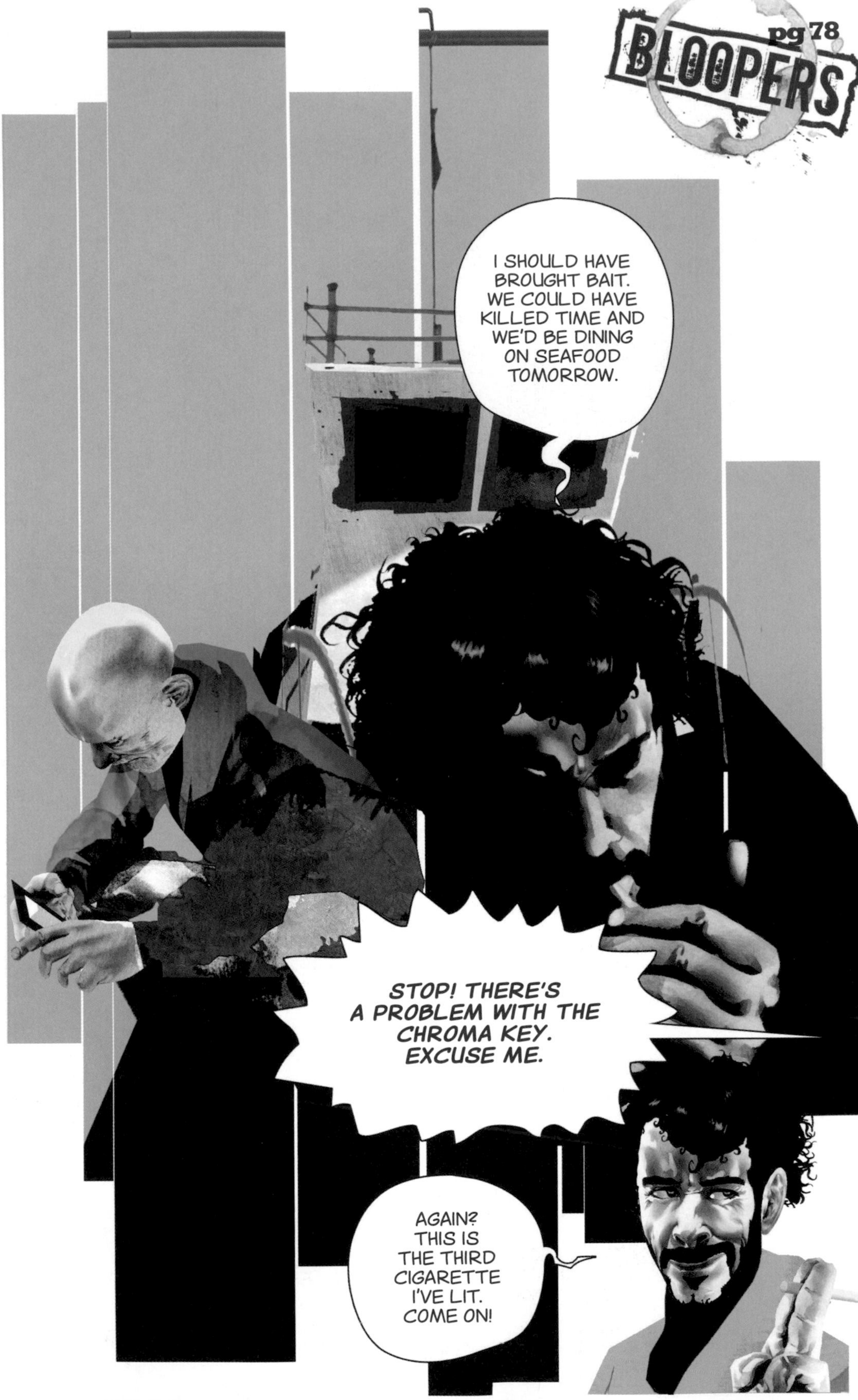
I SHOULD HAVE BROUGHT BAIT. WE COULD HAVE KILLED TIME AND WE'D BE DINING ON SEAFOOD TOMORROW.
STOP! THERE'S A PROBLEM WITH THE CHROMA KEY. EXCUSE ME.
AGAIN? THIS IS THE THIRD CIGARETTE I'VE LIT. COME ON!

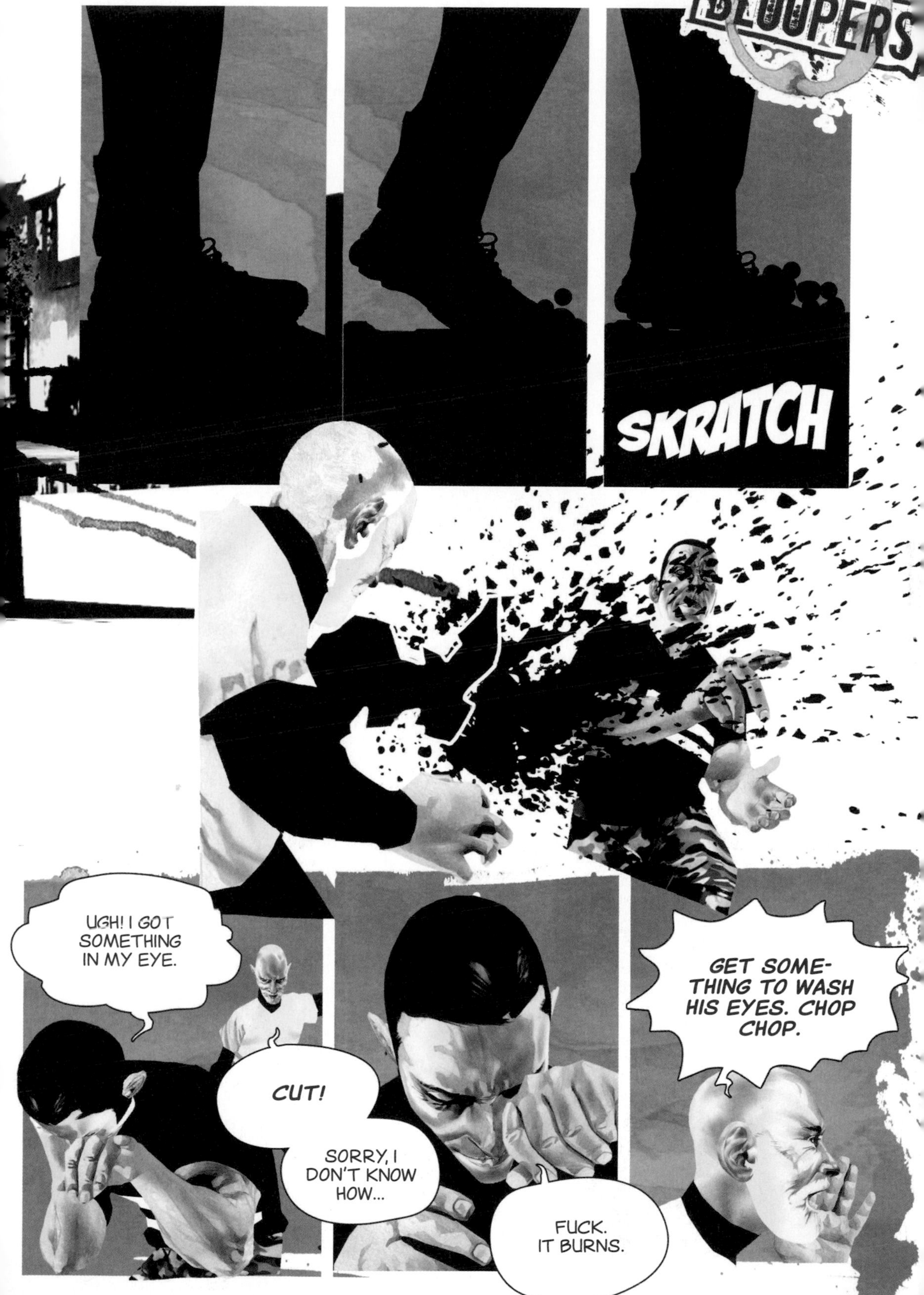
SKRATCH
UGH! I GOT SOMETHING IN MY EYE.
CUT!
SORRY, I DON'T KNOW HOW...
FUCK. IT BURNS.
GET SOMETHING TO WASH HIS EYES. CHOP CHOP.

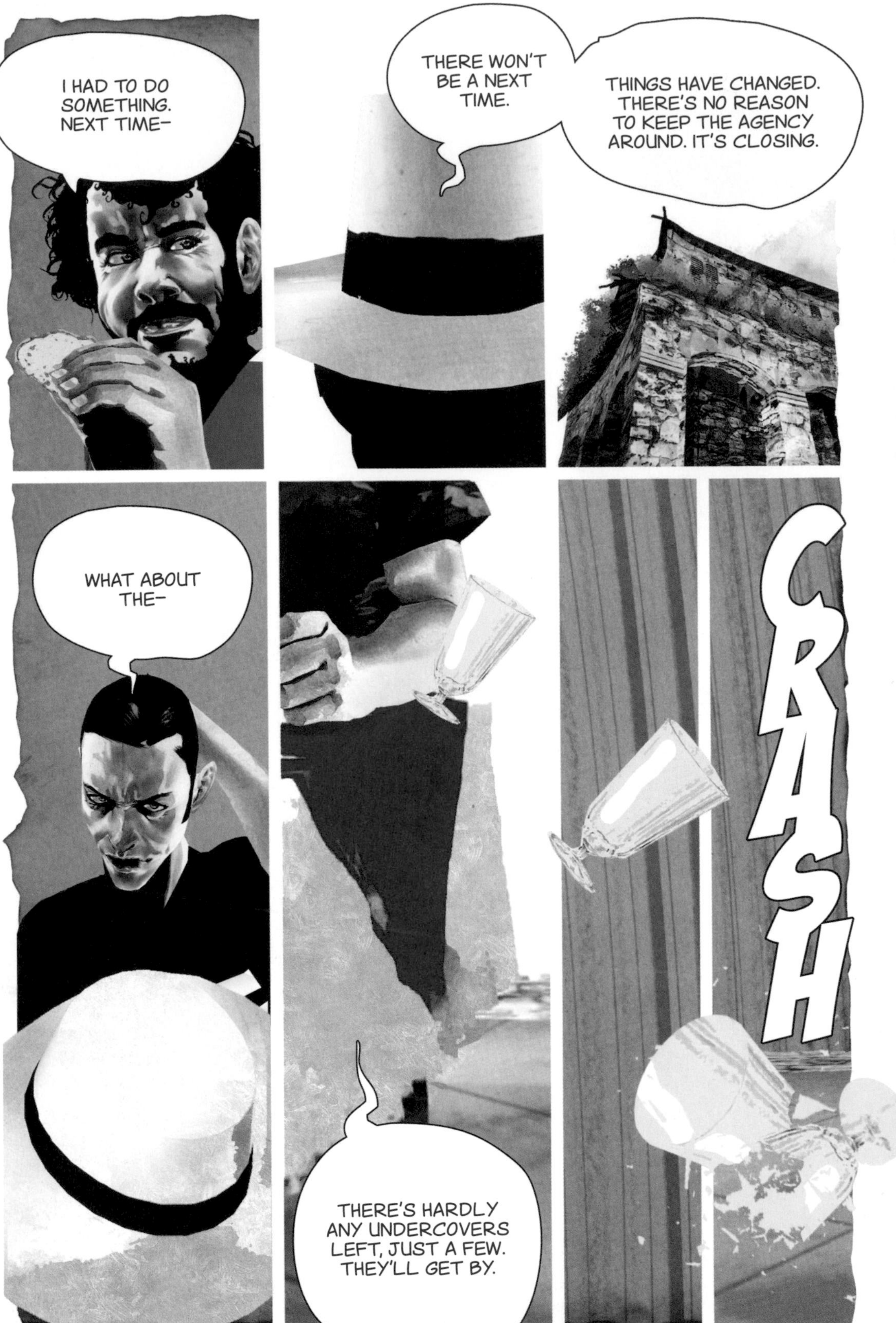
I HAD TO DO SOMETHING. NEXT TIME–
THERE WON'T BE A NEXT TIME.
THINGS HAVE CHANGED. THERE'S NO REASON TO KEEP THE AGENCY AROUND. IT'S CLOSING.
WHAT ABOUT THE–
THERE'S HARDLY ANY UNDERCOVERS LEFT, JUST A FEW. THEY'LL GET BY.
CRASH

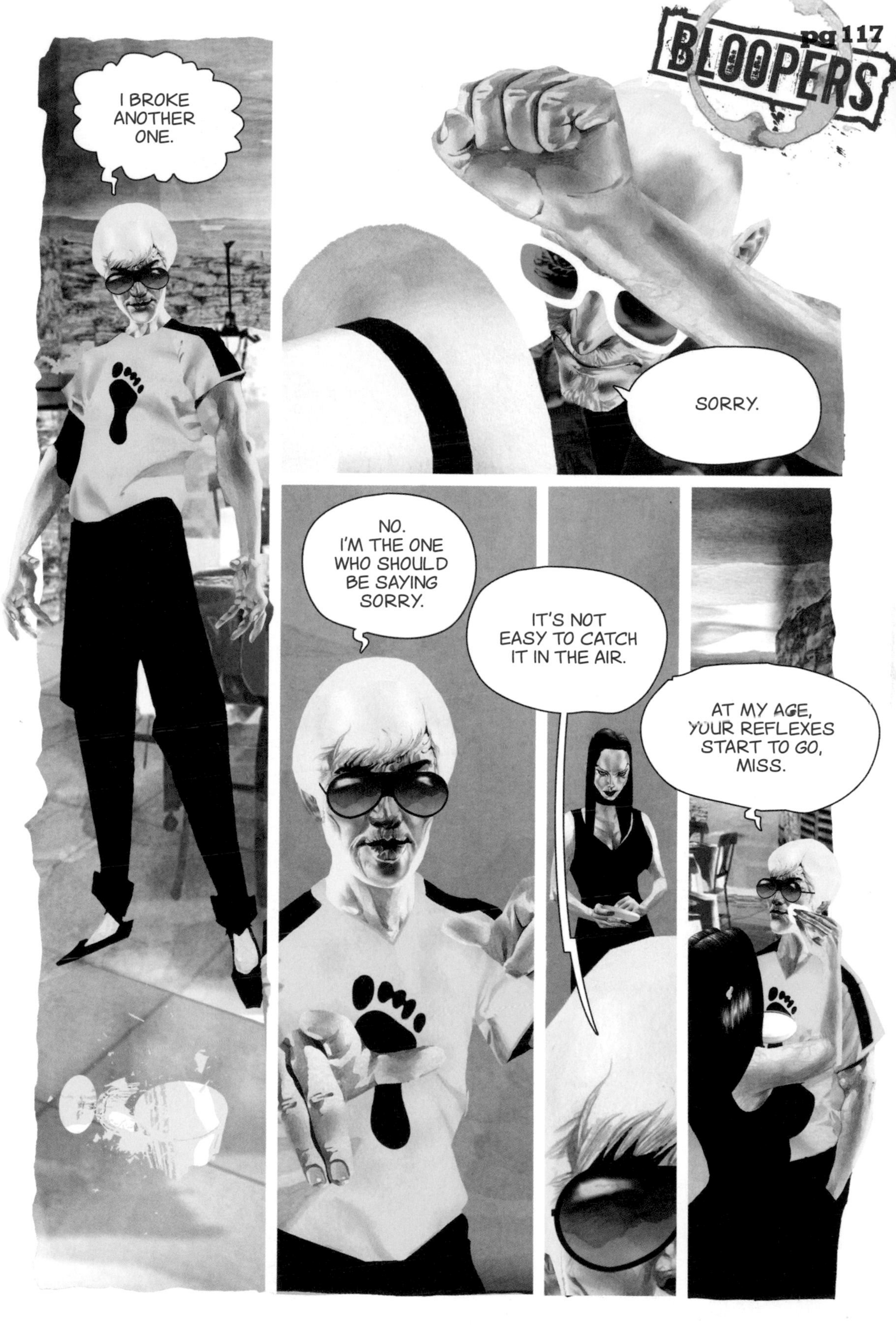

pg 117
BLOOPERS
I BROKE ANOTHER ONE.
SORRY.
NO. I'M THE ONE WHO SHOULD BE SAYING SORRY.
IT'S NOT EASY TO CATCH IT IN THE AIR.
AT MY AGE, YOUR REFLEXES START TO GO, MISS.

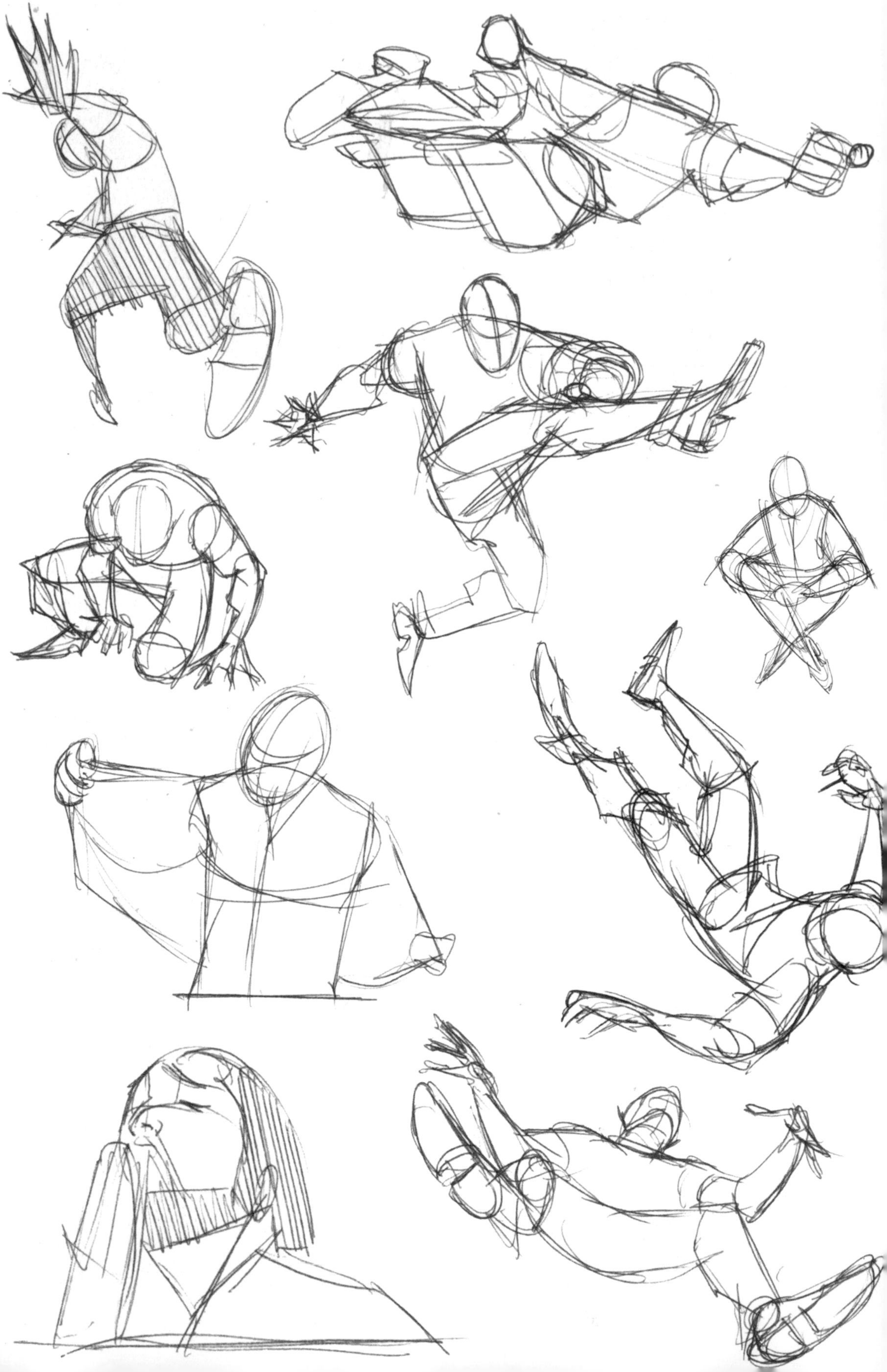

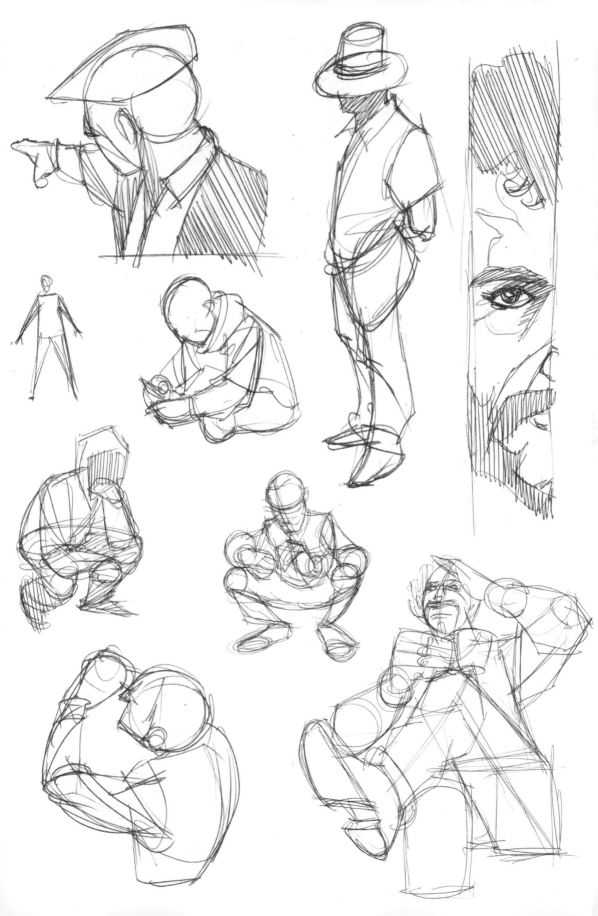

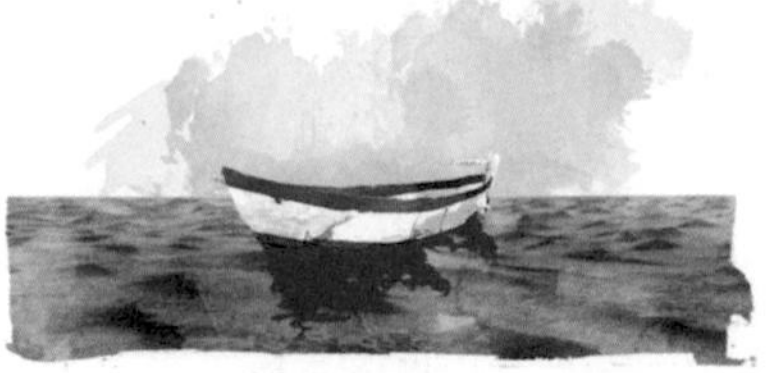
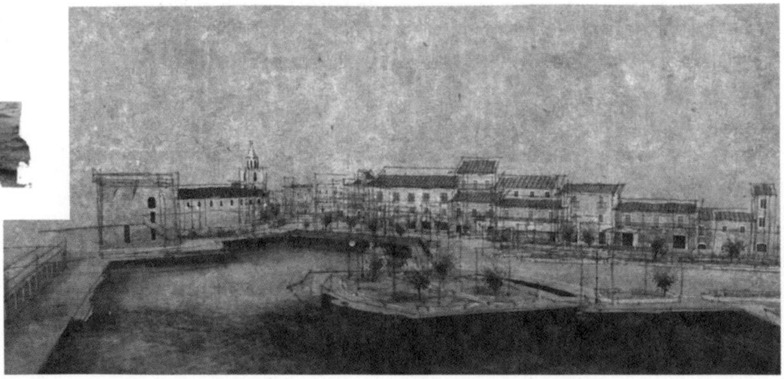
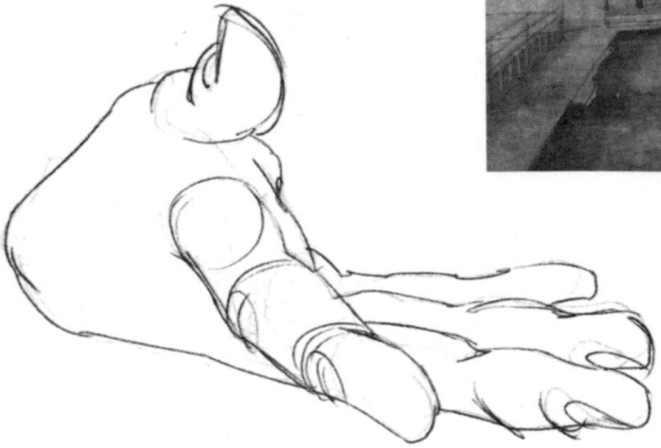
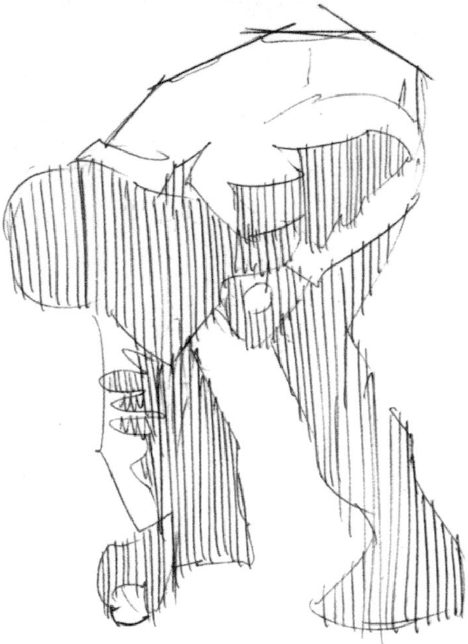
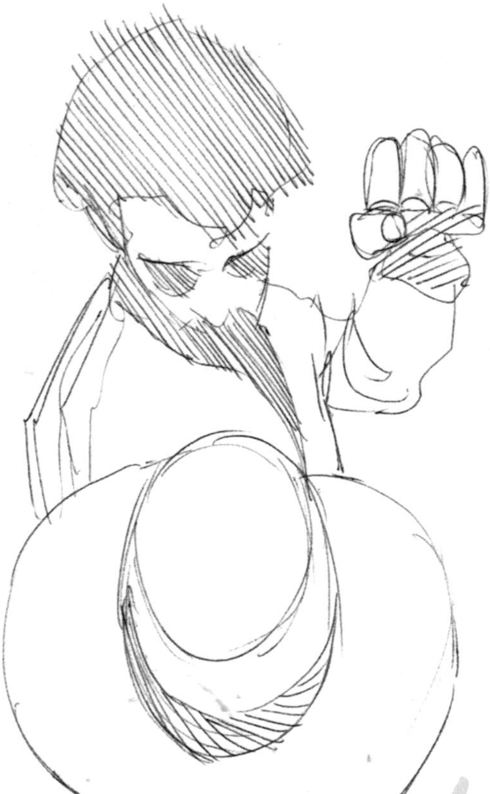
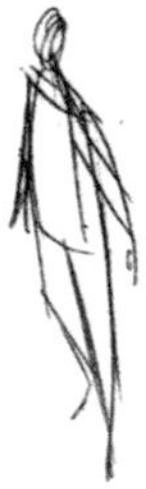
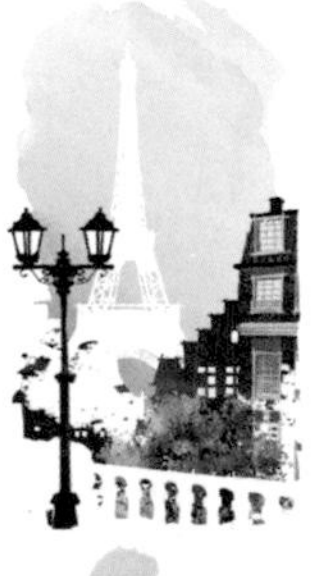
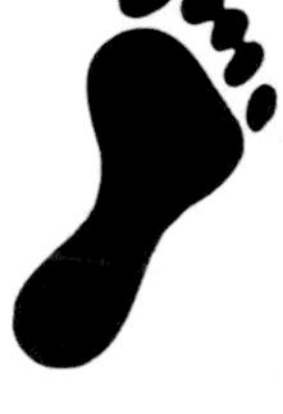
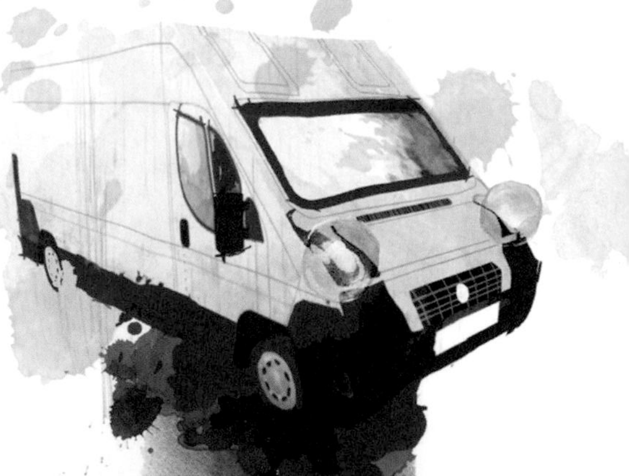
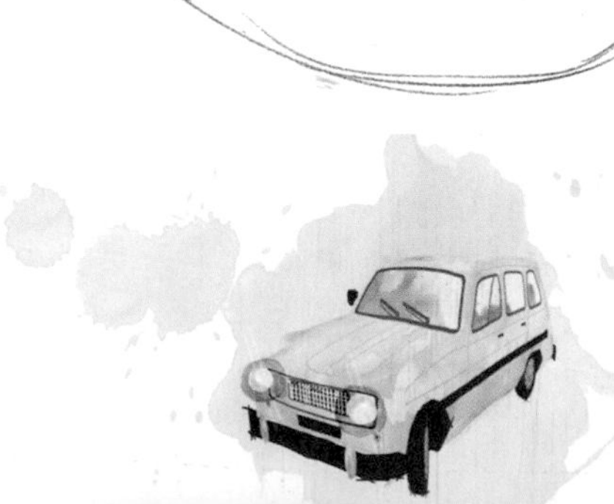

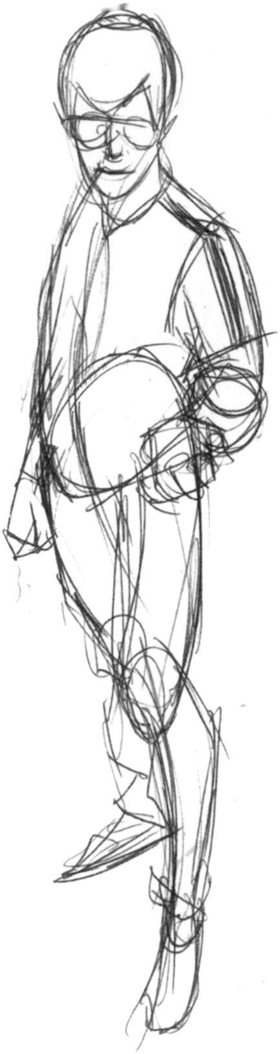
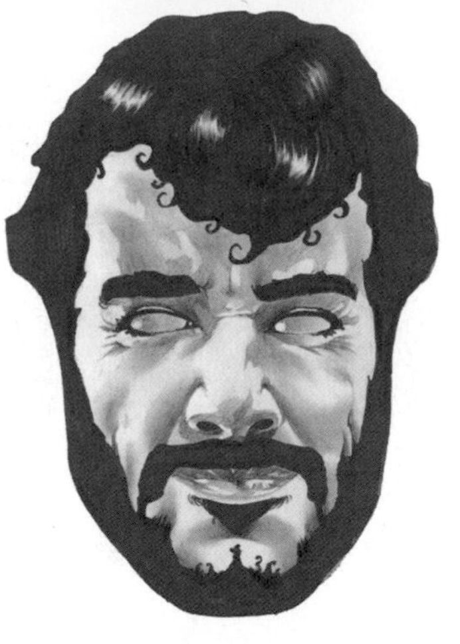
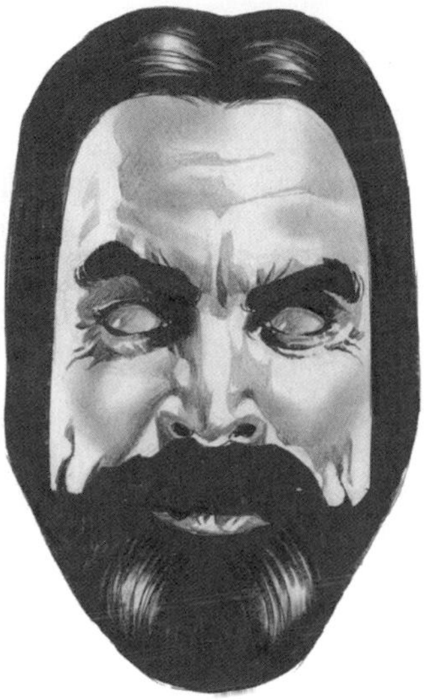
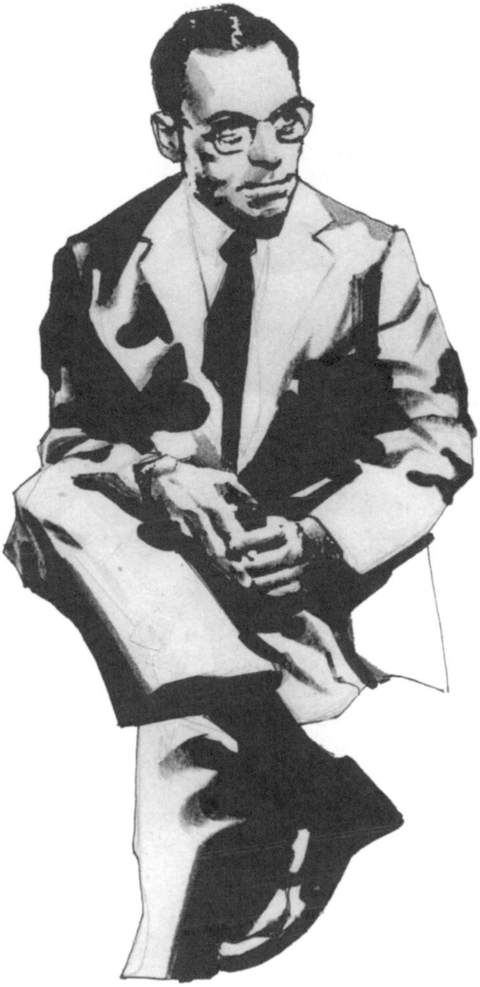
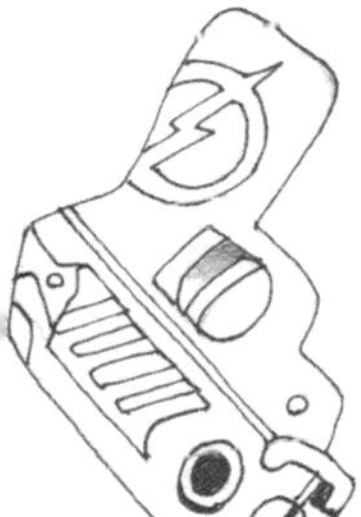
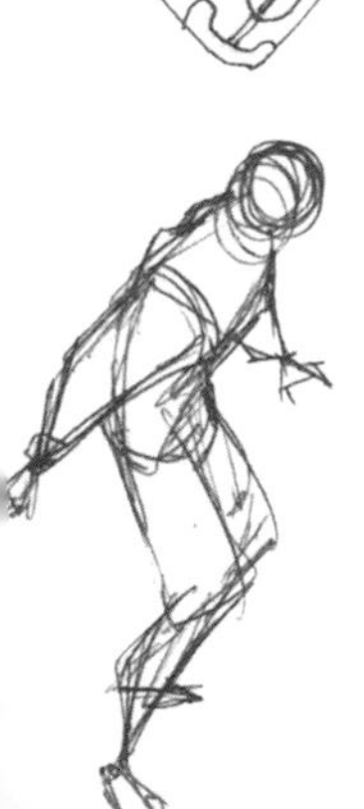
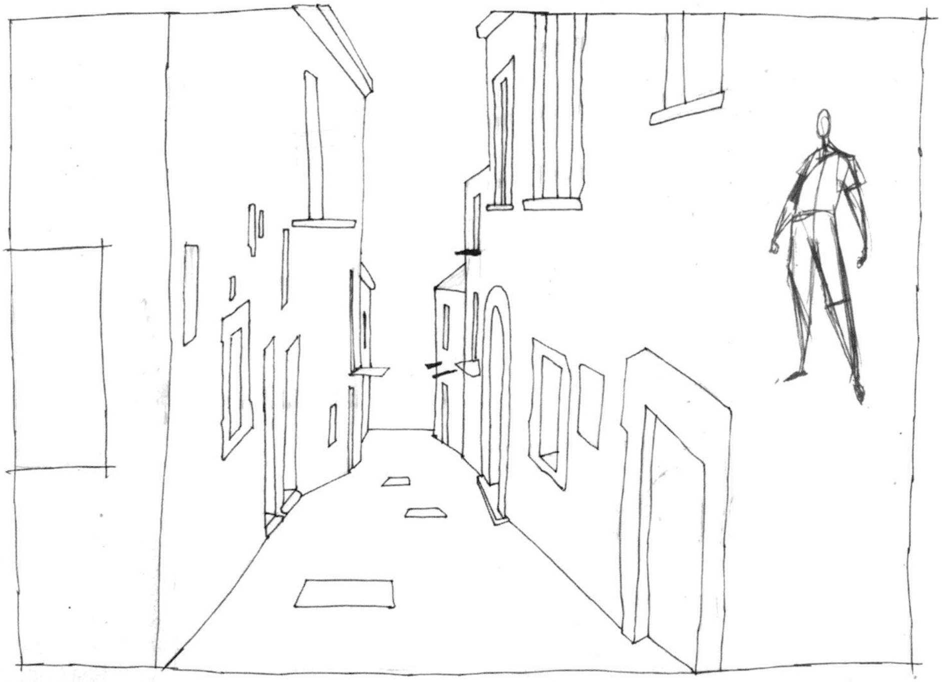

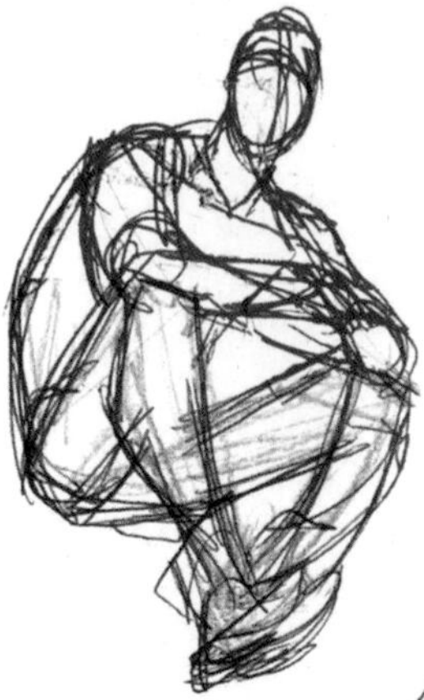
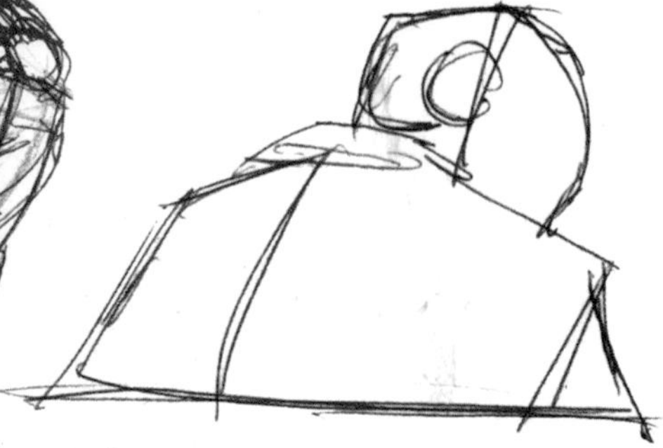
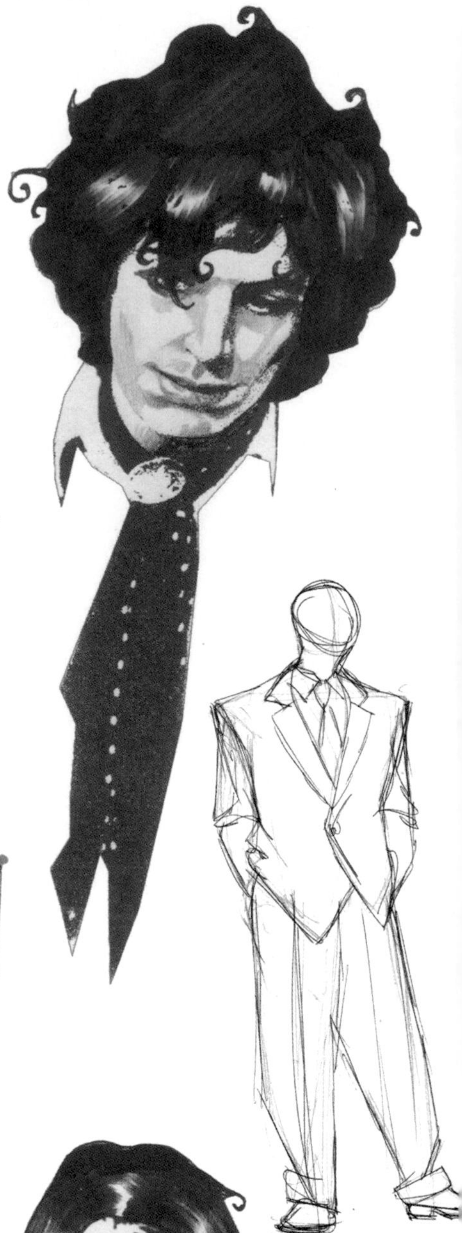
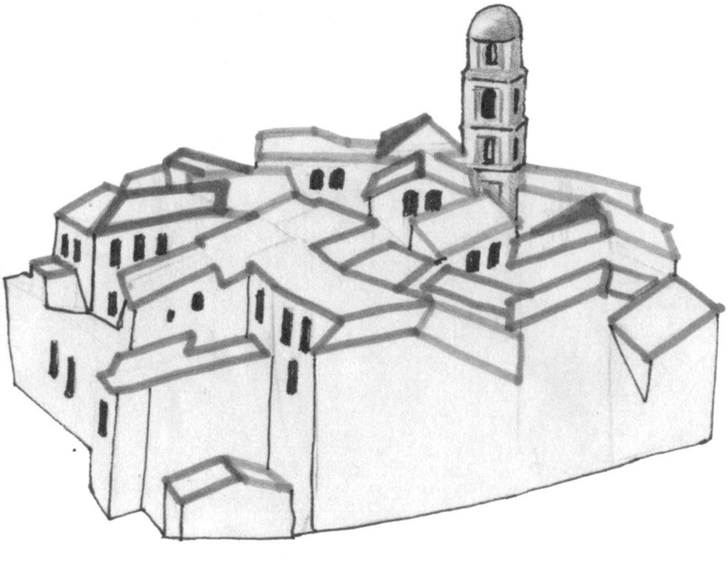
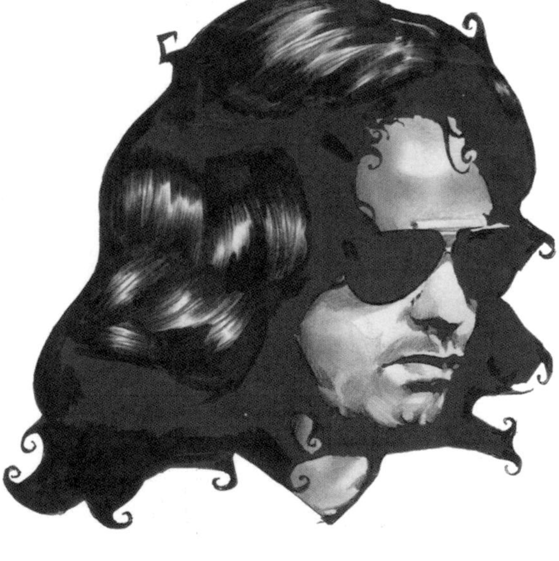
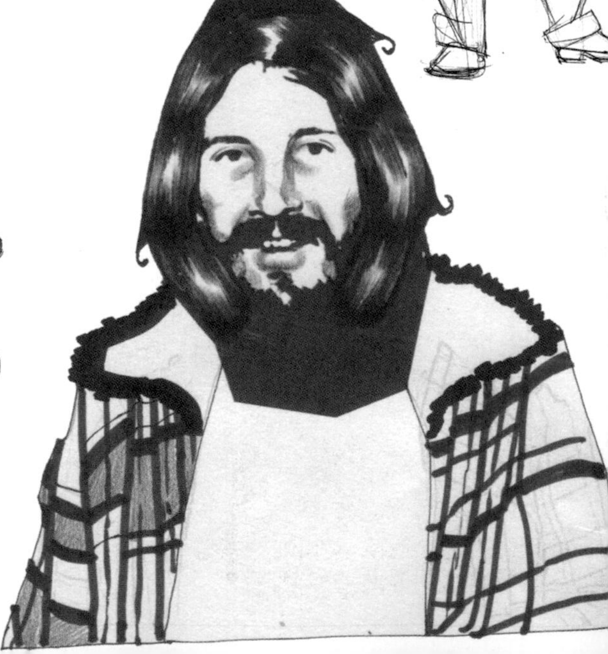

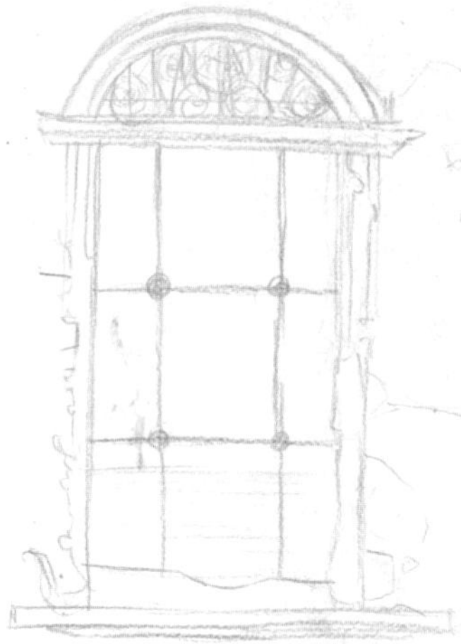

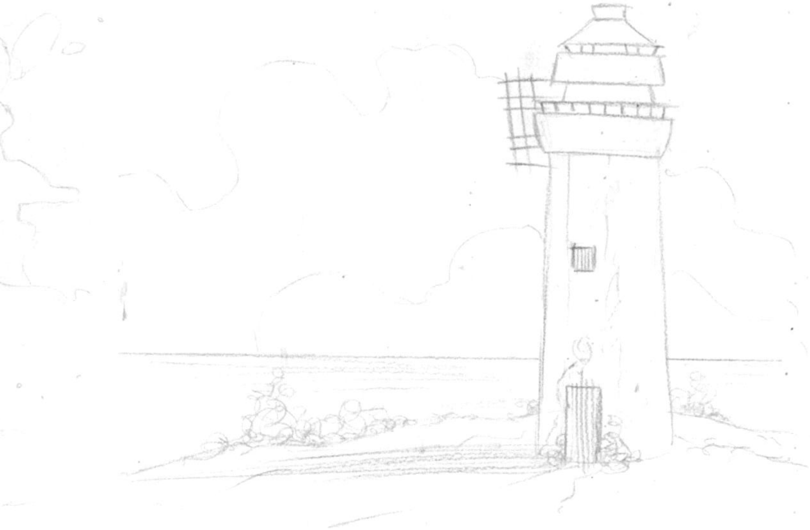

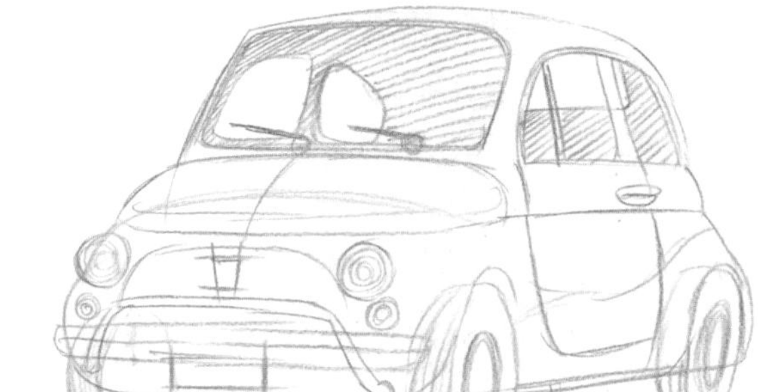

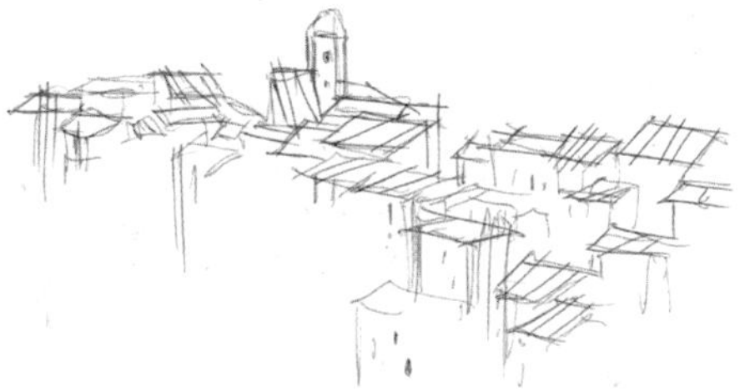

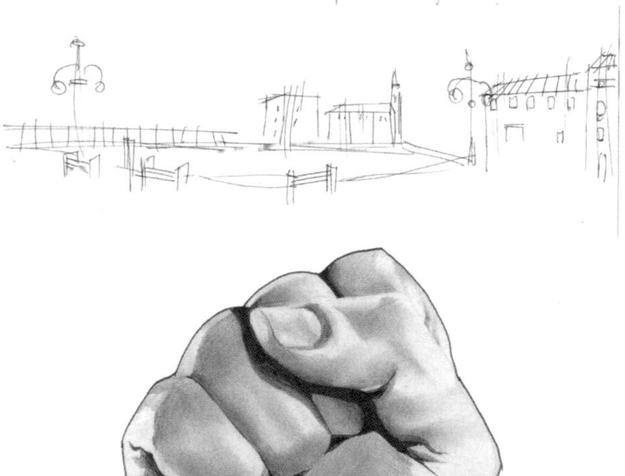

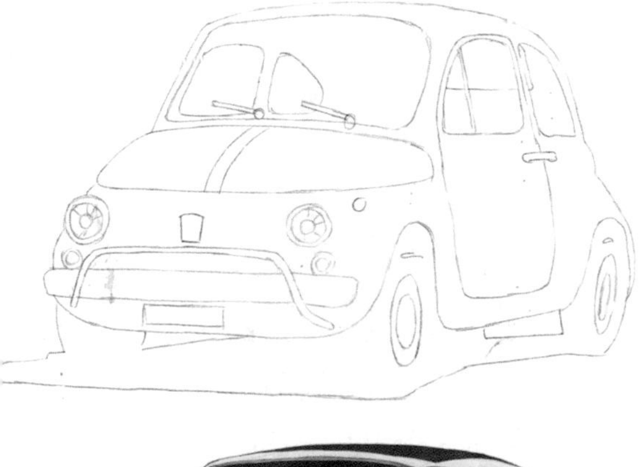

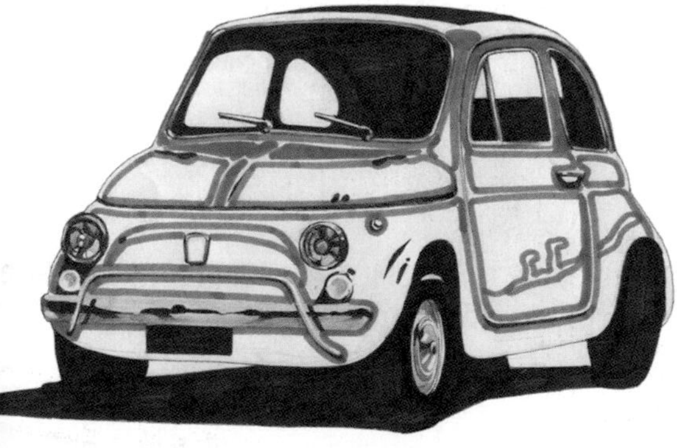

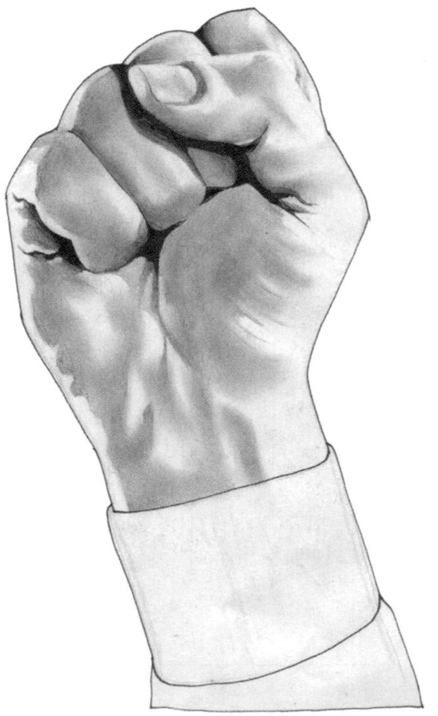

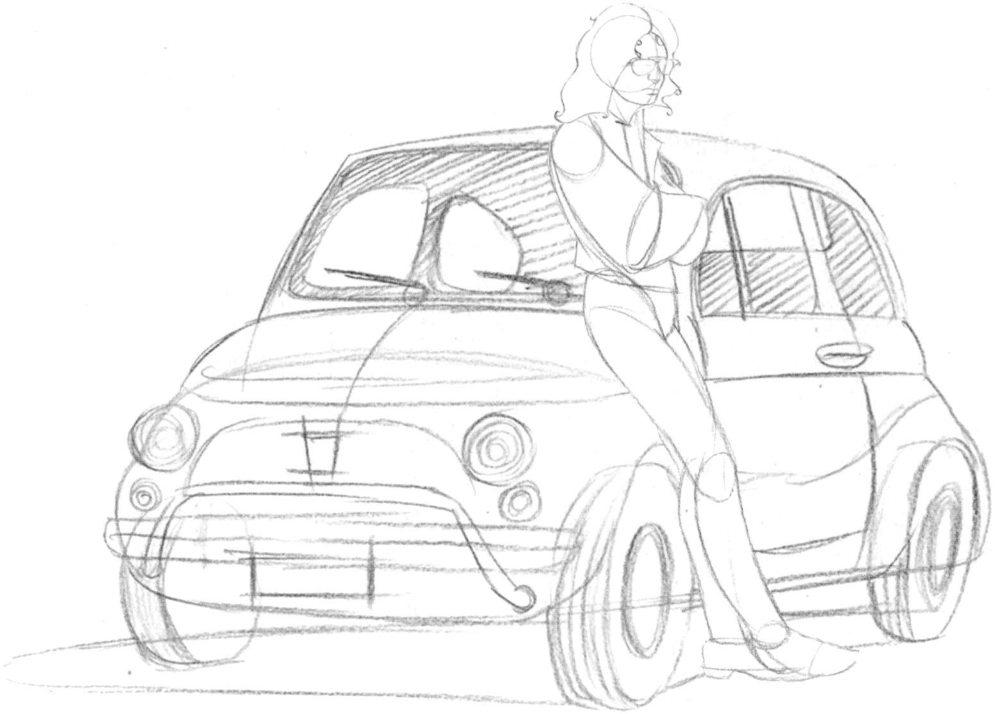

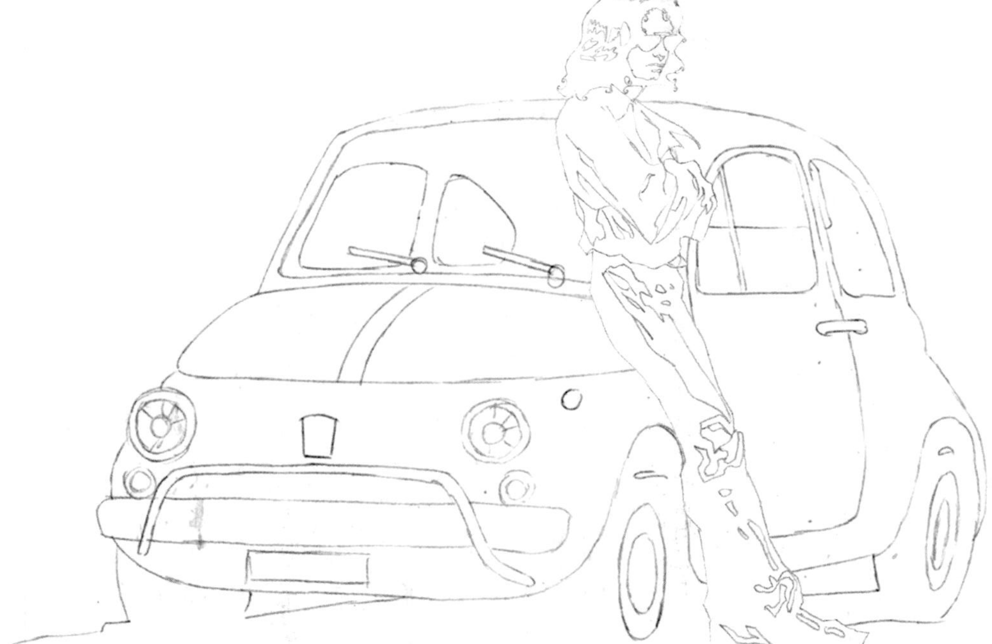